British Political Science: Fifty years of Political Studies

Edited by

Patrick Dunleavy, P. J. Kelly and Michael Moran

Blackwell Publishers

Copyright © Political Studies Association

ISBN 0-631-22412-2

First published 2000

Blackwell Publishers
108 Cowley Road, Oxford, OX4 1JF, UK.

and
350 Main Street,
Maiden, MA 02148, USA.

British Library Cataloguing in Publication Data
A catalogue record for this book is available from the British Library

Library of Congress Cataloging in Publication Data
Cataloging-in-Publication data applied for

100220 7922
T

Printed and bound by Page Brothers, Norwich

BRITISH POLITICAL SCIENCE: FIFTY YEARS OF *POLITICAL STUDIES*

Preface

British political scientists constitute probably the second largest national grouping in the discipline worldwide, after the USA, home of the much larger and still intellectually dominant American associations, APSA and ISA, covering political science and international relations respectively. The British discipline has played a very active and intellectually influential role in the international development of political science, and particularly helped shape the development of European political science since the 1970s.

There have been a number of retrospectives covering the evolution of political science as a formally constituted academic discipline within the UK. In 1975, the twenty-fifth anniversary of the founding of the Political Studies Association (PSA), a range of distinguished authors reflected in specially written pieces for the Association's journal *Political Studies* on the changes over two and a half decades. And in 1999 the British Academy sponsored a substantial volume of retrospectives and reflections (Hayward, 1999).

The idea for a differently slanted celebration of British political science on the fiftieth anniversary of the PSA's foundation and at the start of the new millennium came from the PSA Executive in 1999, especially the then Chairman, Professor Ian Forbes and the long-standing Treasurer, Professor John Benyon. Their suggested approach was to let the authors of the last half century speak directly for the continued relevance of their work, within a reasonably balanced selection covering different areas of the discipline. The material included would be drawn exclusively from the pages of *Political Studies*, the PSA's main journal, and stretch from the journal's very first issues into the 1990s.

It has fallen to us as the current and immediate past editors of *Political Studies* to revisit the journal's now vast and still burgeoning archive of published papers, and to embark on the potentially fraught task of making a selection. We have aimed to provide a reasonable picture of the development of the best work in our discipline over this long vista, and yet to select material from across the period that is still relevant and interesting in the light of contemporary concerns and professional standards. Inevitably there were far more candidate articles for inclusion than we could possibly fit in, and too many important bases for selection for us to conceivably put to use. To meet these pressures we expanded the initially planned number of contributions from ten to eighteen, although at the price of focusing only on highlights of around 5,000 words from each of the authors included. Chapter 1 provides a brief synoptic review of the development of the discipline and explains the rationale we used in our selections.

We hope that the resulting collection will strike intellectual chords with the concerns of today's political scientists, and help a new generation of scholars to better appreciate the evolution of knowledge in their subject area, and the strengths and possible weaknesses of the 'British tradition' of political analysis.

Patrick Dunleavy and *P. J. Kelly*
LSE, London.

Michael Moran
Manchester.

References

Hayward, J., Barry, B. and Brown, A. (eds) (1999) The British Study of Politics in the Twentieth century. Oxford: Oxford University Press for the British Academy, xv + 511, ISBN 0 19 7 26 2066.

Acknowledgement

We thank Simon Bastow and Jane Tinkler for their invaluable help in preparing this volume.

Characterizing the Development of British Political Science

Patrick Dunleavy, P. J. Kelly and Michael Moran

Over the last half century British political science has to some extent been limited but also simultaneously strengthened by two features which have helped shape its distinctive intellectual 'look and feel':

 – the influence of political continuity; and
 – a degree of scepticism and eclecticism in its approach.

Both these factors have at times constrained the professionalization of the British discipline, and sometimes seemed to shape the direction and tempo of intellectual development in unhelpful directions. But they have also contributed strengths to the British way of doing political science, and over time both political continuity and a certain anti-modernist scepticism have decayed as inhibitors and grown more constructive as positive influences. In particular, the essays in this collection demonstrate the extent to which UK political scientists have followed Leopold's advice that: 'The first rule of intelligent tinkering is to keep all the parts'.[1] Far more than in the USA, the British discipline has kept available and interacting with each other all its original elements in a relatively unified set of departments and professional organizations. Since the 1970s especially, British constitutional and intellectual idiosyncracies have diminished under the influence of Europeanization trends, and the discipline has begun to operate more confidently on a wider stage. We review changes in the two influences in turn. The last section of the chapter explains the basis on which we have selected and presented the contributions included here.

1. The Influence of Political Continuity

> The legal constitution of the British state is extremely peculiar.
> *W. J. M. Mackenzie, in 1967*[2]

> There has been little enthusiasm at any time since 1789 in Britain for fundamental constitutional change.
> *Brian Harrison, in 1995*[3]

Amongst liberal democracies, even amongst the 'Westminster system' models created in British-influenced political systems, the UK's unfixed and uncodified constitution for a long time set it apart. No doubt every political system can make claims to 'exceptionalism' in some respect or another, and some more plausibly than others – such as the claims of US exceptionalism founded on the absence of socialism.[4] But the absence of a constitutional founding document or of a codified view of the relationship between citizens and their rulers must by any standards be

Published by Blackwell Publishers, 108 Cowley Road, Oxford OX4 1JF, UK and 350 Main Street, Malden, MA 02148, USA reckoned an important differentiating feature. This relatively unique constitutional structure was founded on the elusive principles of parliamentary sovereignty and the attendant importance of elite consensus on self-restraining behaviour bound by conventions.

This different foundation for the polity, and the long-run ad hoc evolutionary unfolding of the institutions of liberal democracy in Britain, shaped the post-war development of political science in many different ways. Both for empirical analysts and for political theorists it created a professional socialization strongly rooted in national distinctiveness, focusing on some kinds of questions barely considered else-where, and ignoring or downgrading different kinds of questions viewed as funda-mental in other countries. In some areas, notably the analysis of elections and the study of interest groups, the British profession picked up very completely (and largely uncritically) perspectives imported from the USA, the dominant centre for the discipline throughout the post-war period. But in other areas, such as the analysis of law/politics relationships or the systematic study of legislative behav-iour, sub-fields remained either marginal or developed with only a slow tempo by comparison with the voluminous American literatures.

National distinctiveness also sustained for a long time a kind of intellectual con-servatism about theoretical and empirical methodologies in British political science. The discipline held out for a long time against the 'behavioural revolution', as any survey of the 1950s coverage of *Political Studies* serves to demonstrate. When these barriers to new methods cracked in the 1960s, a continuing reluctance to embrace formalism in empirical theory and relative slowness in developing quantitative ap-plications still meant that the discipline had a distinctively 'soft' feel compared with harder-edged work coming from the United States, with more of a UK emphasis upon historical and institutional studies. The founding of the *British Journal of Political Science* in the early 1970s, plus a noticeable change of orientation at *Political Studies* a few years later under the editorship of L. J. Sharpe, helped to counteract these problems and encouraged new generations of scholars to take a different tack. The role of government-funded research councils in supporting more 'big science' studies, not just of elections but also of policy processes, helped to foster new skills and approaches. And in political philosophy the systematization in theoretical efforts flowing from the influence of John Rawls' *A Theory of Justice* had a big influence in the UK, as P. J. Kelly stresses below (pages 10–12). But the impression of a hard/softer contrast between the character of professionalism in the USA and Britain persists to this day. A significant part of this differential in empirical work has been the relative difficulty of measuring decision-making and policy-making attributes in a polity where informal processes and unclear specifications of powers have prevailed.

From the 1973 accession of the UK to the European Economic Community, how-ever, the underlying structure of the British constitution began to change signifi-cantly, and parliamentary sovereignty no longer meant what previous generations of scholars had taken for granted. Britain's constitution remained uncodified, but it progressively became more formalized and the issues surrounding its exceptionalism came to be seen in a different light. The re-emergence of large-scale demands for a written constitution in the late 1980s, partly in response to

Thatcherism, might still be held not to refute the confidently generalizing quote from Brian Harrison which began this section, claiming a 200-year-old stasis on constitutional issues. But certainly the plethora of major institutional changes enacted after the Labour victory in 1997 has now moved the UK to a radically different constitutional footing from the situation in late 1996, and one much closer to patterns in liberal democracies elsewhere. Like all other large European nations the UK is now quasi-federal in structure, with significant devolved parliaments and assemblies in Scotland, Wales, London and (more tenuously) in Northern Ireland. The long dominance of first-past-the-post elections has been decisively cracked, inaugurating a probably long-running co-existence with proportional representation systems, with implications that were already unfolding through the party system and voters' patterns of alignments in the elections of 1999 and 2000, with their record low levels of voter support for the 'two party system'. Citizens' rights (as codified in the European Convention on Human Rights provisions) are now directly embodied into British domestic law and will work through the system over the next ten years. The European Court of Justice provides powerful elements of a constitutional supreme court, able to strike down British legislation. The hereditary principle has been removed from the House of Lords, and a more significant bi-cameralism seems in prospect. And formal 'separation of powers' provisions have appeared in various contexts, notably in the vesting of independent powers over monetary policy in the Bank of England; inside the London metropolitan authority in the relations between the Mayor and the Greater London Assembly; and in the terms of operation of many regulatory bodies set up since the 1980s. As a result of these cumulatively impressive changes Britain looks much more like a 'normal' democracy than it once did.

Above all the development of the European Union (and the broader international standardization of policy-making on subjects like carbon emissions to whaling) has meant that many issues in British politics are now decreasingly capable of being settled on a single-country plane. For better or worse the partial centralization of power away from all EU member states' individual competences has exerted an important if still rather diffuse influence upon UK policy-making styles and institutions. The influence upon British political science has been immense, with a major shift of empirical research away from single-country topics and towards studying the EU level or the comparative politics of Europe. The creation of the European Consortium of Political Research has been especially influential here, alerting large numbers of UK political scientists to European experiences and theoretical perspectives, with particular impact in areas such as the study of party politics and public choice theory. Convictions of national distinctiveness, so clearly evident in the pages of the 1950s or '60s *Political Studies*, are singularly absent in the 1990s volumes. The orientation of British political scientists towards overseas work has shifted markedly away from the focus on the US discipline (and to a lesser degree on Commonwealth countries) characteristic of the early post-war period, with referencing of the US and European literatures especially becoming more even-handed.

2. Scepticism and Eclecticism

> I treat government not as a conscious contrivance, but as a half-instinctive
> product of the effort which human beings make to ward off from them-
> selves certain evils to which they are exposed.
> *Sir J. R. Seeley, 1891*[5]

> If anyone wants the pure science of man in society, I think he [or she]
> has come to the wrong shop for it here.
> *W. J. M. McKenzie, 1951*[6]

These two quotes illuminate a second enduring characteristic of British political
science for much of the post-war period – a reluctance to embrace formally stated
theories which became evident in a certain anti-rationalism in the self-definition
of political science, and a kind of premature closure of intellectual debates about
why institutions are as they are in favour of explanations stressing the ineluctable
diversity of human behaviours, and the importance of personality, chance and
history. What James Scott calls 'the high modernist optic' took root only partially
in British public policy (as in the slum clearance and civilian nuclear power programmes) and became dominant in only a few corners of political science (like the
analysis of voting behaviour).[7] Much of the discipline, for much of the post-war
period, took a rather sceptical stance towards the idea of a unified 'political science'
at all. Many of the major departments (in LSE, Manchester and Essex, for example)
were labelled as 'Government', and the vast bulk of the remainder followed the
PSA and used some non-controversial variant of 'political studies' in their titles and
degree labels.

The intellectual cores of anti-scientism and anti-rationalism in the 1950s and '60s
were clearly Oxford, under the grip of ordinary language philosophy and the LSE
under the influence of Michael Oakeshott. Oakeshott dismissed blue-printing
schemas for human improvement as 'this jump to glory style of politics' and a
product of a too prevalent 'rationalism' in politics. He lauded instead a stance for
the political analyst centring on 'the irony that is prepared to counteract one vice
with another, the raillery that deflates extravagance without itself pretending to
wisdom, the mockery that disperses tension'.[8] Yet as illustrated by the quotes at
the head of this section, it was not just political philosophers nor ideological conservatives alone who favoured a very tempered approach to political analysis.
Seeley, a late nineteenth century pioneering Cambridge political historian determined to systematize his subject matter, was years before his time in his 'rationalist' ambitions to discover regularities in political processes behind disparate
historical narratives. But the influence of the British 'discovery learning' approach
to constitutional development none the less shows through in his stance. And
Mackenzie, the doyen of the Manchester school and leading critic of Oakeshott
amongst empiricists, was similarly modest in his ambitions. In 1951 he disarmingly
called his own field public administration 'the application to a complex of practical
problems of fag ends of a great many different sciences'. A decade and a half later
his still unsurpassed survey, *Politics and Social Science*, exhaustively ransacked every
neighbouring discipline for ideas and perspectives to bring to bear in political
analysis.[9]

A somewhat compensating trend was that for many years British political science remained less specialized and more eclectic than its US counterpart. The relatively small size of the majority of departments encouraged colleagues to collaborate across different subject boundaries, while undergraduate curricula were typically broad. In the early post-war period empirical scholars in the mould of Harold Laski, Mackenzie, Peter Self and others kept an active interest in and contributed to debates at the interface between political theory and applied analysis. And political theorists were important players as critics of empirical analysis.

Both aspects of the British professional stance (eclecticism and relative unity) changed a good deal in the second half of our period, from the 1970s on. Specialist groups and journals focused on sub-fields became more important in the 1980s and '90s, and with them professional standards began to internationalize more. And as cross-country collaboration expanded, it became both easier and more important for colleagues to write for and talk primarily with people in the same sub-field in other departments within the UK, or within Europe, or overseas. Linkages between different parts of the British discipline have remained more important than in the USA, because specialization has been less hyper-developed. But integrating effects are now more modestly scaled than once they were. The modern division of labour may no longer allow, say, a public administration expert to emulate Mackenzie's omni-competence in social theory. But political theorists, for instance, have still been able to reconcile and accommodate the increasingly different analytical, normative and historical projects present in their field, retaining a common culture and a still integrated debate, as P. J. Kelly argues in his introduction to the political theory chapters below.

A certain eclecticism remains built-in to the intellectual sub-structure of the discipline, but now in a more intellectually productive way. British political science has always been a pluralist field. Normally there has been a predominance of institutionalist empirical work and liberal political theory, but there have also been vivid sub-cultures, of conservatives, of hard-line big science modernizers, of Marxist and other left perspectives, of comparativists, from time to time public choice-influenced approaches, and most recently post-structuralist, green and feminist perspectives. Far more than the USA, political science is now set up in the UK as an inherently multi-theoretical discipline, in which alternative well-developed interpretative frameworks vie with each other for hegemony or advantage.[10] Acute observers have lamented some corollaries – such as the profession's inability to agree on a 'book of the year' to serve as a common reference point noted by Brian Barry in the mid 1970s, or the non-emergence of 'gurus' on a par with the most influential US figures.[11] And some British debates have shown a recurring 'foundational' tendency which has to some extent inhibited the development of 'normal science' processes, the cumulation of an accepted body of knowledge and the focusing of debate upon relatively specific, derived implications of each basic orientation. Critics from a different perspective often want to go back and dig up the founding assumptions, chopping at the roots of whole sub-fields and approaches, rather than just debating new findings or extensions. But the power of critique also remains a strong force for good in the British discipline. Vigorous 'generalist' journals and conferences provide an acute public barometer of the health of different areas and perspectives, and maintain a sharp competitive edge that might get lost in a more segmented and specialized structure. If anything, the arrival of new government-sponsored bureaucratic methods of trying to assess both research outputs and teaching quality from the 1990s strengthened disciplinary unity and peer group processes in political science, whatever its other substantial costs.

3. The Basis for this Selection

Looking back over a half century of published work is both a humbling and a revealing task. The strengths of British political science showed through in our first 'long' list of possible candidates for inclusion, which stretched to 241 papers. We considered a large number of possible bases for winnowing down this rich variety to a mere ten or so papers, and almost immediately concluded that we must cover more authors for slightly less space to help ease our selection problems. We next moved to a 'short' list of around 40 papers, and then within that group we looked for a pattern of papers which would do three things.

1. We wanted to cover the key areas of the discipline, which we boiled down to the three categories which now form the Part structure of this book: political theory, a field where *Political Studies* has always been strong; British politics, where UK authors of course have a comparative advantage; and comparative politics and empirical theory, where the bulk of new approaches have concentrated.

2. We also needed to find work from different eras which has to some extent stood the test of time, and remains fresh and interesting for contemporary readers. This criterion undoubtedly bore down hardest on empirical articles, many of which covered topics now hard for current readers to re-capture, or used methods which would not now count as systematic enough. By contrast, a great many political thought and political theory pieces often stood up well on this test, necessitating a rather more drastic selection here.

3. We also wanted to capture the diversity of the discipline, something of the ebbs and flows of debate, of the interests and intensities amongst schools of thought which enliven professional life. In some respects our selection succeeds in doing this, for it includes some notable practitioners of political science with very different modes of operating. In other respects finding diversity was a hard task. Our final set of authors is mainly British, but we have included several distinguished overseas contributors to show their important role also in UK debates. However, our set of authors is far less diverse in gender terms than we would have liked – for the inescapable reason that the contributors in *Political Studies* for much of its life have been overwhelmingly male. Since the mid-1970s this highly undesirable position has changed, of course, albeit far too slowly. But two of the seven strong papers selected from these more recent times are by women authors.

We are acutely aware at the end of this process that what is assembled here is only *a* selection from the *Political Studies* legacy, one of many possible selections that might have been produced by a different set of editors or the use of different criteria. We could have pulled together just the most cited articles from the journal or those most influential in their day. We could have polled members of the PSA or created a jury and gone with a selection based on votes. We could have looked more mechanically for the 'best' articles from each defined sub-period or sub-field.

We did not follow these courses for many reasons, but primarily because we feared that they would lead us to a selection based on the reputation of author names or the presumed content of papers diagnosed from their titles, rather than a selection based on genuinely re-reading the papers with an eye to what seems to have lasted well and can still speak to current readers in a fresh way. But even in these terms the richness of the *Political Studies* archive left us with many papers of virtually equivalent merit and an irreduceable arbitrariness in what was included and what was left out.

So the sense in which this selection constitutes the 'best of' fifty years of *Political Studies* is a highly contingent one. We trust that readers will find here material to provoke them to re-access both the full versions of these authors' work, and to think about and discuss the surrounding literatures with which they were engaged. In many fields of human endeavour, the chance to re-appraise traditions has been used to stimulate new advances and progressions. The fiftieth anniversary of the Political Studies Association affords British political scientists an important opportunity of this kind, and we hope that this collection can help to enrich this re-appraisal.

Notes

1 Aldo Leopold cited in James C. Scott, *Seeing Like a State: How Certain Schemes to Improve the Human Condition have Failed*, New Haven: Yale University Press, 1998, p. 345.

2 W. J. M. Mackenzie, *Politics and Social Science*, Harmondsworth: Penguin, 1967, p. 347.

3 B. Harrison, *The Transformation of British Politics, 1860–1995*, Oxford: Oxford University Press, 1995, p. 5.

4 See B. Shaffer S. M. Lipset (ed),

5 J. R. Seeley, *Introduction to Political Science: Two Series of Lectures*, London: Macmillan, 1896, p. 129.

6 W. J. M. McKenzie, *Explorations in Government*, London: Macmillan, 1975, p. 16.

7 James C. Scott, *Seeing Like a State: How Certain Schemes to Improve the Human Condition have Failed*, New Haven: Yale University Press, 1998, p. 345.

8 M. Oakeshott, 'On being a conservative' in R. Kirk (ed.), *The Conservative Reader*, Harmondsworth: Penguin 1982, pp. 589, 597.

9 W. J. M. Mackenzie, *Politics and Social Science*, Harmondsworth: Penguin, 1967, p. 347.

10 See, for example, P. Dunleavy and B. O'Leary, *Theories of the State: the Politics of Liberal Democracy*, Basingstoke: Macmillan, 1987.

11 B. Barry, 'Review article: exit, voice and loyalty', *British Journal of Political Science*, 14, 1, 79–107.

POLITICAL THEORY

Introduction *by P. J. Kelly*

The interest in political theory has been a persistent feature of both *Political Studies* and the practice of political science in Britain over the last fifty years. A cursory glance at the cumulative index of the journal would show the significant place of political theory in all its forms within the British science of politics. It would also show the enormous variety and diversity within British political theory, the deeply contested character of the method and point of normative and historical approaches to political theorizing and the key role played by British political theorists in the evolution of internationally significant developments or theories. I want to say something about each of these three features of British political theory over the last half-century, as reflected in the journal.

Political theory has always been at the heart of the study of politics in Britain but it has only emerged as a distinct component of political studies in the last half century, roughly coinciding with the history of the journal. In the early part of the twentieth century, at least up until 1950, political theory was central to the study of politics, but there were very few 'political theorists' as such. The early champions of political studies in Britain such as Graham Wallas, Ernest Barker, Harold Laski, George Catlin and Douglas Cole were all political theorists of sorts, but they also saw themselves as 'political scientists' engaged in the wider search for knowledge concerning political phenomena. Indeed each would probably reject the designation of 'political theorist' if this were supposed to designate an interest narrower than what is covered by the remit of *Political Studies*. None of the above fits into any of the contemporary categories of 'normative' or 'positive' or 'historical' political theorist (see the selection from Cole). Each used 'great texts' or traditions of political ideas as a way of analysing and explaining political phenomena or prescribing political change. And each remained an advocate of the centrality of studying political ideas as part of an education in Government or Political Science. That said, the study of political ideas or 'great texts' was not intended as a process of recovering some timeless wisdom. Most simply used the great texts of political theory as a way of entering into discussing issues of the nature, character and function of government. The 'great texts' were not used as a 'moral' resource in the way advocated by American advocates of the tradition of political philosophy such as Leo Strauss. The canon of political thought was often as much concerned with issues that fall under the contemporary sub-disciplines of public-administration, institutions, and comparative politics as with what now concerns 'normative' political thought.

The emergence of political theory as a distinct subject of enquiry developed slowly in the 1950s, partly as a response to the progressive expansion of the British university system and the consequent development of degree schemes in political science and government which distinguished themselves from courses offered by sociologists, economists, historians and philosophers. Other important formative influences were a dramatic increase in contact with the more methodologically self-conscious American political science. Among philosophers a slow abandonment of the most austere variants of logical positivism and Oxford ordinary language philosophy, both of which had seemed to undermine the possibility of normative political thought as practised up until the time of Henry Sidgwick at the turn of the twentieth century, opened new possibilities for political theory. Whereas most members of the Political Studies Association would still have been expected to teach both political ideas and institutions to undergraduate students their research interests were becoming more methodologically focused and therefore more specialized.

Perhaps the two landmark developments in political theory in the 1960s were the emergence of normative political theory and the history of political thought as distinct activities. Brian Barry's *Political Argument* (1965) building on philosophy and economics defended the credibility of 'normative' enquiry even in circumstances of disagreement about fundamental political values. Barry's work was soon supplemented by the import of John Rawls' *A Theory of Justice*. Although an American work, through the influence of theorists such as Barry, Rawls' work and the project it initiated soon came to occupy a dominant position in political theorizing in Britain. All the major departments of political science have 'normative' theorists on the staff.

The influence of Barry and Rawls was to give a harder more rigorous and philosophical character to political theory than can be found in predecessors such as Isaiah Berlin (see the selection from Steiner). However, the hegemony of the liberal paradigm was not universally acclaimed. The Rawls/Barry agenda did not merely attract internal criticism from libertarians and communitarians, but it also raised the profile of alternative radical and continental critiques ranging from Adorno and Habermas in German critical theory to French post structuralism. Anyone who thinks that normative political theory in the Barry/Rawls mode has crowded out any other voices need only check the volume and diversity of critical non anglophone political theory that has been consistently published in the journal since the late 1960s (see the selections from Coole and Rose).

The other significant development to shape political theory in Britain was the emergence of a methodologically distinct 'historical' approach to political ideas. The origins of the 'history of political thought' movement are varied and complex. In part it emerged as a response to the growth of 'positivist' approaches to political science, partly also as a response to reductionist neo-Marxist accounts of political ideology of the sort found in Laski or his student C.B. Macpherson. The 'history of political thought' movement also developed as a response to the resurgence of 'normative' political theory. As 'philosophers' such as Rawls recovered and 'used' the contract tradition, or Nozick and Steiner 'used' Lockean theories of basic rights, some theorists began to question the propriety of such uses and misuses of the political ideas of the past. The 'historians' have contributed two important strands to British political thought and its international significance. First they have added enormously to the quality of our understanding of particular thinkers and traditions (see the selections from Dunn). Second, the methodological writings of the Cambridge 'trinity' of Skinner, Dunn and Pocock have challenged not only the way in which we understand the use of past political thinkers but also the way in which we understand thought and action. This latter development has significant implications for the whole of political theory and political science as well as more narrow 'historical' enquiries into particular political thinkers.

Whilst the 'historical' turn appeared, at first sight to threaten the place of the 'history' of political thought within the political science curriculum – after all, why should the 'history' of political thought not be done in History departments? – all of the major political science departments continue to house 'historians' of political thought. Furthermore, *Political Studies* continues to attract high quality submissions in the field notwithstanding the proliferation of specialist journals.

Despite the significant changes in the structure of political science and political theory over the last half-century, the British study of political science has managed to retain much of its diversity and plurality. Political theorists, whether continental or anglophone, post-structuralist; or analytical, normative or 'historian', manage to coexist side by side in most major departments. And whilst they may regard each other's project as 'hegemonic' they also manage to inform, challenge and influence each other in ever more subtle and sophisticated ways.

What is Socialism?

G. D. H. Cole

All Souls College, Oxford

In the first issues of *Political Studies*, with the cold war at its height and the British welfare state newly established in something like its final form, Cole wrote a two-part manifesto for a multi-volume history of socialism on which he was then working. His theme was to make a sharp distinction between the growth and dominance of Marxist-Leninist forms of socialism on the one hand and the importance of 'utopian', 'ethical' and 'constitutional' strands on the other. His clear polemical aim was to rescue these latter to his mind defensible and preferable forms of socialism from any guilt by association with Soviet communism. The delicate irony of Cole pronouncing on socialism from the sheltered confines of All Souls College, Oxford was compounded by his scholarly method – the complete two-part article has not a single footnote!

What is Socialism? There have been so many notions of it; but if the name has any real meaning there must be some common element, however elusive it may be. The word has been in frequent use for upwards of a century in both French and English: in which of the two countries it originated is still uncertain. It seems to have been used first – apart from a single earlier use in Italian in an entirely different sense – at some time in the second half of the 1820s, and to have passed quickly into fairly general use to describe certain theories or systems of social organization. 'Socialists' were the persons who advocated these theories or systems. Alternatively such persons were called 'Owenites', or 'Fourierists', or 'Saint-Simonians', or by a variety of other names derived either from the originators of particular systems or from the names these originators gave to them – for example, 'Harmonists', or 'Associationists,' or 'Icarians' – this last after Cabet's projected Utopia, described in his *Voyage en Icarie* (1840). Jérôme Blanqui, the economist, brother of the better-known revolutionary, Auguste Blanqui, dubbed them all 'Utopians': Karl Marx took up the word, and grouped them in the *Communist Manifesto* of 1848 as 'Utopian Socialists', by way of distinguishing their doctrines from his own 'Scientific Socialism'. Thereafter there were said to be two sorts of 'Socialism' – 'Utopian' and 'Scientific'. To these was soon to be added a third kind, Libertarian or Anarchist, of which in their several ways Proudhon and Bakunin were the pioneers. Later still came a fourth kind, often called 'Fabian' or Evolutionary Socialism, differentiated from Marx's Scientific Socialism by its belief in what is termed 'gradualism' – the creed of most of the western Labour and Socialist parties of today. What had all these kinds of Socialism in common, to be called by the same name? The answer, in brief, is – hostility to *laissez-faire* and economic competition, and belief in some sort of collective or co-operative action as a means of improving the condition of the many poor.

The 'Utopian' Socialists whom Marx claimed to supersede were all essentially moralists. They set out, some with more and some with less regard for time and place, to prescribe the conditions needed for the establishment of the 'good society', or of 'good societies' which would enable men to escape the evils of the actual societies in which they were living. It was a common view of all of them that existing societies were corrupt and corrupting to their citizens, and that the possibility of living a good life depended on devising and establishing a right structure of human relations.

Thus the 'Socialists' of the early part of the nineteenth century were moral reformers who held that the clue to moral reformation was to be sought in the reformation of the social order. They were 'Socialists', first and foremost, because they put the main stress on social arrangements as the operative causes of good and bad living, and of individual virtue or vice. They tended to regard evil conduct as a consequence less of individual sins or shortcomings than of a bad, 'unnatural' environment. Get the environment right, they said, and most men will behave decently and reasonably in their mutual affairs. They differed, indeed, to some extent concerning the process by which the change in individual behaviour would come about.

'Utopian Socialism', then, made its début as a plan for a system of social organization designed to further human happiness and well-being by the facilitating of good behaviour. All its proponents agreed that existing societies, far from doing this, gave most men strong temptations to act anti-socially. They differed in the stresses they put on different aspects of the evils of society as it was; some of them denounced 'privilege' as the principal cause of social ills, others 'competition'. The former pointed out how the system of privilege for a limited group within society was inconsistent with the fundamentally equal right of all men to pursue happiness and well-being, because it involved a structure of preferential 'rights' and therewith a denial of the rights of the many in deference to the claims of the few. Some – for example Saint-Simon – also argued that it was manifestly wrong for privilege, if it were to be accorded at all, to go to the unproductive (*les oisifs*) at the expense of the productive (*les industriels*). Others, such as Owen and the 'left-Ricardian' economists who preceded Marx, stressed chiefly the evils of competition, as encouraging men to contend against men, instead of fostering habits of mutual co-operation in a common pursuit of the good life. Which of these arguments got most emphasis depended largely on the kind of society the reformers were thinking of as needing to be overthrown. Against the *ancien régime* it was natural to stress the iniquities of privilege: against the rising capitalist system the evils of competition in money-making. Wherever the stress was put, the 'Socialists' were at one in denouncing the exploitation of the real producers of wealth by the ruling classes, and in demanding that in the new society co-operation, and not mutual antagonism and conflict, should be the guiding principle of social organization.

It has sometimes been said that the 'Utopian' Socialists differed from their successors in having no notion of Socialism as a 'class-issue'. Where most of the early Socialists differed from the Marxists who became the inspirers of later Socialist movements was not in being unaware of class distinctions but in resting their case on arguments of justice and human brotherhood rather than on a conception of class-*power*. Marx's 'Scientific' Socialism was an attempt to demonstrate the certainty of the conquest of power by the working class quite apart from any consideration of what *ought* to happen, in a moral sense. Of course, Marx, as much as any other Socialist, believed class-exploitation, class-privilege, and class-monopoly to be morally bad, and wanted them to be swept away in the interests of human well-being. But he claimed that this was bound to occur, whether he wanted it or not, because of the inexorable movement of economic forces which were *fundamentally independent* of men's wills. This *was* his 'scientific' doctrine, resting on his Materialist Conception of History, which altogether excluded considerations of right and wrong. Marx believed in a natural law of social evolution which involved, as men's knowledge of productive techniques advanced, a growing 'socialization' of the processes of production. This, he held, carried with it a corresponding evolution in the field of human relations, destined to result in a complete democratization of economic affairs and in the achievement of a classless society. The way in which this must come about, he held, was the way of class-conflict, because no privileged class would ever yield up its superiority except under pressure from the class or classes it had been holding in subordination. Thus the progress of society from worse to better depended, not on appeals to goodwill or reason, but on the development of the power of the subjected class that stood next below the existing class of rulers. This conception of power as the key to the social problem did not mean that there were no moral issues at stake: it did mean that the moral aspect was irrelevant from the stand-point of predicting the course of events.

Herein lay indeed a sharp contrast; for all the 'Utopians' believed that, apart from considerations of power, it was possible to affect the future by appealing to reason and conscience. Among the 'Utopians', Saint-Simon had the keenest sense of historical development and was most clearly in the succession of the great eighteenth-century philosophers of the Enlightenment.

This difference had important consequences. The Marxists, on the other hand, thought that the main task was that of arousing the workers to a sense of their class-power, and that this would hasten the advent of the new classless society. Saint-Simon thought men were bound, by a law of nature, to become more enlightened, and that his efforts could only hasten and make more efficient a development that was bound to occur in any case. Marx thought that the evolution of the 'powers of production' was bound to carry the proletariat to victory, but that the victory could be hastened and made more efficient by stimulating the proletariat's confidence in its historic mission.

The Marxist version of Socialism was fully proclaimed in 1848 in the *Communist Manifesto*; but it had little influence on the European revolutions of that year, and after their defeat Socialism went for a time almost into eclipse. In Great Britain, Chartism slowly flickered out, despite Ernest Jones's efforts to recreate it on Marxian foundations during the 1850s: Paris, which had been the great centre of Socialist ideas and movements, relapsed under Napoleon III into a quiescence partly accounted for by the dispersal in exile or prison of most of its leaders. Revival did not come, on any significant scale, till the 1860s: when it did come, Germany, rather than France, occupied for a time the leading position, with the followers of Marx and of Lassalle contending for the control of the developing working-class movement. In this contest the question of the Socialist attitude to the State came to play a vitally important part. Marx regarded the capitalist State, which in Germany, and especially in Prussia, was also the semi-feudal State of the older privileged classes, as an enemy to be fought with and over-thrown. Lassalle and his followers, on the other hand, looked on the State as a mechanism that could be transformed by the establishment of manhood suffrage into an instrument of social progress: they demanded that the State should place capital at the disposal of the organized workers for the establishment of free, co-operative productive enterprises.

Marx's instrument for this rebuilding was the First International – the International Working Men's Association which was founded in London in 1864. This was an amorphous body, centrally directed from London by a council made up largely of British trade unionists who sympathized with revolutions abroad without having any use for them at home, and for the rest of foreign exiles in London who were mostly prepared to accept Marx's leadership. The sections of the International which were founded in other countries, except Germany, were much less amenable to Marx's influence: the French section was dominated by followers of Proudhon, with a minority of Blanquists and only a sprinkling of Marxists. The resolutions passed at the International's early congresses were the outcome of a mixture of influences: Marx kept control of the central organization only because the British trade-union leaders, little interested in niceties of doctrine and regarding the whole affair as concerning mainly the continental working classes, gave him, up to 1871, almost a free hand. Within the International there soon developed a bitter conflict between Marxists and Anarchists, with other tendencies playing only a secondary role.

Then came the Franco-Prussian War, the collapse of Napoleon's empire, and the proclamation of the shortlived Paris Commune.

Marxism did not, however, die after the fall of the Paris Commune: it entered speedily on a new phase, which was in effect the birth of the Social Democratic movement. The establishment of the German Empire, with a Reichstag elected on a wide popular franchise, transformed the conditions of political action in Germany and made the division of the German Socialists into two rival parties an unwarrantable barrier to electoral success, which the new franchise rendered for the first time possible. Under pressure of this electoral consideration, Lassallians and Eisenachers patched up their quarrels, and in 1875 formed at Gotha a united German Social Democratic party; and this party became the model for the establishment of new Socialist electoral parties in one continental country after another. Up to that time the franchise had almost everywhere been so restricted as to give working-class parties practically no chance of electoral success. But after the British Reform Act of 1867, the German Constitution of 1870, and the establishment in France of the Third Republic, electoral rights were extended in other countries, and it became possible to organize Socialist parties on a parliamentary basis, or rather with the contesting of parliamentary seats as one of their principal objectives. Such a policy was in practice as irreconcilable with the maintenance of Marx's attitude towards the existing State as it was with the Anarchism of Bakunin. In theory, it is no doubt possible for a working-class party to contest parliamentary elections without putting forward any projects of partial reform within the existing social and political order, and to use elections – and representatives, should any get elected on such terms – merely as means of propaganda for thorough-going Socialism. In practice, such a line is possible only where the executive Government is entirely irresponsible to Parliament, and there is no chance of getting valuable reforms by parliamentary means. In the west, the Socialists could hope to get votes only if, in addition to their long-run Socialist objectives, they put before the electors immediate programmes of reform within the existing political and economic system.

The German Social Democratic party of 1875, though it largely adopted Marxism as a theoretical creed, in effect accepted this necessity, without which no fusion with the Lassallians would have been possible.

What the Germans had done was not to repudiate Marx's doctrine of the class-struggle or his Materialist Conception of History but, while accepting these, to deny the conclusion he had drawn from them concerning the nature of the State and the appropriate political means of advancing from a capitalist to a Socialist society. They had treated his view of the State as having been rendered obsolescent by the establishment of a wide franchise, and had set out to capture the State rather than to overthrow it utterly and put a new proletarian State in its place. The full consequences of the change appeared only gradually; and in Germany they were delayed by Bismarck's Anti-Socialist law of 1878, which forced the Socialists back to underground activities. But with the repeal of this law in 1890 and the establishment of the rights of organization and propaganda, the transformation of the party went on apace. At Erfurt, in 1891, it explicitly adopted, side by side with its ultimate programme, an immediate programme of social reform. Removing the Lassallian demand for State aid in the establishment of workers' co-operatives, and redrafting the economic part of its programme in such a way as to assert its entire loyalty to Marxism, the German Social Democratic party turned, as far as the still largely autocratic constitution of Germany (and still more of Prussia) would allow it, into a constitutional party commanding a wide following concerned mainly with reform rather than with revolution. Eduard Bernstein, in his famous attempt to procure a 'revision' of the Marxist doctrine in the late 1890s, wished to make the change explicit, at the cost of openly discarding a number of Marx's more disputable doctrines ('increasing misery' of the workers, impending collapse of capitalism through its own inner 'contradictions', and the sharp division of the whole people into contending classes of exploiters and exploited). He was defeated and reprimanded; but in practice the German Social Democratic party followed more and more closely the line he had recommended to it.

The Social Democratic parties in other countries which were modelled on the German original went largely the same way. In Great Britain Hyndman's Social Democratic Federation remained too weak ever to need to make a clear choice: it was *superseded* as a political electoral force in the 1890s by Keir Hardie's Independent Labour party. In France the Social Democrats (Jules Guesde's *Parti Ouvrier*) constituted only one element in a Socialist political movement made up of a number of different tendencies – Blanquist, Proudhonist, Marxist, and others. The rival groups did not combine until 1905, and then only under the severe pressure of the turmoils arising out of the *affaire Dreyfus*. When they did unite, under the leadership of Jean Jaurès, their attitude to the State had much more in common with Lassalle's than with Marx's and the doctrine of outright hostility to the *bourgeois* State was sustained only by the Syndicalist *Confédération Générale du Travail*, which insisted on complete trade-union aloofness from parliamentary action.

Thus Social Democracy, which had begun as a revolutionary political movement based on a full acceptance of Marxist theory, turned under the influence of the franchise extension and the growth of parliamentary government more and more into a non-revolutionary agitation for reform and into an attempt to take over, instead of destroying, the machinery of the State. In Great Britain there was no corresponding development only because the climate of opinion among the workers was highly unfavourable to the reception of Marxian ideas. In almost all the continental countries organized religion was closely associated with political conservatism, and the working-class movements grew up in deep hostility to the Churches. In Great Britain, on the other hand, Nonconformist religion had a strong hold on the workers, as well as on the middle classes, and was traditionally associated with political Liberalism. Nonconformity served for a considerable time as a force causing political Labourism to develop inside the Liberal party, and served to prevent it from taking on any anti-religious character. Hyndman's Social Democratic Federation, which was anti-religious in the continental manner, came up against a blank wall when it attempted to convert to Socialism the main body of the British working class. The Independent Labour party was able to push it aside largely because, far from setting itself against religion, it set out to harness the ethical impulses associated with religion to the Socialist cause. On such a basis there could be no acceptance of the materialist philosophy of Marxism, though, of course, some elements of the Marxist doctrine influenced Keir Hardie and his collaborators. In the hands of the Fabian Society and of the Independent Labour party and its successor, the Labour party, British Socialism grew up as a non-Marxist demand for social justice, with the Sermon on the Mount, rather than *Das Kapital* or the *Communist Manifesto*, as its ultimate court of appeal.

There was, however, a second force at work in Great Britain; and this made on the whole for the same result. The conception of the course of history as determined finally by the forces of economic development was linked by Marx to the conception of the class-struggle as involving the revolutionary displacement of one governing class by another as the economic conditions became ripe. But an economic conception of history is equally reconcilable with an evolutionary, or gradualist, conception of social development. There is nothing contrary to logic in supposing that, as economic conditions change, political and social conditions change with them gradually, and not by revolutionary upheaval. Marx had dismissed this possibility, partly because of his Hegelian way of thought and partly because he held that no governing class would ever yield up its power without fighting its hardest to retain it. As against this view the Fabians, who also held a broadly economic conception of historical evolution, argued that under conditions of extended suffrage and responsible government the electorate could use its power to extract one concession after another from the ruling class, and to claim an increasing share in political authority for any representatives it chose to elect. Thus, they argued, the existing State could by a gradual process be transformed into a 'Welfare State', and a working-class party could be carried to political power by a sequence of electoral successes. This presupposed that the old governing class would not at any point decide to fight in arms in defence of its authority; and the Fabians held that in a parliamentary State enjoying responsible government it would in practice be very difficult for the governing class at any stage to defy the constitution. In the climate of British opinion, with its long tradition of responsible government and of gradual advance towards democratic control, this view seemed to fit the situation very much better than any more revolutionary theory – indeed, the evidently unrevolutionary attitude of the working class made any other notion untenable as a basis for mass political action.

Accordingly, British Labour and German Social Democracy had arrived, by the early years of the present century, at broadly the same conclusion, though they had travelled to it by widely different roads. The conditions of parliamentary campaigning under a wide franchise had, moreover, tended in both cases to establish in the minds of the party leaders a conception of democracy very different from Marx's. By 'democracy' Marx meant the proletariat, and no one else. He assumed that the proletariat stood for the majority; but he thought in terms, not of majorities and minorities, but of *classes* contending for power. Under a parliamentary system, however, the factor that counts is the vote of the individual elector, to whatever class he belongs. A parliamentary Socialist party cannot woo the proletariat alone: it has to get all the votes it can, from any source; and its leaders therefore think instinctively in terms not of classes but of majorities and minorities of individual voters. They are led to accept a conception of 'democracy', as meaning majority rule, which is entirely at variance with Marx's conception of it as class-rule. Thus Socialism, which in its early Marxian period had espoused the notion of the coming 'dictatorship of the proletariat', reverted later in the west of Europe, as the conditions of political action changed, to a conception much more closely akin to that of the 'Utopian' Socialists whose attitude I have discussed earlier in this essay. They were appealing, not to a single class – even if they did look to the workers for the bulk of their support – but to all persons of goodwill, and were appealing on grounds of ethics and justice, rather than as the exponents of a 'scientific' doctrine of inevitability and 'historic mission'.

The Leninist Marxism which emerged during the early years of the Bolshevik régime was, in a literal sense, faithful in almost every particular – save one – to Marx's doctrine. The one outstanding difference was that Lenin revised Marx's theory by asserting that it was possible for the proletariat, instead of first helping the *bourgeoisie* into power and then turning upon them after their victory, to take power at once and carry through the necessary process of capitalist development under proletarian control. This was Lenin's theory of 'State Capitalism', and it was definitely a departure from what Marx had held. Besides this, there was a more subtle difference. Marx had spoken of the 'dictatorship of the proletariat' as a necessary stage in the transition to a classless society. Lenin, made the 'dictatorship' the very corner-stone of his theory, and interpreted it as signifying in effect the dictatorship of the Communist party as the only true representative of the proletariat and the only interpreter of its historic mission. The role of the 'party', merely adumbrated in certain passages of the *Communist Manifesto*, was worked up into a complete theory of class-leadership. Lenin always insisted that the party must so act as to carry the mass sentiment of the workers – including the poorer peasants – along with it: it was to 'dictate', not *to* the workers, but on their behalf. If the 'party' alone had a correct understanding of the processes of historical evolution and of the workers' part in them, it alone was in a position to tell the workers what to do in their own interest. According to Marx's determinist doctrine there could be only one right course, marked out by the development of the economic forces. Accordingly there had to be a central determination of party policy to ensure that this one right course should be followed. 'Democratic central-ism', the laying down at the centre, after debate within the party, of a line which every party member must accept without further question, logically followed. The party became a dictatorship over the workers, and, within the party, the structure became more and more hierarchical and the determination of policy, under stress of continual danger to the régime, more and more a matter for the central leadership. Purges and convictions of 'deviationists' followed as a necessary sequel; for, when once the party leadership had decided a thing, all questioning of it came to be regarded as treason to the working class.

Most of these developments of Communist theory came only after Lenin's death. They were largely the work of Stalin, who had not, like Lenin, any understanding of western Socialism. Lenin, as an old Bolshevik, had been essentially a 'westernizer', looking to the industrial proletariat to be the principal agent for lifting Russia out of its primitive backwardness. Stalin, too, wanted to push on with industrialization, as a means of defence against western capitalism; but in his eyes the west had nothing to teach the Russians except in the technological field. In his essential ideas Stalin remained eastern; and under his influence Marxism was transformed into an oriental doctrine, untinged with any respect for the cultural, as distinct from the purely technological, achievements of the west.

This thoroughgoing 'revision' of Marxist doctrine was, of course, greatly fostered by western mishandling of the new Russia, both between the two world wars and after 1945. The countries of western Europe did their best between the wars to wreck the Soviet Union or to treat it as a pariah; and after 1945, when western Europe was too weak to continue along the same lines, anti-Communist *hysteria* took a strong hold on the United States, powerfully reinforcing the bent of Stalinism, already strong enough, towards the isolation of the Soviet peoples from contact with western movements and ideas. There were attempts after 1918 to rebuild a united Socialist International, broad enough to comprehend both Com-munists and western Social Democratic and Labour parties – and parallel attempts to create a comprehensive Trade Union International. On the trade union side, these efforts were resumed after 1945, with temporary apparent success. But neither between the wars nor after 1945 was there ever any real prospect of a united movement. The western parties and trade unions had fully accepted the policy of constitutional action, of a gradual capture of the State, and meantime of its use as an agent of social welfare, and of ballot-box democracy as the only legitimate road of advance towards a Socialist society. The Soviet party and its satellites, on the other hand, believed in the necessity of world revolution, in the impending down-fall of capitalist society because of its inner contradictions, and in a one-party system which had nothing in common with the multi-party systems of the western countries. There was no bridging such gulfs.

[The] Socialist movement, which began as an idealistic drive for social justice and for co-operation, instead of competition, as the right foundation for human relations in the new era ushered in by the great French Revolution, has today become divided into two separate movements, resting on deeply antagonistic philosophies. This divorce was heralded by Marx, when he set out to establish a new 'Scientific Socialism' based on the concept of class-power. But western Marxism, under the conditions of political and economic development in the advanced capitalist countries during the second half of the nineteenth century, lost much of its revolutionary character, and therewith reverted more and more to ethical appeals for social justice, even while its votaries continued to recite the Marxist slogans of class-war. The revival of the older Marxism occurred, not primarily in the west, but in those parts of Europe to which Marx's diagnosis continued to apply because of their economic backwardness and of the starker conditions of class-antagonism which went with it. From these backward countries the older Marxism – with a difference due to its change of habitat – streamed back into the west between the wars as the difficulties of western capitalism multiplied, and as stalemate, or worse, overtook the leading Social Democratic parties of continental Europe. For a moment, in 1945, it looked as if, under the leadership of the victorious British Labour party, the western Social Democratic parties might be able so to rally their forces as to sweep their political antagonists, largely tainted as they were with war-time 'collaboration', from the field, and to establish in the western countries the foundations of a democratic parliamentary Socialist régime. But British Labour was neither alive enough to the possibilities nor internationally minded enough to give the required lead; and the possibility of a victorious Social-ist 'Third Force' in world affairs, if it ever existed, speedily disappeared. It began to look as if, as a great international force, Social Democracy had shot its bolt, despite its sustained strength in Great Britain and in the Scandinavian countries.

Moreover, after the Second World War, Socialism ceased to be, as it had been previously, an essentially European movement, with no more than outposts else-where. The rising tide of nationalism in Asia and in the colonial territories of the European powers in other continents fitted in much more easily with Communism than with parliamentary Socialism, which was a creed devised to fit the conditions of advanced countries possessing responsible government. The Communists set out everywhere to exploit to the full the discontents of the nationalist movements, by denouncing the imperialist practices of the capitalist countries. Communism gained the day in China, and troubled the British, the French, and the Americans (in Korea) with colonial wars which dissipated their resources. Communism was a ready article for export to a great many countries for which parliamentary Social-ism had no message the main body of the people could even begin to understand. Indeed, the parliamentary Socialists, forced on to the defensive, found themselves the reluctant allies of their political opponents in a reliance on American aid which involved their enlistment in a world-struggle between the world's two remaining great Powers – the United States and the Soviet Union – a struggle in which the issue was primarily between capitalism and Communism, with Social Democracy as third man out.

Yet Communism, even if it be a necessary stage in the transition from capitalism to a new social order in eastern Europe, in China, and in other countries in which effective reconstruction of society can hardly begin without a revolutionary change, is manifestly inappropriate to the needs either of the United States or of the advanced countries of western Europe. These countries have far too com-plicated a class-structure for the simple class-theory of the *Communist Manifesto* to fit their conditions, or for their peoples to want thoroughgoing revolution on a class basis as a means to change. Communism will not prevail in western Europe unless the Russians install it by sheer force in war: it cannot under any conditions prevail in the United States. The Communist *World* Revolution is not going to happen: it cannot happen in face of American immunity to its appeal. In the west, except as an outcome of war, capitalism cannot be replaced except by some form of Social Democracy; and if Social Democracy is too weak to replace it, the continuance of capitalism, however it may be modified in secondary respects, is assured for a long time to come. It shows no sign of speedy collapse under pressure of its own 'contradictions' – such as Marx, and later Lenin, expected to occur.

Socialism, then, is no longer a single movement, making it a single direction. In the west it is – as the first forms of Socialism were – fundamentally a drive towards social justice and equality, rather than a class quest for power. It can, of course, no more avoid having to think in terms of power as well as of morals than Communism, for all its insistence on the factor of power, can avoid invoking the aid of ethical appeals. The Communist needs to feel that his cause is righteous, as well as historically determined: the western Socialist needs to feel that the workers are behind him, as well as that his cause is good. Both are aiming, in a sense, at the same thing – a classless society – and both believe in collective action as the means of advancing towards it. Both regard private property in the essential instruments of production as inconsistent with the absence of class-distinctions: both in some sense want to 'socialize' men's minds by socializing their environment. But whereas the Communist seeks these ends by means of class action and regards the dictatorship of a class as a necessary step towards their attainment, the western Socialist looks to the winning of an electoral majority, however composed, and repudiates dictatorship as inconsistent with his conception of the democratic principle. Western Socialism acts on the assumption of a basic social solidarity which holds the community together: Communism denies this solidarity in any society which has not been through its social revolution and eliminated feudal and capitalist privilege. The two conceptions are related to two different kinds of society. In Great Britain, as in the United States, in Switzerland, in Scandinavia, in Canada and Australia, and to a less extent in Belgium and Holland, this underlying social solidarity is a fact based on a long historical experience. Even in France and in Germany the same tradition exists, though it is partly counteracted by other factors. But in Russia and over most of eastern Europe this solidarity has not existed in the past, and is barely intelligible to those whose thinking is based on the history of these countries. Accordingly, the conception of an overriding class loyalty, transcending national loyalty, meets with no such obstacles in eastern as in western Europe; and a Socialism that dismisses nationalism (except when it is being exploited as a means of stimulating 'anti-imperialist' revolt) as a petty *bourgeois* concept is able to make its realistic way. What has still to be seen is what will happen in the long run in those parts of the world in which Communism and nationalism are now appearing as uneasy allies.

Nationalism and the sense of social solidarity are, however, by no means necessarily the same. Nationalism can be, and often is, the creed of a group or class within a nation, rather than of the nation as a whole. Marx spoke of it as if he supposed it was always of this limited kind, because his entire philosophy involved treating every concept as in the last resort a class-concept. It is of course true that in class-ridden societies the ruling classes often identify themselves with the nation; and Marx was in fact largely right about the nationalist movements of his own day – though not wholly so in relation to France, where the revolutionary tradition of national unity was strong. But there can exist, without a nationalist movement in a political sense, an attitude of social solidarity permeating a whole people, or at any rate cutting right across class-differences, in such a way as to limit very greatly the possibilities of fundamental class-conflict. Such a sentiment can exist, I think, only in societies which are either very static, so that habit suffices to hold them together, or very mobile, so that the classes they contain are continually shifting both in their nature and in respect of the individuals composing them. In the former type of society everyone has his station and knows it: in the latter, even if class is still a prominent category, status is no longer definite or unchangeable, and does not mark men off into sharply separated groups. It is in the intermediate types of society, in which there is a conflict between a static and a mobile sector, that the sense of social solidarity is least likely to be strong.

Such a conflict exists to a great extent in those economically backward countries which have been recently subjected to the impact of industrialism. As long as this impact remains mainly foreign it gives rise to forms of nationalist rejection of the foreigner which create a sentiment of union; but as soon as the forces of change come to be largely internal – through the development of native capitalism, native trade unionism, and so on – this unity tends to disappear, not being rooted in any deep social solidarity but simply in hostility to foreign influence. The Communist leaders are aware of this: they realize that, in taking sides with 'nationalism' directed against foreign influence, they are helping to create the conditions in which national unity will give place to class-conflict as the mobile elements in the societies concerned are brought into direct conflict with the static elements and as this conflict in turn is replaced, with the victory of the former, by a conflict between capitalist and worker.

Social Democratic thought cannot grapple easily with problems of this order, because it is an emanation of liberalism, based on the conditions of countries in which the static elements in the social structure have had to give way to the mobile elements – in other words, where capitalism has already subordinated the feudal elements to its own needs. Paradoxically, it is precisely in those countries in which *bourgeoisie* and *proletariat* are most free to fight each other and have least need to combine in order to fight against aristocratic privilege that these contending classes are least disposed to push their quarrel to extremes, because, far from becoming more uniform, they become more diverse and interpenetrated. But this state of affairs exists in a high degree only in a very limited number of countries; and I am afraid the conclusion has to be that the Social Democratic form of Socialism is for the present of equally limited applicability in the world. It is not applicable to countries in which a fundamental revolution – for example, in the land system – is a necessary starting-point for real social change: nor is it applicable after such a revolution until there has been time for the post-revolutionary settlement to have become stabilized and generally accepted, so that the dominance of power-considerations which is a necessary accompaniment of revolution can wear off. Only stable societies possessing a sense of solidarity can in practice give ethical factors priority over considerations of power.

This essay is an attempt to answer the question 'What is Socialism?' in terms of the present day. It contains nothing that even pretends to be a definition of Socialism, either as it exists today or in the light of its history. Socialism cannot be defined in a sentence or a paragraph because it is fundamentally not a system but a movement which has taken, and will doubtless continue to take, diverse forms both from country to country and under the influence of particular theorists and practical exponents. It can be, up to a point, described and characterized, but not defined. Thus, one essential element in it is the stress laid on the need for collective regulation of social and economic affairs, and therewith its rejection of the entire philosophy of *laissez-faire*. But Socialism is not alone in rejecting *laissez-faire*: there are plenty of 'plannists' who are among its most violent opponents. A second element is its thoroughgoing hostility to class-divisions and its aspiration towards a 'classless society'. This it shares with the Anarchists and Syndicalists, but, I think, no one else, though there is, of course, a kind of radical individualism that is sometimes allied with it in the struggle against 'class-privilege'. Thirdly, Socialism traditionally stands for 'democracy'; but democracy can be conceived of in so many different ways that the word, by itself, is not of much help. It does, however, provide the necessary clue to the deep division that exists today between Communism and Socialism of the western countries. For Communism, the class itself is the unit in terms of which all political structures are to be assessed; and accordingly democracy is the rule of a class – of the working class as the representative champion of the unprivileged. For western Socialists, on the other hand, the individual is the final repository of ethical values, and democracy involves majority rule coupled with respect for individual rights. Western Socialism, in the last analysis, is 'Utopian' rather than 'Scientific'. It is conceived of as a means to the good life for the individuals who make up human societies, and not as a destined outcome of a predetermined historical evolution that lies outside the individual's control.

POLITICAL STUDIES: 2000, 26–33

Justice and the Interpretation
of Locke's Political Theory

John Dunn

King's College, Cambridge

One of the major trends in the study of the history of political ideas in Britain since the 1960s has been a return to contextualism, grounding the analysis of major political philosophers in a full analysis of the ideas and currents of their period – in contrast to earlier approaches which treated 'great books' as 'standing outside time'. John Dunn's work is often associated with the school of Cambridge historians including Quentin Skinner and J. G. A. Pocock who have done most to encourage the contextualist approach. But Dunn's message here is also engaged with a much broader study of politics, going beyond the historical enterprise of recovering meaning from past texts. Political ideas in his view are not of merely antiquarian interest, but have contemporary importance. Dunn sets out to criticize the authenticity of the interpretation of Locke that is supposed to underpin modern libertarian theories of justice, such as that of Robert Nozick. Getting history right, Dunn argues, can change the questions that we ask and the assumptions that we make.

The two most powerful and incisive recent interpretations of Locke's political philosophy have been produced by men who feel a shared antipathy to contemporary liberalism and contemporary capitalism and who ascribe to Locke a deep affinity with these unsavoury developments. Both see him indeed as incarnating that authentic 'spirit of capitalism' which is the source of all that is most repulsive in contemporary civilization. Since there was a certain initial novelty to this interpretation – and since it was, as Strauss[1] and Macpherson[2] so often emphasize, so far from the delicately roseate picture which contemporary liberal democrats liked to have of their historic forebears – fairly strenuous interpretation of the texts has been needed to sustain it. This operation has shed an enormous amount of light on the complicated intellectual context in which Locke wrote and the notably heterogeneous set of conceptions which he attempted to integrate. But the shedding of this light has been regarded as, in some degree, incidental to the assignment of confirming the truth of this interpretative doctrine. We are not left by it with the picture of a figure in a state of sharp tension between mediaeval and capitalist social ethics, between collectivism and individualism, the organic community and the market.

True, there is some significant divergence of tactics between Strauss and Macpherson over the proper procedures for simplification. Macpherson accepts the existence of a real conflict of values within the thought and indeed ascribes it to the transitional character of the society in which Locke lived. But this apparent qualification turns out in practice usually to be a case of *reculer pour mieux sauter*. Although he is not averse to taking shelter behind the acknowledgement of Locke's inconsistencies, these qualifications lose much of their salience in the course of his subsequent exposition and we end up with the *Reasonableness of Christianity* as an exercise in social control and with the virtual disappearance of the Christian obligation to charity. For Strauss, on the other hand, matters are simpler. Any incoherences in Locke's thought indicate not intellectual confusions, still less any real ambivalence of feeling. They merely point to the cunning concealment of his univocal allegiance to the more heterodox (and vicious) doctrine. The kind of intellectual cryptography which is the heart of Strauss's historical method can sometimes yield – and undoubtedly has yielded in the case of his studies of Locke – historical insights of remarkable power, but its employment is necessarily capricious. For, if it were to be employed consistently, if the principle used in the section on Locke were universalized, it could never be the case that one could know that men felt genuine conflicts of value – unless they were very *stupid*. In other words the central precept of the Straussian position is wildly intellectualist. It implies that historical changes in values only happen in the minds of stupid men and that the great philosophers never come upon the scene until the materials for the construction of a complete new synthesis become available. Quite apart from the difficulty of maintaining any such belief, it makes it hopelessly obscure how one could ever have sufficient reason to allocate someone to the category of great philosopher. Of course, we all know how *in fact* this category is developed – the indispensable conservative and fictive function of the university curriculum. But that merely indicates the arbitrary character of the use to which Strauss puts the notion.

It so happens that Locke is a peculiarly implausible candidate for such interpretation – not because of his robust and reckless courage – but simply because of the sort of information which we have available in abundance about him. Some of Strauss's constructions – the hilarious idea that in the *Two Treatises of Government* Locke must have been significantly concerned with persuading the deists, (those inveterate disciples of Filmer?) – are implausible at a level of historical specificity which ignores all the evidence of the private papers. But these latter impugn the reality not just of individual elements of the interpretation but of the entire construction. It is not that many, indeed most, of the elements of the construction are not correct – they are – but that the criteria of truth and falsity implied in the analysis are not in any way satisfactorily related to the body of historical evidence. The huge bulk of the Locke papers makes it possible to examine the historical development of a man's mind in a fashion almost unique for the period, from his informal and private jottings in notebooks, some of them even in shorthand, and not just from published works or correspondence with their inevitable ambiguities of intention. When confronted with this evidence, Strauss's interpretation often can simply not be sustained.

The fulcrum of the Strauss/Macpherson position is an interpretation of the role of justice in Locke's politics. The purpose of the theory is claimed to be the justification and protection of bourgeois property rights and the freeing of these from the constraints of traditional natural law theory, more specifically from the duty of charity. This operation is effected by the reduction of the concept of justice, the key term in the evaluation of human social existence, to the guarantee of property rights, embodied in positive law and secured by the constitutional apparatus of the modern bourgeois State. Human duty which used to be a construct out of the needs of all men becomes merely a construct of the legally-articulated political power of private capital. The virtue of charity which used to be a constituent of justice is covertly elided or explicitly rejected. Men confront each other as discrete organisms, incapable of sympathy and devoid of moral claims upon each other, united merely by the utility of their social division of labour in 'the joyless quest for joy'.

This unflattering portrait has naturally provoked some little hostility from the exponents of more traditional views of Locke; and one major assault upon it, by Raymond Polin, has set out Locke's thought as an integrated system, arranged around the central ontological category of the justice of God.[3] Here justice is not merely the value of bourgeois legality. It subsumes all other human values beneath it and becomes the central norm of human experience. Much of Polin's exposition is also of a very high order and in many ways it is historically better-judged than its demonological opponent – even if Locke at times seems to be forced into an oddly Kantian mould. But both interpretations, assume a degree of integration in Locke's thought which can be shown, as a matter of historical fact, simply not to have been there. Both substitute a theoretical unity for an actual ambivalence.

Locke's first extensive references to justice come in his *Essays on the Law of Nature*. Aristotle's definition of natural justice in the *Nicomachaean Ethios* is adduced as evidence for the existence of a natural law. Justitia, together with pudicitia, castitas, and pietas erga parentes, appears as a paradigm of a central ethical value which is rejected by some whole human societies, as a proof of the failure of the traditional argument for the natural law from the universal consent of mankind. He takes the incompatibility between social inequality and the natural rights and interests of individuals, and the consequent injustice of most social orders, maintained by Carneades, as the essence of the theory that natural law is a function of individual human utility and subjects this theory to extended refutation. He claims that any virtue, like for instance justice, is complementary to every other virtue and not antagonistic, as is frequently the case with interests. Finally, justice is asserted to be inconceivable without property.

Certain definite conclusions can be drawn from these discussions. Firstly, justice is conceived of, primarily, if not exclusively, as an attribute of the distribution of goods among human beings. Secondly, the right distribution of these goods is held to be that which maintains the property or ownership of the proprietors or owners. Justice, then, is a dependent function of ownership. All goods are to be conceived as the property of God and their individual human ownership as a revocable grant from God. Theft, either inside or outside a community, is the paradigm of injustice. A prime function of natural law is precisely to guarantee the security of these distributive arrangements. If the law of nature were reducible to self-interest the conditions of scarcity in which human beings live, the inelasticity of supply and the consequence that every appropriation is necessarily performed at the expense of others, would mean that it was self-contradictory. There is a permanent conflict between human duty and human interest in the world and it is the function of the law of nature to mediate this conflict.

There is nothing very remarkable about the reduction of justice to the guarantee of property. It is a perfectly traditional extrapolation from the notion contained in Ulpian's famous axiom, and it is compatible with a wide range of substantive interpretations. It is, however, notably more restricted in its interpretation than the form in which the concept appears in Aristotle or Bodin, where it is seen as a sociologically differentiated articulation of the entire political and social system of a society, or in an Anglican theologian like Jeremy Taylor where it is one of the structural categories of the individual moral life. Even Hobbes provides a logically more comprehensive analysis, though this is presented as a simple extrapolation from the duty to perform covenants made. Perhaps more remarkable, however, than this indeterminacy of Locke's treatment is the blandness of its positivist implications. Any conceivable critical purchase which the idea might have in its Aristotelian or even Bodinian versions is avoided by the simpliste formulations but the social proprieties are not ruffled by any explicit corresponding reduction of property rights to an exclusive basis in positive law. In the distribution of goods among men, whatever is is right but need not gracelessly, in the manner of Hobbes or Spinoza, be *said* to be so. Nor clearly enough did Locke *exactly* think it to be so. In his first writings on toleration he had insisted on the necessary power of the sovereign over all the possessions of the subject, and implicitly rejected any natural right to property. Property is thought of as essentially a private right, to be used, *ceteris paribus*, entirely at the will of the proprietor, but, as a private right, liable to be altered or abolished at any time by the order of the magistrate. He was perfectly prepared to concede the possibility, in principle, that the magistrate's power might be used for the expropriation of the citizens and it seems likely that he would have regarded some acts of legal expropriation as intrinsically thefts (and hence contrary to natural law). But it is not clear that he could give any account of the impropriety of such appropriation which would make sense and the development in the *Essays on the Law of Nature* of the discrepancy between individual interests and positive property-rights renders his position even harder to defend coherently.

When Locke subsequently attempts again to define justice he recurs to this account in terms of property. But he also employs the term in a much looser way, without apparent embarrassment as a synonym for fairness or legality. In the 1667 *Essay on Toleration*, for instance, he argued that any encroachment of the magistrate upon the moral behaviour of individuals, except where this threatened the public welfare was an injustice. At this point an important asymmetry appears in his political theory between the rights of the sovereign and the duties of the subject. Passive obedience remained just as much a duty as it had been in the early writings; but the *right* of the magistrate was now confined to the execution of his duty to advance the general welfare, more particularly by securing men's properties. His rights in this endeavour were extensive, limited only by the precise form of the duty to preserve mankind as much as may be. They included the right to alter property arrangements in any way which served the general welfare; and his subjects had no authority to challenge his decision. But his right (his *jus*) was no longer coextensive with his will, but rather with his duty. Not that the latter had changed in character; but its slight shift in jural relevance was of dramatic import-ance. Tyranny became a focus of positive, instead of quasi-moral, authority. The subjects might owe it obedience but they no longer owed it any supine moral subservience. Injustice became a possible accusation for them to level aggressively against the ruler. They might lack the standing to confront him in the field of politics (though the constitutional pieties could provide a convenient focus for evasion here) but they had acquired at least the authority to *judge* him morally in the exercise of his power.

With the 1671 Drafts of the *Essay* Locke's epistemological interests became more sharply focused and justice continued to appear frequently as an example of a moral concept. Like other virtues, men are said to be more familiar with it as a word, a sound, than they are with its precise meaning. This is not surprising, since it is a relational idea not a simple idea of sensation, an action referred to a rule, frequently in practice a highly complex description of an action, referred to a rule, and not a simple behavioural constant. It is a notion which men acquire from the language of commendation and reprobation prevalent in their community but learning it in this way provides them with a merely verbal knowledge. It is only in so far as it is amalgamated with a set of legal sanctions propounded by a sovereign, human or divine, that it acquires obligatory force upon human actions. This tension between conventional moral values and effective legal sanctions, terrestrial or transcendent, is henceforth a continuing theme of Locke's ethical thought. The epistemological inquiries seem to have been initially designed to bring these together in a deductive ethical system. The effort was necessarily not very successful and the treatment of human justice in his writings continued to bifurcate with increasing sharpness into conventional English usage of the time and the perfect moral language, the former when a substantive moral point is to be made, the latter when the issue is more the philosophical character of moral reasoning. When discussing the proper limits of political authority, as in the 1667 *Essay*, or the offensive character of religious penal laws, justice is given an interpretation which could only be linked to property in a very extended sense indeed. But where the deductive and non-empirical character of moral reasoning is being asserted, it is initially given no interpretation at all and subsequently stated to be logically dependent upon the idea of property. The difficulties posed by this dilemma arise over both the terms in the relationship. Justice is predicated by Locke of a wide range of human acts in accordance with his contemporary moral vocabulary. These can only be made compatible with the deductive property analysis by making the usage of property purely formal – that is, by making it axiomatic that anything which is owed to a man, anything to which he has a 'title', a claim, is his property. There is nothing in itself improper about this – it *is* analytically true that whatever is owed to an individual is owed to an individual. What makes this tautology interesting is what makes it intellectually (and in the end perhaps morally) pernicious. Because justice is a function of property, does it not follow that what is a man's property is necessarily just? Plainly you could use the words that way. But since property right is in fact a function of positive law, since people, including Locke himself at times, do not use the words that way, this would seem to mean that all positive law property-distributions are necessarily just. Even at his most authoritarian, Locke seems never to have adopted such an obsequious posture.

But how, when it came to the construction, or for that matter the reprinting, of a political theory could this dilemma be resolved? Most plausibly, perhaps, by making the legitimacy of positive laws contingent upon (though not of course constituted by) the observance of property rights. Laws which infringed property rights were void. But would not this mean that for instance all taxes as such were necessarily legally void? This dilemma too could be resolved by the benign legacy of English constitutionalism. Due constitutional procedures mediate between the unequivocal right to enjoy one's own, the right of property and the sociological prerequisites for its continued enjoyment, the necessity for property to be regulated and guaranteed by positive law. Logically, it cannot be claimed that they mediate with any great success. They delineate a path of possible compatibility for conflicting human claims, not a necessary harmony. The logical function of the chapter on property in the Second Treatise is undoubtedly to indicate this path and this function is shown magnificently in Macpherson's reading. But to interpret its logical function, as Macpherson seems to, as the biographical cause for its presence is to ignore Locke's stated aim in the chapter in question and to forget the character of the entire rest of the book. To have written the whole of the *Two Treatises* when what one really had to say was chapter V of the Second Treatise, would have shown a literary and philosophical ineptitude of staggering proportions. But it is not just the historical inconsequence of the reading which is in question; it is also its philo- sophical adequacy. It is precisely in the consequences which Macpherson draws from his interpretation, the assertion of the morally unfettered nature of property rights, that it becomes most exposed. For this consequence could only follow if it were the case that chapter V were intended to demonstrate a necessary harmony of conflicting human claims – and not merely their possible compatibility. The crucial test for this interpretation must be the status of charity. Medieval conceptions of property rights made them functional in basis, contingent on the performance of social duties, pre-eminently the duty of charity. Charity was a right on the part of the needy and a duty on the part of the wealthy. Such it remained for Locke. Justice and Charity, it is true, are no longer equivalent. Justice, equity, the just price, now make one set of demands and charity makes another. The political world is a world of convention and justice in an attribute of conventions (though not all conventions, of course, are just). But within the world of conventions there remains a world of nature, the world God gave to man; and in this world every man has the right, which can be voided only by his own misbehaviour, to a suffi- cient and commodious living. In this world, at any point, the rights of men may conflict. Justice is a right like other rights, neither pre-eminent nor derivative.

It is predicated of many different situations and from many different points of view, punishment, exchange, equity, law, property. Only in Locke's last great work, *The Reasonableness of Christianity*, does it come to have a more comprehensive and unitary content – and there for a very simple reason. For, in this work, Locke is concerned not with social morality but with individual salvation, not with how a man ought to act, with virtue and vice, but with what he must do to be saved, not with individual moral response to divine demands, the covenant of works, but with individual religious response to divine intimations, the covenant of faith. Here he confronts not men's struggle to meet the meagre demands of social acceptability but their abject failure in the sight of a God, in which no man living is justified. Righteousness (the life of the just man and its rewards) is presented solely as an achievement of faith, a gift from God, which through his charity men can earn by their efforts as they could never earn it by their performance. And this righteous- ness is clearly no matter of the observance of equity and the uninhibited exaction of the market price in conditions of scarcity. We do not know exactly how Locke regarded the queasy parabola of compatibility between the demands of unlimited appropriation and the demands of God, which he had elaborated in chapter V of the Second Treatise, how far he was aware of the precariousness of the line, or how far he was convinced (or wished to be convinced) by the energy of his own punning. We do not know just what social situations (if any) he saw it as, or intended it for, justifying, at the time at which he wrote it or later. What we do know is that, when he turned away from the exigencies of political tactics and the puzzlements of intellectual polemic to lay out the sole possible way for a man to live well, he made no attempt to elaborate on the adequacies of contemporary moral insight and approbation. For a man, as he had once said, 'immersed in the body and beset with material objects' a man 'under the difficulties of his nature, beset with temptations and hedged in with prevailing custom', there was no security within the sanctions of conventional morality. Only the direct intervention of the deity in history, the personal sacrifice of the Son of God, could justify a man. When Locke's thought moves away from the pragmatic demands of politics or the education of an English gentleman and away too from the construction of a massive intellectual synthesis, to the problem of how, in the world, a man can be good, it is not the spiritual resources of capitalism to which he turns. When justice is a weapon in political manoeuvre, a value in the training of a conventional youth or a philosophical example, the moral qualities of seventeenth-century English society suffice to define it. But when justice appears as *the* rule of life, the rule under which all other rules can be subsumed, the central theme of individual human aspiration, he has recourse to a more transcendent standard. Where the justice of the prevailing commercial code gives way to the justice of human moral adequacy, the demands of capitalism yield to the demands (and the provisions) of God.

In this point the whole meaning of his life comes into focus. From his earliest performance as an intellectual he had struggled to show the reasons for the ways in which he knew that men should live. But the reasons had early taken on their own autonomy and proved recalcitrant to all the moulding intellectual energy devoted to their reconstruction. In the great teased-out web of thought which records this failure, we have left to us the epistemological foundations of the Enlightenment, a formidable legacy. But as the endlessly stretched threads still failed to come together and tossed insecurely in the turbulences of the world, the exhaustion of a lifetime demanded a more secure identity and a less contingent shelter. If unease was the mode of all human experience and Reason a standard which the world could never embody, the next world must be drawn in sharply and immediately to redress the balance of this one. It is possible to describe the consequence harshly enough, the private failure of nerve, the surrender of the old man, sick, mean, suspicious, exhausted, and tetchy. But it was more than the sanctification of individual abjectness. For by projecting his deprivation out into the transcendent categories of Reason he gave it fixity and clarity – the honesty and intellectual force of the struggle guaranteed that. And if the myth which made this reason active in men's lives, which alone could make it immanent in the world, were to lose its power, the deprivation etched out in its categories would demand the remaking of the world. It is because the Reason which is elaborated in Locke's works is in the last resort, and in all intellectual supineness, the Reasonableness of Christianity and not the rationality of capitalist appropriation, that it carried always within it, for a de-mystified world, the potential of Revolution. And because the myth which it embodied promised to men a world of ease and not merely one of consumption, it carries this same potential still today.

Notes

1   L. Strauss, *Natural Right and History*. Chicago: University of Chicago Press, 1953.

2   C. B. Macpherson, *The Political Theory of Possessive Individualism*. Oxford: Oxford University Press, 1962.

3   R. Polin, *La Politique Morale de John Locke*. Paris: Presses Universitaires de France, 1960.

The Vocabulary of a Modern European State

Michael Oakeshott

Despite shaping the education of many British political theorists for more than a generation, Oakeshott was sceptical about the intellectual credentials of both normative political theory and (especially) political science. His stance made him a singular political philosopher, often conventionally located as a conservative theorist but difficult to place within any single research project, while his work effortlessly conveyed an impression of extensive learning and strong intellectual standards within an always idiosyncratic process of reflection. This article, itself a relatively unusual form of publication for Oakeshott, is a 'meditation' on a set of terms associated with the modern form of 'state' – conceived as a complex unity of authoritative offices, a set of mechanisms for enforcing decisions or outcomes, and a mode of people associating with each other. Avoiding anything so vulgar as a theory Oakeshott's meditation reflects the linguistic turn of much political philosophy. The original article (which was published in two parts in succeeding issues of the journal) also contained an equally erudite reflection on the concept of power.

I am concerned here with the words and expressions used in recognizing the character and identifying the characteristics of a modern European state and its like elsewhere in the world.

The somewhat novel associations of human beings which came to be called modern states emerged slowly, prefigured in earlier European history. The manners in which they emerged were as diverse as the local conditions from which they sprang were various; their fortunes were uneven, their durability unequal. They were the outcomes of conquest, the extinction of palatine independencies in feudal realms, the consolidation of fiefs, purchases, the marriage settlements of rulers, multiple treaties, rebellion and secession. Their boundaries were often the lines upon which contingent hostilities came to rest and their human components were determined by the contingencies of earlier territorial settlement. Each was a piece of inhabited territory with a government: land (often ill-defined), people (often miscellaneous) and a ruling authority (usually in the course of seeking recognition). Each was the outcome of human choices to do this rather than that in contingent situations. In some (those of more recent appearance) there has been evidence of a design not merely to do something but to create a 'State'; in a few there is evidence of a grand design. Even the most substantial was a ramshackle construction and has remained so. But although the differences which distinguished one from another were large and have never been extinguished, they came to be recognized as versions of, or as approximations to an emergent ideal character. From one point of view the history of modern Europe is the story of the emergence and dissolution of these associations; what used to be called the rise and fall of states. From another point of view it is the story of the emergence of a novel mode of association, of the exploration of the ambiguities of its character and of the reflective engagement to understand it. And in the course of time a state became eligible for the sort of enquiry Aristotle devoted to the ideal character called a *polis* or that which Maitland devoted to Township and Borough, enquiries concerned with practices and procedures but also with beliefs.

In these circumstances, the word 'State' (and its equivalent in other languages) was added to the European vocabulary of association and, after some hesitation began to be used alongside older expressions (such as 'realm' or 'principality') to denote these emergent associations. It began as a metaphor; like the word 'nation' in its modern meaning it pointed to an ideal character and identified it only in terms of its similarity to what was already familiar. A state was some sort of an 'estate', a tract of land and a condition of its inhabitants. But in order to describe this character, to recognize its most important characteristics, to distinguish between various forms of them and to specify the beliefs entailed, an extensive vocabulary had to be invoked or invented.

Many of its terms were invented and first used in relation to long defunct human associations thought to be in some sense precursors of modern states – an ancient Greek *polis*, a Biblical nation, a Persian or a Roman Empire, a medieval realm; and although in modern use something of their former meanings survives, they have acquired extended or contracted meanings which have sometimes been reflected in qualifying adjectives. Others of these terms (such as 'community', 'corporation', 'partnership' etc.) have been taken from the vocabulary of other kinds of association, religious or commercial. Words of common discourse (such as 'constitution' and 'constitutional') have been appropriated, given more precise meanings and put to use in order to specify emergent distinctions. Indeed, the whole European vocabulary of association has been ransacked for suitable expressions with which to describe and to appraise the formal character of a modern European state.

This character was puzzling and has never ceased to excite wonder as well as enquiry. But it was early perceived to have three main characteristics, each of which has acquired a vocabulary appropriate to itself: an office of authority, an apparatus of power, and a mode of association. But for a variety of reasons expressions (often etymologically distinguished) which properly belong to one of these vocabularies have been given a place which they cannot intelligibly occupy in one or both of the others. Commonly this confusion has been the outcome of inadvertence, a failure to observe the categorical differences between these characteristics and a consequent misunderstanding of their relationships to one another: the authority of an office confused with its engagements and with an apparatus of power, and all three confused with a mode of association. Elsewhere it has represented a denial of these differences or a design to recommend a certain understanding of one of these characteristics by using an expression which had come to carry with it respect or approval in connexion with another – for, of course, most of these words have acquired recommendatory or deprecatory as well as descriptive meanings and the discourse in which these vocabularies are used has always been concerned both with identification and with approval or disapproval. On other occasions a scanty vocabulary in respect of one of these characteristics has been enlarged not by appropriate invention but by inappropriate borrowing from another. Some words have acquired two distinct meanings and are thus eligible to occupy a proper place in more than one of these vocabularies, so long as these meanings are distinguished. And since consideration of these matters became a commonplace engagement which anyone may undertake, the terms of these vocabularies have for long enough been at the mercy of often negligent users. The words 'politics' and 'political', for example, already ambiguous in the Aristotelian vocabulary, are now merely rhetorical expressions, powerless to identify anything in particular. In these circumstances of considerable confusion some attempt to sort out these vocabularies may be worthwhile.

The second characteristic of a modern European state to be considered is the apparatus of governing annexed to the authoritative office of rule; that is, an instrument for implementing, not formulating and issuing, prescriptive utterances. The consideration here is neither authority, nor engagements but power.

The word 'power' may mean merely 'force' (such as that of wind or water), or it may denote the energy a man may intentionally exert to destroy, to manipulate or to overcome the resistance of an object (or of another man considered merely as an object), but in human affairs it stands for the ability to procure with certainty a wished-for response in the conduct of another. It has to do with substantive conduct; and since it is a relationship between human beings and depends upon both the ability and the disposition of the respondent to perform the wished-for action, this certainty can never be absolute and power can never be irresistible. The considerations in terms of which the wished-for response is sought have nothing to do with a shared understanding of the parties concerned as to its worth or its propriety (its character as a subscription to a recognized rule or procedure); they are neither more nor less than the beliefs of the respondent about the consequences to himself of compliance or non-compliance with the demand. Thus, there is a relationship of power between one who makes a demand threatening the respondent with some harmful consequence if he does not comply and a respondent who understands this and nothing else to be the case and who fears the threatened harmful consequence both because of his aversion from it and because he believes that there is the intention and the resources to implement the threat; or, between one whose demand is joined with the promise of a satisfaction to the respondent which he is so far unwilling to forego that he regards it as a need, which he has no other means of obtaining and which he believes there is the intention and the resources to provide; or, in a situation in which such fear of injury and such want elevated into need are combined. He who neither fears anything nor needs anything cannot be drawn into this relationship. Taken by itself this is a rare relationship which the absence of any conditions save instrumental considerations concerned with the satisfaction of substantive wants identifies as non-moral, or unconcerned with *mores*. But where it is moralized (that is, where the demand is made by one who occupies an office and is recognized also to have an antecedent right to make it) it may subsist as a subordinate consideration in imposing or subscribing to an obligation.

It is often suggested that all human association must be supposed to begin in the relationship of a potentate (or a class of potentates) and those over whom he or they exercise power, this being the only 'natural' (biological?) relationship; or that historical evidence goes to show that such a beginning is a not uncommon occurrence, the only alternative being a supposed spontaneous co-operative association. But it is safe to say that, in general, there is little to be said in favour of these speculative suggestions; and as an account of the emergence of modern European states, nothing at all. It is true that the early rulers of many of these states stood in some such power relationship to some of their 'new' subjects, and that Hobbes was provoked to consider the possibility of the emergence of a *civitas* out of the power relationship of conqueror and conquered, but no state emerged in this manner. The conquerors were always the occupants of some office of authority; mere potentates (such as Cesare Borgia whose power derived from the wealth of the papacy) were few and failed to establish themselves as rulers of states. In the total absence of the recognition of authority, power was never enough to create and maintain an association of human beings.

Nevertheless, the resources of power at the disposal of an office of rule are a consideration independent of its authority. An apparatus of power cannot, of course, endow such an office with authority; and although a recognition of its authority may be expected somewhat to diminish resistance to the obligations it imposes (and thus marginally reduce the occasion to exert power), it falls far short of securing continuous and exact subscription to demands of which no subject is required to approve. Machiavelli, believing that there were some simple devices by means of which power might be acquired, explored this consideration in respect of the rulers of the 'new' principalities of Italy. Their authority being regrettably minimal, they must make the best use of their also slender resources of power if they were to survive. And the situation of the rulers of the emergent states of Europe was not dissimilar. Their authority was not so considerable that the undertaking to maintain and enhance it could safely be neglected. Indeed, from then until now this has been one of their major (and not notably successful) concerns. And to create an efficient apparatus of power commensurate with their undertakings has been the second of their concerns, entered upon in the sixteenth century and continuously pursued. It constitutes the administrative histories of these states and it has evoked a sparce vocabulary concerned with the identification of the features of an apparatus of power common (for the most part) to all modern states.

The formal character of the power of an office of rule in a modern European state is no different from that exercised by any other human agency. A government is powerful in respect of the same considerations as any other human organization is powerful: in virtue of being able to formulate its demands clearly and make them known in utterances which reach and are readily understood by those who are to respond, to enlist their continuous support or to compel their continuous acquiescence, to act rapidly, economically and with the likelihood of achieving the wished-for outcome as little hindered as may be by the intrusion of unwanted consequences; in virtue of being able to collect the revenue it is authorized to collect and use its resources to employ efficient agents – advisors, directors, secretaries, deputies, administrators, registrars, accountants, inspectors, confidential agents, clerks, typists, messengers, porters, caretakers, warders, custodians, mechanics and assistants of all kinds; in virtue of having the use of instruments and procedures for collecting, recording, filing, retrieving, disseminating or concealing information of all sorts; and so on. This apparatus, the activities which go on in its component councils, committees, offices, *bureaux* etc., the expertise and the routines of those employed in them, the filing cabinets, the indexes, the safes, the telephones, the computers they use – none of it is different from what is to be found elsewhere. Indeed, this properly called 'machinery of government' emerged from the application of commercial techniques to the rudimentary administrative procedures and instruments of medieval kings and ecclesiastical chancelleries, and it now represents the participation of governments in procedures, instruments and devices of power all of which are at the disposal of anyone who can afford to use them. Nor is this apparatus of governing distinguished in being a notably unconditional exercise of power. Its employment is no less specified than that of a commercial corporation, and while it may enjoy certain immunities and a not inconsiderable opportunity of concealing malpractice, it may be subject to special conditions and the conduct of its officers is not exempt from the obligation to subscribe to the ordinary rules of the association. It is, however, unique in having the authorized monopoly of certain sources of power, the chief of which are military force and the power to execute the judgments of a court of law: a modern European state gives no recognition to private armies or private prisons.

This characteristic of a modern state, the authorized apparatus of power at the disposal of its office of government, is, then, a distinguishable and an independent characteristic. Power is not identifiable with authority and it is not even among the considerations in terms of which an office of government is recognized to have authority. The difference is categorial. The contingent features of its apparatus of power are neither formally nor substantively related to the constitutional shape of the office of rule. The continuous expansion of the apparatus of power at the disposal of all modern governments, in virtue of which the least powerful is better equipped with the means of implementing its designs than the most powerful of earlier times, is not a reflection of constitutional change, it relates merely to the increase in the ability to control men and things characteristic of the five centuries of modern European history. And the multiplicity of constitutional shapes characteristic of modern Europe is not matched by *corresponding* differences in organizations of power. There are, indeed, differences and what they relate to I shall consider later; but they do not relate to differences of constitutional shape.

The apparatus of power annexed to an office of government is, for the most part, understood and spoken about in terms of an appropriate vocabulary of expressions designed to identify its features and to specify its organization. Few of them are unique to this apparatus: factories and even universities, no less than associations recognized as states, are said to be 'policed', and a so-called 'chain of command' is commonplace. It is true that the only verbal invention of modern times designed to identify an apparatus of power annexed to an office of government is the bastard expression 'bureaucracy' which etymologically suggests that it belongs, like 'democracy' or 'oligarchy', to the vocabulary of authority. But only the already muddled are deceived into mistaking it for the name of a constitutional shape. The genuine and not inconsiderable confusion springs from three, not necessarily related, failures to recognize categorical distinctions. First, there is the common failure to distinguish between power and authority which reveals itself in the belief that there is a positive or negative relationship of identity or correspondence between the constitutional shape of an office of rule and the features of the apparatus of power annexed to it. Thus, it is thought that the *lettre de cachet* is a characteristically king-shaped feature, or it is said: 'The year is 1984. England has its concentration camps. Democracy has disappeared.' This, of course, is contingent muddle. There was nothing uniquely king-shaped about the apparatus of power which Thomas Cromwell began to assemble in sixteenth-century England, and nothing either 'republican' or 'protectorial' about Oliver's major-generals. But its fatality so far as intelligible discourse is concerned lies in its being categorical muddle. Secondly, there is the belief that an office of government is itself nothing other than an apparatus of power designed to control human conduct by means of the employment or the threat of employment of physical compulsion. This mis-understanding of an office of government, in order to conceal the nakedness of its error, has evoked the disposition to use expressions which belong to the vocabu-lary of authority – words denoting constitutional shapes, and particularly the word 'sovereign' – to identify or to qualify organizations or features of organizations of power, with the consequent intellectual confusion. And, no doubt, both these confusions owe something to that misappropriation of constitutional expressions in which they are used to identify methods of government understood in terms of the substantive character of their prescriptions, the interests they promote or protect and the satisfactions they distribute. When 'democracy' means a method of gov-ernment designed to reflect the will or promote the interests of the majority it is but a small additional perversion to make it mean an apparatus of power with this engagement. Thirdly, there is the categorical misunderstanding of the apparatus of power in which power is denied the character of a relationship between human beings and is understood as a dynamic process in terms of pushes and pulls, pres-sure and resistance to pressure, friction, velocity of 'communication' and causal linkages. In short, the exploration of the theme of power, like that of authority, in relation to a modern European state has been an encounter of considerable confusion.

The third aspect of a modern European state is its character as an association of human beings. The consideration here is neither the authority of an office of government (its constitutional shape) nor the apparatus of power annexed to it, but the terms and conditions of a human relationship; not the *causa foederis* but the *modus foederis* of an association.

Human association is always in terms of beliefs and of ascertainable conditions; it cannot be understood in the terms of mechanics or chemistry, and there can be no unconditional human association such as the current use of the words 'social' and 'society' suggests. Where it is the outcome of a choice to be associated these conditions are at once the understood terms of association and the terms of a self-understanding of the associates; for example, the relationship of persons who choose to be associated in respect of the pursuit of an identified common purpose and consequently understand themselves, in this connexion, as voluntary servants of this undertaking. Where, on the other hand, there is a recognition of being related but without a choice to be related, the persons concerned recognize their situation in terms of a name (both common and proper) identifying the association and themselves in terms of some understanding of what is expected of them: 'I am a Cherokee and this is what it means'. And if (as in tribal association) the absence of the relationship is an unknown situation, this may be as far as the associates, as associates, are disposed to go in understanding it and themselves. A modern Euro-pean state in its emergence was for most of the associates both an unchosen asso-ciation and one of not inconsiderable novelty. Its proper name might or might not be familiar, but the word 'state' identified an unavoidable association of almost unknown character and of a character still in the making. Consequently, to explore the character of this relationship, to consider not only what in fact it was but also what it might become and perhaps what it should be made to become, was an engagement which might invoke the attention of anyone whose curiosity or ambition went beyond a wish to know what might be expected of him from day to day.

The resources available for pursuing this enquiry were not negligible. The emergence of a state was not always so abrupt as to destroy the worth of analogy with what went before in trying to understand it. This was particularly the case in England where the character of the *communis regni* had long been a matter of reflection and where the conviction that *lex facit regnum* was not only strong enough to mediate the passage to modernity but, surviving some antinomian adventures, remained to distinguish English thought on this subject until well into the nineteenth century. Elsewhere, the past delivered a message which pointed, but without notable conviction, in a different direction, or one so hesitant that it afforded nothing much in the way of guidance. Here consideration of the mode of association identified by the word 'state' became a more speculative enquiry. But those who undertook it seriously had at their disposal some ideas and some words in which to do so. Indeed, current ways of thinking may be said to have presented them with an alternative. A state might be recognized as what was known as a *societas*; that is, human beings associated solely in being related to one another in terms of their common acknowledgement of the authority of rules of conduct ('law'). Or it might be recognized as what was then known as a *universitas* or corporation aggregate; that is, human beings associated in terms of their joint pursuit or promotion of a chosen substantive purpose or interest. And here some specification of the purpose would be called for. But although there were writers well aware of a difference between this enquiry into a state as a mode of association and others such as those concerned with the authority of its office of government or with its apparatus of power and who were not ignorant of this distinction between modes of association, the enquiry itself was soon plunged into confusion from which it has never recovered.

The ever-changing features of this confusion are too many to catalogue; I will mention only a few. First, the distinction between a *societas* (or as it came later to be called, a 'civil association') and a *universitas* (or a corporation aggregate) was familiar, but when it was recruited for use in this enquiry about a state it proved to be elusive. In particular, the erroneous conviction that all human association must be in terms of a common substantive purpose suggested that this distinction, if it specified anything, specified merely a difference between purposes. And the proponents of a state as a *societas* too often mistook their concern for that of presenting *societas* as a kind of purposive association. Moreover, the observation that rules of conduct are a feature of both these modes of association, together with the neglect of the difference between the instrumental rules of purposive association and the non-instrumental rules of a *societas*, reinforced the obscurity of the distinction. And further, the notion of *universitas* had to be emancipated from certain disqualifying features (its voluntary character and its character as the creature of legal authority) before it could be used in relation to a modern state. Secondly, the significance of this distinction was considerably reduced and the temptation to blur it increased by the observation that a modern European state as it emerged from a medieval realm or from a patrimonial estate exhibited features which suggested both these modes of association; the proportions might vary, but nowhere was it manifestly the one to the total exclusion of the other. Thirdly, the recognition that it was circumstantially impossible for a particular state to survive as a purposive association in one idiom was often mistaken for the conclusion that it could not sustain this character in any idiom. For example, the conviction of the *politiques* that France could not survive as a *universitas* in a religious idiom was too hastily translated into the conclusion that it must become and be understood to be a civil association.

But the confusion which has overtaken this enquiry has not sprung from the indistinctness, the inadequacy or the inappropriateness of the modes of association canvassed (either as descriptions or as recommendations) in relation to modern European states. It is a confusion between this enquiry, concerned with a state as a mode of association, and the other categorically different enquiry concerned with the authority of an office of government. And its chief sources have been, first, the disposition to conduct it in words which belong to the inappropriate vocabulary of authority; secondly, when an appropriate vocabulary of its own was invented, the disposition to regard its terms as constitutional or authority words; and thirdly, the intrusion of terms – such as the word 'nation' – which purport to disclose conditions of association but which specify no mode of association.

The categorical distinction between the terms of association and the authority of the office of government has been obscured on account of a confusion between the constitutional shape of an office of government and another quite different aspect of such an office which *is* necessarily related to the mode of association, namely, the character of its engagement. Thus, governing an association devoted to the pursuit of a substantive purpose, in which the associates are related in terms of the joint pursuit of this purpose, is necessarily a managerial engagement. Its government, however it may be constituted, is concerned with the exploitation of the appropriate resources of the association in the furtherance of its purpose, with the actions and utterances in which the associates shall currently pursue their joint purpose and with rules of conduct recognized to be instrumental to the undertaking. And governing an association which has no substantive purpose, in which the associates are not related in terms of any common undertaking, cannot be managerial engagement; there are no resources to be exploited and no conduct to be directed so that it contributes to the success of an undertaking. The engagement of its government, however it may be constituted, is nothing other than the care and custody of the necessarily non-instrumental rules which are the terms of association. In short, the mode of association and the engagement of its government are necessarily related; to enquire into or to specify the one is to enquire into or to specify the other. But there is no such relationship between the constitutional shape of an office of government and the character of its engagement, and hence none between the terms in which such an office is recognized to have authority and the terms in which the associates are joined. There is nothing whatever in the character of either a *societas* or a *universitas* which requires its government to have a democratic, an oligarchic or any other particular shape. And the electoral rules which may encapsulate beliefs about the terms in which an office of government may be recognized to have authority do nothing to specify the engagements of those who legitimately occupy it.

Nevertheless, much of the enquiry concerned with a modern state in respect of its mode of association has been conducted in the language of constitutional shapes. Montesquieu, for example, a writer more consciously concerned than most others with this enquiry, used the word *monarchie* to denote a state understood as a *societas* and *république* for a state understood as a *universitas*, its substantive purpose being specified as *la vertu*. Of course, he did not think that a civil association must have a king-shaped office of government or that a state as a purposive association required some sort of republican shaped government, but the confusion is neither unique nor innocuous. Those who now use the word 'democracy' to stand for a constitutional shape, a method of governing, an apparatus of power and a mode of association follow in his footsteps; they may not confuse themselves but they are agents of confusion. And the new expressions which have been invented and the old which have been seconded to describe or to recommend a state in respect of its terms of association and a government in respect of its engagement have not been conspicuously successful either in avoiding this confusion or in specifying what they purport to specify.

The traditional expressions available to modern writers with which to identify a purposive association and its ruler in respect of his managerial engagement were 'lordship' (*seigneurie*) and 'lord' (*seigneur*). And for a long time the expression 'seigneurial government' was used analogically to identify the engagement of the ruler of a state understood as an enterprise association. No doubt these words owed their place in this European vocabulary to the fact that all kings were also *Seigneurs*, but since no king was recognized to be a *seigneur* in respect of his kingdom, the expression 'seigneurial government' was commonly used to describe Turkish or Muscovite rule. Its meaning, however, was soon obscured. A totally inappropriate quality of 'absoluteness' (whether of authority or of power was never made clear) was attributed to it, and it was confused with 'despotism', that is, with an office of rule in respect of its authority. But in spite of their analogical cogency the words 'lordship' and 'lord' were abandoned as identifications of a state as an enterprise association and government as a managerial engagement on account of the disrepute into which they fell. The preferred expression came to be 'enlightened government'. In this expression, beginning as a self-description of the engagement of an ambitious king and standing in the end for the management by Baconian or St Simonian *illuminati* of a state understood as a development corporation, the idea of a state as a *universitas* declared its modernity. But it did not escape categorical ambiguity. An 'enlightened' régime as such was commonly spoken of as a 'despotism' (that is, as a constitutional shape), and the enlightenment of the *illuminati* was recognized, in a supposedly Platonic idiom, not only as a description of their engagement but also of the terms of the authority of their office. Of the subsequent expressions used to identify or to recommend a state as a *universitas* – socialism, national socialism, fascism, totalitarianism, communism etc. – none have escaped this ambiguity and the cogency of some has depended upon it. Each is connected with an allegedly appropriate office of authority, although it may be suspected that the expressions used to identify this corresponding constitutional shape (democracy, social democracy, the authority of a 'leader' or of a 'Party' or that of a *völkisch* or 'proletarian' character) are method-of-governing words masquerading as authority words. And it must be confessed that the most recent addition to this vocabulary of purposive association and managerial government, the word 'teleocracy', is not an altogether happy invention: it is etymologically unfortunate in suggesting that the end pursued is itself the terms in which its office of government could be alleged to have authority. And this, of course, is impossible.

A state understood as a *societas* and the appropriate engagement of its office of government was obscured and compromised at the outset by its alleged connexion with a king-shaped office of authority, and it was later further obscured in the muddle which related it to a so-called 'capitalist' economy. And, for long enough to do it almost irreparable damage, those who explored its character were mispersuaded that it, also, must be a purposive association and devoted themselves to a specification of its purpose. But the expressions in which it came to be identified – 'civil association' and *der Rechtsstaat*, for example – revealed themselves vulnerable to other ambiguities. What the word 'civil' signifies here had lost its precision long before it was destroyed in being equated with 'desired' or 'desirable' in the common use of the expression 'civil rights'. The word 'law' does not itself disclose the categorical difference between the instrumental rules of a *universitas* and the noninstrumental, moral rules of a *societas*, and it is often not made to do so in the writings of those who have explored the idea of a *Rechsstaat*. And the expression 'nomocracy' may be thought to suffer from something of the same sort of defect in this connexion as 'teleocracy' does in the other.

Moreover, the enquiry concerning the character of a state as a mode of association has suffered damage in being conducted in empty, irrelevant or ambiguous terms. the word 'social' is empty (alleged association without any specific terms of association), and the word 'liberal' has been emptied of any exact meaning in relation to the engagement of an office of government; neither is capable of identifying any mode of association. A distinction between modes of association has been sought in the obscure and certainly irrelevant distinction between a 'pluralistic' association and a 'sovereign' office of government. And the enquiry has been conducted in such ambiguous terms as 'freedom' or the distinction between 'public' and 'private', each of which has, or may be alleged to have, a precise meaning in respect of different modes of association but are worthless for specifying a mode of association unless and until that meaning is spelled out and detached from any reference to the constitutional shapes of offices of government.

For example, both a *universitas* and a *societas* may each be identified in terms of a characteristic 'freedom', but not in terms of a distinction between a so-called 'positive' and 'negative' freedom, and not in terms of the contingent shape of an office of government or the quality of its authority. The 'sovereign' quality of the authority of the office has no bearing upon the characteristic 'freedom' of a mode of association. To specify a mode of human association in terms of 'freedom' is to identify the manner in which it preserves the link between belief and conduct. Thus, an associate joined with others in the pursuit of a common substantive purpose is 'free' if and because his situation is one of his own choosing and because he can extricate himself from it by a choice of his own. Freedom here is conceptually tied to the choice to be and to remain associated. And herein lies the main hindrance to the idea of a *state* as at once 'free' association and enterprise association. But where the mode of association is that of *societas*, the 'freedom' of an associate lies precisely in the absence of any common substantive purpose. The terms of association here are the acknowledgement of an obligation to recognize the authority of rules which prescribe, not satisfactions to be sought or actions to be performed, but non-instrumental (that is, moral) conditions to be subscribed to in seeking self-chosen satisfaction and in performing self-chosen actions; an obligation which is not denied in non-subscription, a subscription which is an understanding of the conditions prescribed by the rule and is itself a self-chosen performance, and conditions of which he is not, as an associate, required to approve.

But aside from these difficulties concerned with the specification of alternative understandings of the character of a modern state as an association of human beings, the consideration of this theme has been hampered by other embarrass-ments. As it emerged, a modern state was beyond doubt an ambiguous association, a strange and perhaps unstable mixture of civil and enterprise association. To make it intelligible in this character was an adventure in historical understanding. But the explicitly political questions were concerned with what it might or should be made to become. At first it seemed likely that these questions would be answered without having been directly asked: a state was destined to become what the ambitions of rulers of all sorts, with their attention turned upon other matters, might inadvertently make of it. Their attempts to grapple with what was known as 'the problems of the poor' or their military adventures might inadvertently turn it into a *universitas* of some sort. Nevertheless, these questions became a matter of serious concern. This concern was somewhat compromised by being ill-distinguished from a concern with the terms in which an office of government might be acknow-ledged to have authority, but it was more severely hindered by uncertainty and confusion about the considerations in terms of which these questions might be answered. Thus, some time ago, it began to be distracted by the doctrine that the becoming of a modern state was an evolutionary process about which something might be known but little or nothing done, and by the report of those who had studied the process itself and were well-informed about its direction that a state was an association on its way to becoming an unambiguous *universitas* in the idiom of a development corporation. From this interruption it has not yet fully recovered. And I call it an interruption because human associations are not processes but prac-tices intelligible and acceptable in terms of the self-understanding of the associates.

How is Critical Theory Possible? Theodor W. Adorno and Concept Formation in Sociology

Gillian Rose

University of Sussex

The late 1960s and 1970s brought a substantial widening of the intellectual currents influencing UK political science, with an opening particularly to European and Marxist-influenced currents in theory terms and a more general shift towards political sociology research linked to larger themes of state formation and transformation in empirical research. Rose's paper reflects this newer current, focusing on the work of Adorno (a key member of the Frankfurt school) and asking how his critical theory assault on established ways of acquiring knowledge of society can survive his own critique. How can an independent view of contemporary society be formulated in a situation where social structures so extensively determine the production of knowledge? Rose's treatment of this key problem is quite difficult but foreshadows later parallel themes raised by critics of post-modernism.

Adorno's criticism of sociologies which employ 'total' concepts is [...] contrasted with his own central dependence on the concept of totality. Even though Adorno's concepts, are 'total' in a way which could make his own position less compelling, I offer an interpretation of that position which meets this challenge. Lastly, I consider Adorno's discussion of the concepts 'static' and 'dynamic' as sociological categories and his discussion of the problem of value judgements and the concept of 'value' as a sociological category in order to show his principles in action.

Adorno [does not] accept Marx's ideas as an *a priori* theory of society, but rather [as] *presenting a dialectic*: instances of how various modes of cognition, including Marxist and non-dialectical social sciences, each of which if taken in isolation would be inadequate and distorting, might be confronted with each other precisely on the basis of an awareness of their individual limitations, in order to yield an insight into social processes. This is the movement of knowledge in the second sense – cognition by means of the analysis of reified theories and concepts. Adorno calls this approach 'the immanent method'.

The Concept of Totality and 'Total' Concepts

Adorno is fighting on several fronts: against the sociology of knowledge and its 'total' concept of ideology; against systems, philosophical and sociological, which claim to capture reality totally in their concepts; against positivisms and formalisms which give priority to the unity of methodological devices at the expense of the object to be known.

© *Political Studies Association, 2000.*
Published by Blackwell Publishers, 108 Cowley Road, Oxford OX4 1JF, UK and 350 Main Street, Malden, MA 02148, USA

Yet does not the immanent method itself depend on 'total' concepts? Adorno considers that the working class is no longer the 'universal class' in that it does not possess even the possibility of developing knowledge of its role as the class which really could act in the name of the whole society. There is no longer a possibility of privileged knowledge in this sense. The status of knowledge *sui generis* is attributed instead to intellectual and artistic phenomena: 'The only way to pass philosophically into social categories is by deciphering the truth content of philosophical ones'. Adorno substitutes his 'immanent method' for any class analysis or any relating of superstructural phenomena to class structure. The state of society is derived from an understanding of intellectual and artistic phenomena, not by locating them in a social structure which is independently known. Such phenomena are thus granted a 'total' status. Their validity is not diminished by their class character. They themselves offer the possibility of attaining universal knowledge, knowledge of the whole society and of all its possibilities.

Adorno quite explicitly depends on the concept of totality. 'Totality' is the perspective according to which he believes that every individual social phenomenon must be conceived. He is also committed to the substantive thesis of the increasingly complete reification of the mind and of society. Can he therefore avoid the charge which he makes against the sociology of knowledge that it 'calls everything in question and criticizes nothing', or that 'the causes of human suffering ... will be glossed over in the lament over reification'? There is, however, a difference between the 'total' concept of ideology which Adorno indicts as a methodological device and his own thesis of the *totalization* of ideology. Adorno's views are not analogous to the traditional Marxist understanding of art, law and other superstructural phenomena. They are analogous to Marx's critique of political economy. For Marx political economy both revealed and distorted the true social relations of men, while his thought and ultimately that of the proletarian class had a chance of understanding the true relations. For Adorno there is only one ideology, bourgeois ideology, which both reveals and distorts those relations. His criticism of total concepts and his own use of the concept of totality are consistent with the definitions of the concept and the object.

Total Concepts

Adorno criticizes relativisms, absolutisms, and positivisms. By 'the sociology of knowledge' he understands a mode of cognition which uses the concept of ideology in a relative manner, that is, which describes any intellectual phenomenon or consciousness of society as determined by its social location or interest. In the 'sociology of knowledge' the concept of ideology does not have a notion of true or false consciousness. Adorno claims that, 'The concept of ideology is only meaningful in relation to the truth or untruth of what it covers'. Thus the concept of ideology developed in the 'sociology of knowledge' is not fulfilled by what it is being used to cover. This is Adorno's general notion of ideology: any concept or idea or set of ideas which is used as if it were rationally identical with its object. The relativist concept of ideology has no heuristic value, because it prevents the understanding of 'socially necessary illusion', because the concept seems to cover its object. For only if the necessity of the illusion is understood, can the non-illusory conditions be derived and the conditions that produced the illusion be perceived. This is the immanent method: 'Socially necessary illusion can only be spoken of relative to what would not be illusion, hence only relative to what has its index in that illusion.' The sociology of knowledge has taken the dialectical concept of ideology from Marx and translated it into a classificatory one. Adorno considers that criticizing relativism is the most important task for non-identity thinking: 'Drastic criticism of relativism is the paradigm of determinate negation'.

In criticizing positivism, Adorno distinguishes between 'critical sociology' and sociology as ordinarily understood. Critical sociology or theory is oriented to the idea of society as a subject in spite of all experience of reification, and critical sociology gives direct expression to that experience. Non-critical sociology, on the other hand, accepts reification, repeats it in its methods, and thereby loses the perspective according to which society and its laws reveal themselves. For sociology in general has a double character: as the subject of all knowledge, precisely as the bearer of logical universality, it is at the same time the object. It is this fundamental perspective which positive (non-critical) sociology ignores. Society is subjective because it refers to the men who form it. Its principle of organization refers to subjective consciousness. Its most universal form of abstraction – logic – refers to an essentially intersubjective consciousness. Society is objective because of its underlying structure, because its own subjectivity is not transparent to it, because it has no total subject and because its organization prevents the formation of one. Positive sociology is unable to perceive this. It treats society as if it were an object which can be defined from the outside, even though it is potentially a self-determining subject. Literally positive sociology objectifies (*vergegenständlicht*) that which causes objectification and by which objectification may be explained. Such substitution of society as subject by society as object constitutes the reified consciousness of sociology. It is not recognized that, by turning to the subject as to an object standing opposed and alien to itself, the subject as the object of sociology becomes an Other. Thus society's objectivity is aberrant. Adorno is not merely saying that it follows from the double nature of society as subject and object of knowledge that any mode of cognition which operates solely on the basis of society as object takes what is in effect a determining process to be a predetermined object. His thesis that the object is untransparent to subjectivity is also a thesis about the condition of society. The concept of the object (society) is not fulfilled by the object to which positivist sociology applies it. In this way positive sociology constitutes its object and proceeds to classify it and describe it, attributing properties to it as if it were an object in itself, instead of examining the processes of its formation. This is reified sociology. Adorno does not deny that this sociology has its *fundament in re*, that such sociology describes the *appearance* of society correctly.

Adorno criticizes systems of absolute knowledge which claim that they express or cover everything in their concepts: 'The slightest remnant of non-identity sufficed to deny an identity conceived as total'. They are systems which incorporate a principle of universal explanation (*umfassendes Erklärungsprinzip*). They include everything in concepts, which are conceived substantively and not, though this is often assumed, as mere conceptual tools. This results from a desire to control the world. Comte, for example, explicitly claimed that his sociology was constructed on the basis of a desire for control (*Herrschaftsanspruch*). Durkheim's sociology has similar aims. Notions such as collective consciousness and society as a reality *sui generis* are total and comprehensive principles for explaining everything, which in Adorno's opinion explain nothing.

The Concept of Totality

The 'total' concepts of non-dialectical sociologies can themselves be derived from the increasingly total society and, vice versa, that society can be derived from them. Adorno's refusal to define concepts is consistent with his aim and with his criticism of other sociologies. He seeks to avoid 'constructing' the object by the categories of the science, and wishes also to avoid attributing static, invariant qualities to the object. He shuns investigating 'an object with an instrument which its own construction decides in advance just what the object is – a simple case of circularity'. Adorno omits definitions, because to define a concept would be to stipulate what the object is, which would be to imply that the concept must be rationally identical with its object. Instead Adorno advocates an approach which involves taking certain concepts as given and perceiving the non-identity inherent in their use. This is not a case of circularity in the sense he indicts. Concepts 'constitute' their objects only in the sense in which the objects may be derived from the non-identity in the concept: 'Dialectically, knowledge of the non-identical lies exactly in that it also identifies but to a greater extent and in a different way from identity thinking'. Adorno has a further positive expression of the reason for not defining concepts. He frequently quotes Nietzsche who said that 'all those concepts in which a total process is semiotically [*semiotisch*] embraced escape definition; only that is definable which has no history'. The concept of society is such a concept *par excellence*.

The concepts of totality, essence and appearance, universal and particular, abstract and concrete are the concepts which yield the dialectical perspective. They are intrinsically interrelated. Any society is a totality from the perspective of its interchange with the natural world (*Stoffwechsel mit der Natur*), an interchange which results in fundamental processes within any society by which it 'produces and reproduces itself'. Society is a totality in which all individuals are dependent on the totality which they form. The totality is determined by the basic mechanisms of interchange and exchange, to which Adorno refers, instead of specifying the mode of production, as Marx had done. Because this notion of totality does not imply that society is a reality *sui generis*, it is not a holist view of society. Individuals and individual phenomena 'express' the universal; they are not merely particulars denoted by it. The individual is at the same time universal and particular.

Critical cognition of society emphasizes the processes of mediation between the totality and the individual – and the essence and the appearance – without diminishing the reality of any of these. The concept of totality is thus the *same* as the concept of the mediation of the particular. Where capitalism is concerned, the task of critical sociology is 'to disclose the mediations of objective categories'. This is another way of stating the basic characteristic of non-identity thinking. To perceive the mediation of the individual by the totality and of the appearance by the essence, is to perceive how the existence of individuals, or the façade of society, does not fulfil its concepts, how unequal things are made equal by the prevailing form of commodity exchange and by the corresponding conceptual apparatus of that society. Because dialectic, in Adorno's words, 'strives to master theoretically in its procedure the antinomial relation of the universal and particular', his concept of totality is not a superordinating category. Totality in Adorno's usage is neither a 'comprehensive principle of explanation' nor an 'arbitrary globalism' (*unverbindlich Globalen*). On the contrary, because it is another way of reaching the non-identical in the relation between concept and object, the concept of totality is not a heuristic device at all. It is substantively critical.

Adorno is also committed to the thesis that capitalist society has become more total. This is the substantive thesis that society increasingly controls and constrains individuals. The critical perspective of totality is still relevant. It 'seeks to save or help to bring forth what does not obey the totality, what contradicts it or what first forms itself as the potential of individuation which does not yet exist'. This is the double meaning of the concept of totality, or it is to say that the concept both applies and does not apply. Adorno calls this the applying and not applying of a concept a contradiction. He argues that such contradiction must not be eliminated for the sake of an ideal theory without contradictions. This does not, however, involve a denial of the law of non-contradiction.

Durkheim made the totality of society, conceived substantively, into the *essence* of society, while for Adorno the task is to look at the processes of mediation by means of which the totality comes to *appear* to be the essence of the social:

> Totality is, provocatively formulated, society as thing-in-itself with all the guilt of reifications. Precisely because this thing-in-itself is not the total social subject although its heteronomous nature continues, it has a moment of indissolubility which Durkheim onesidedly explained as the essence of the social.[1]

Society is taken mistakenly to be an object-in-itself. Another way to make these distinctions is to say that the concept of totality must not be ontologized or made into a primeval reality (*zu einem ansichseienden Ersten gemacht werden darf*). This does not deny that the concept of totality refers to a real social totality. It is to emphasize that this totality is not invariant, fixed; and that it is not rationally identical with its concept.

Adorno believes that by comparison with early capitalism, the present mode of production does not produce visibly distinguishable social classes. This is due to the increasing power of capital in the spheres of mind and public opinion. Adorno's concepts are 'total' in the sense that he is criticizing the appearance of society and our universally prevalent paradigmatic mode of thinking and is opposing another albeit immanent dimension to these features of society, a dimension which cannot even be *imputed* to an ideal-typical class consciousness, as Lukács had done in 1924. His concepts are 'total', too, because he does not oppose to the concepts of the façade his own theoretical concepts, but 'transcends the concept by means of the concept' or *thinks* the non-identity in the concept and object. Yet the thesis of the totalized society results in concepts which, if 'total', are still critical, and which operate differently from the 'total' concept of ideology. Adorno's concepts are immanent, while the 'total' concept of ideology is 'transcendent': 'it calls culture as a whole into question from outside under the general notion of ideology'.

While Adorno's propositions about totality can be unpacked to show a reference to the exchange mechanism, there is in his writings a crucial shift away from Marx in the status granted to concepts. The thesis that human needs are not totally con-trolled is equivalent to saying that the 'use-value of commodities has lost its last spontaneous [*naturwüchsig*] self-evidence' or, 'If commodities consist of exchange value and use-value, then in advanced capitalist society an illusion of pure use-value, as displayed by cultural goods, has been substituted for pure exchange value. This exchange value has deceptively taken over the function of use-value'. Adorno believes that there is no satisfactory theory of advanced capitalist society because there is no longer a satisfactory theory of value. The difficulties in grounding the formation of classes without a theory of surplus value are prohibitive. There is no free market and hence no genuine exchange in the sense of Marx's description of a 'fair' exchange: 'Everything is one [*Alles ist eins*] ... today the forces of production and the relations of production are one ... material production, distribution, con-sumption are ruled together'. *Prima facie*, a Durkheimian model of society emerges: 'The still unindividuated tribal spirit of primitive societies, pressed by the civilized ones to reproduce itself in them, is planned and released by postindividual collect-ivism'. The 'total control' of social relations implies that exchange relations no longer depend on 'freely alienable' forces of production. Such a totally controlled society would conform more to the model of a primitive or customary status society. Identity thinking, as described by Adorno, has affinities with Durkheim's insight into the way society endows us with concepts and imposes their hold on us. However, Adorno stresses that it is quite different to postulate total control in a pre-individualistic and post-individualistic society: 'I am not maintaining anything similar to the tendency in cultural anthropology to transfer by means of a specified system of coordinates, the centralizing and total character of many primitive societies to western civilization. Even when one cherishes so few illusions as I do about the gravitations towards total forms and the decline of the individual, the differences between a pre-individual and a post-individual society are still decisive'.

In fact Adorno's emphasis on the compulsive nature of concepts is critical in another sense besides the perception of their non-identity. It is critical in the basic description of their imposition, but in a Nietzschean not a Durkheimian manner: '... this social character of categories of thought is not, as Durkheim asserts, an expression of social solidarity, but evidence of the inscrutable unity of society and domination'[2] It was Nietzsche's view that our concepts are instruments arising from a will to identity. Similarly Adorno says, 'The will to identity works in each synthesis'. In his hands, too, it becomes a short step from Marx's idea of commodity fetishism as a necessary illusion (*notwendiger Schein*), to the very Nietzschean idea that 'Illusion is the most *efficacious* reality'.

Adorno quotes Nietzsche on the reason why concepts are understood to be invariant: '... the higher must not grow out of the lower, it must not be grown [out of something else] at all ... Moral: everything of the first rank must be *causa sui*. The origin out of something else is regarded as an objection, as a sign of question-able value. All highest values are of the first rank, none of the highest notions – the notion of what is, of the unconditioned, of the true, of the perfect – none of these can have become [i.e. undergone a process of formation]; each must consequently be *causa sui*'.[3] Adorno comments that this mode of thinking 'arises from real domination'. The idea that concepts hide their origins, that they are masks is taken over by Adorno from Nietzsche, too: 'The object, the positive expression of non-identity, is a terminological mask'.[4]

Adorno concedes that identity thinking is the only conceivable mode of thinking. This idea is fundamental to Nietzsche's description and criticism of thought. Adorno thus confronts the difficult question: how is it possible to think differently about man and society in the way that the Marxist theory of man and society demands? How can we do this if, as J. Mepham has said, 'ideology is not a collection of discrete falsehoods but a matrix of thought firmly grounded in the forms of our social life and organized within a set of interdependent categories? We are not aware of these systematically generative interconnections because our awareness is grounded through them'.[5] Non-identity thinking in this case can be no more than 'a groping for the preponderance of the object',[6] for the conditions of rational identity.

Sociological Concepts – Exemplars: Static and Dynamic

Adorno's ideas may be seen in operation in his discussions of *Static and Dynamic as Sociological Categories*, and of the problem of values in sociology. These concepts provide a significant contrast, because in using them Adorno demonstrates the critical perspective by analysing the reified categories of static and dynamic while rejecting as a 'heteronomous reification' the concept of value whether it means value-judgement or value of a thing.

The discussion of static and dynamic substantiates Adorno's claims that critical theory retains concepts without making them into a rigid schema, and without sanctioning them either immediately or ultimately. The categories of other sociologies are shown to contain antinomies and thus to transcend themselves. The state of society can be derived from them and they can be derived from that condition.

The idea of dividing knowledge of society into two branches, social statics and social dynamics, originated in Comte's works and extends into twentieth century sociology. Social phenomena which arise from basic human needs fall under static categories and obey static laws, while all social forms which correspond to specific types of socialization are dynamic. This reduces dynamic moments to an inferior status, while the selection of the major categories as static ones amounts to a substantive thesis of social invariants and the omission of anything which is not invariant. This is the ontological imperialism of identity thinking which occurs even when the mode of thinking confines itself ostensibly to classification. The classificatory concepts are attributed to the society. The determinate existent is 'added together' out of the general concepts. The object is thought to exist in itself, whereas what has happened is that the mind, eager for order, has composed social facts out of static and dynamic components.

A view of the totality, of the mediation of each category, will show how these categories developed. This is the critical approach: to show how categories have arisen by deriving them from the historical process. It is to see that these concepts are not fulfilled by the object they cover, to see the non-identity in the concept. In this case the historical process is commodity exchange. The commodity falls under the abstract formula of social static and hence appears to exist in itself. It has not been examined: it has simply arisen from the process of exchange. Marx himself was seeking to prevent the absolutizing of social conditions that occurs when static categories are constructed; his polemic against Proudhon can be applied to Comtean sociology equally well. The dualism for which he reproached Proudhon between eternal ideas as categories of pure reason and 'men and their practical life' agrees in method as well as content with the dualism of static and dynamic. These abstractions also describe a real social situation. Thus both in Marx's and in Adorno's dialectic a theory of invariants has its place – the place of a negative ontology.

Value as a Heteronomous Reification

Adorno discusses both the question of value-judgements and the question of the value of a thing in his introduction to the German translation of Durkheim's *Sociology and Philosophy*. Adorno points out antinomies or immanent contradictions in Durkheim's ideas, often by showing that although many of Durkheim's positions are similar to Hegel's, Durkheim fails to develop their dialectical, critical implications.

Adorno argues that there is a contradiction in Durkheim's views on evaluation in sociology. However, this particular contradiction does not reveal the non-identity in the concept and the object. It involves a rejection of the concept as a concept which has the possibility of the autonomous status that obtains when the concept is rationally identical with its object. The concept of values in science is thus denied a genuine cognitive role. Adorno's point is not that judgements of existence and judgements of value are inseparable. It is that the very question of their separability or inseparability is illegitimate. This follows from the basic characterisation of paradigmatic thinking as identity thinking: 'The claim to truth and the rejection of untruth of the simple logical judgement is already constituted in the procedure which the cliché allots to values separated from their base'.[7] The 'claim to truth' is the utopian moment intrinsic to the concept, that is, rational identity with its object. There is no 'concept' of 'values'. All there can be is 'a concrete process of cognition where what is decided by the confrontation of the thing with what it claims to be by itself according to its concept, is thus decided by immanent criticism'. Adorno grants that Durkheim himself believed, 'There are not two ways of thinking and judging, one for establishing existence and one for its estimation'. Durkheim was thus inconsistent on the question of evaluation.

When Durkheim discusses the value of a thing, Adorno argues that Durkheim's failure to refer to the economic structure of society leads him to such positions as 'Luxuries are by nature costly'. Value is attributed to a thing as a property. This statement occurs in a passage where Durkheim is clearly rejecting it; he says that if values were determined by utility, the value accorded to luxuries becomes inexplicable and luxuries appear to be costly by nature – a patent absurdity. Durkheim describes this position and others as sharing a 'fundamental principle'. They 'all equally presuppose that the value of a thing is inherent in and expresses the nature of that thing'. These theories of value conceive of value as determined by a particular attribute such as utility or social function. When Durkheim further discusses *judgements* of value, which he interprets as ideals and their corresponding value systems, it is possible to give him a much more radical interpretation. Durkheim specifically rejects a Kantian separation of the ideal and the real. The desire and will for an ideal to be real are intrinsic to the ideal. 'If man conceives ideals and indeed cannot help conceiving and becoming attached to them, it is because he is a social being'.[8] 'The ideal is not simply something lacking and desired ... it is to be thought of rather as looming impersonally over the individual wills that move it'.[9] Furthermore Durkheim approaches Adorno's position that identificatory judgements contain a utopian moment: 'Concepts are equally constructions of the mind and consequently ideals ... *all* judgements bring ideals to play. There cannot be more than one faculty of judgement'.[10] Adorno's position is much closer to Durkheim's than he concedes. Even though Durkheim's commitment to the latency of subjective ideals is not the same as Adorno's commitment to the rational utopian moment, both of these commitments share the glaring fault that they can equally well be construed utopianly or conservatively because they are so formal. To say that they are formal is to say that the content of the utopian moment is lacking, although in Adorno's case there is no logical objection to a perspective of the rational identity of the concept and object.

Adorno remarks, too, that Durkheim's circumscription of the possibility of initiating social change is similar to Hegel's opinion on the same matter, when he says that 'in any case we cannot aspire to a morality other than that which is related to the state of our society' – an idea which may be given a utopian or conservative interpretation. Finally, Durkheim denies that sociology 'has a fetish for facts', and says that it 'moves in the field of ideals which, however, it does not construct but deals with as a science'. This sounds almost like critical theory. The dissimilarities between Adorno and Durkheim are of course more striking than such apparent similarities – similarities which may, however, reveal antinomies in Adorno's own thought.

Conclusion: The Immanent Method

Thus there are some concepts which are legitimate as long as there is a need for an 'ontology of the wrong state of affairs', (for example, static/dynamic) and others which are heteronomous reifications (for example, value). These latter have no genuine non-reified application, and no utopian moment accessible to non-identity thinking. We have seen how the non-reified concept is derived from the reified one, and hence how the latter's relation to the underlying historical processes is established. But does the utopian moment have only a formal status? Is it merely the logical perspective from which any given social reality may be correctly described, or does it have any specifiable content? Is it a 'wishful image', or is it a 'concrete possibility'? Utopia is not a vision of any static, reconciled condition; this would be a return to the identity vision of German idealism. In some places the utopian moment seems to collapse into the pragmatic moment of thought, since all activity involves 'the production of something which was a conception but not yet a fact'. And what is 'not yet' Adorno describes as the utopian moment. For Adorno history has come to a halt: the forces of production cannot break through the mode of production. If the forces and countervailing mode were more fully specified, this impasse might provide a criterion for an 'imputable' utopia. 'To want substance in cognition is to want utopia'. 'Utopia' is another way of naming the thesis that non-dialectical thought is closed thought, because it implies that the object is already captured. To see that the object is not captured is to see utopia.

Critical theory does not proceed by postulating relationships among independently defined variables, nor does it proceed by conceiving oppositions which dissolve into each other to yield a new concept, which gives rise in turn to yet another opposition. Concepts are conceived from the outset so that their interconnections hold. These connections are presupposed. It is not a matter of 'proving' them. It is a matter of presenting them so that they are intelligible and cogent. The question of circularity is thus irrelevant.

'Theory is the telos, not the vehicle of sociology'. Critical theory is the conscious-ness of antinomies which makes the necessity of the antinomies it discovers transparent. The procedure for doing so is the immanent method. This method, paradoxically, makes non-dialectical sociologies into vehicles for the dialectical presentation of the critical perspective. The procedure is immanent, because it takes the objective idea of a work, whether it is sociological, musical, or literary, and 'confronts it with the norms which it has crystallised itself', 'naming what the consistency or inconsistency of the work itself expresses of the structure of the existent … [and transforming] this into a heightened perception of the thing itself'. Does Adorno avoid the twin pitfalls of being even more authoritarian than those he indicts, on the one hand, and on the other, of emptiness in spite of his plea for content?

Adorno's thought is as antinomial as the various modes of thinking he criticizes. It is entwined in its own impossibility. It amounts to the inherently paradoxical attempt to state a non-systematic objectivism objectivistically and without a system. This is its importance. The object is the subject returning to itself. This is presented from the point of view of the object – i.e. objectivistically, not merely objectively – but this is not done by eliminating the subject. That would be an objectivism in the derogatory sense of a determinist approach which eliminates one pole of the dialectic – the subject. But a further contingent paradox is that the attempt is bound to fail because of the extent of the reification of the mind and of society. All that can be done is to present the awareness of the limitations of the attempt – 'the mind tearing at its bonds' – and offer a method.

Notes

1 T. W. Adorno, *Introduction to the Battle over Positivism in German Sociology, Gesammelte Schriften*, vol. 8. Frankfurt: Suhrkamp, 1969, pp. 292–3.

2 T. W. Adorno and M. Horkheimer, *Dialectic of Enlightenment*, trans. J. Cumming. London: Allen Lane, 1973, p. 23.

3 T. W. Adorno, *Metacriticism of Epistemology, Gesammelte Schriften*, vol. 5. Frankfurt: Suhrkamp, 1956, pp. 25–6.

4 T. W. Adorno, *Negative Dialectics, Gesammelte Schriften*, vol. 6. Frankfurt: Suhrkamp, 1966, p. 192.

5 J. Mepham, 'The theory of ideology in capital', *Cultural Studies*, 6, 1974, p. 113.

6 Adorno, *Negative Dialectics*, p. 183.

7 T. W. Adorno, *Introduction to Emile Durkheim's 'Sociology and Philosophy', Gesammelte Schriften*, vol. 8. Frankfurt: Suhrkamp, 1969, p. 259.

8 E. Durkheim, *Sociology and Philosophy* trans. D. F. Pocock. London: Allen Lane, 1953, p. 95.

9 Durkheim, *Sociology and Philosophy*, p. 93.

10 Durkheim, *Sociology and Philosophy*, p. 95.

Liberty and Equality

Hillel Steiner

University of Manchester

In a period when most political philosophers followed John Rawls' turn towards contractualism, Steiner developed his own theory of distributive justice as based on rights. He also uses a libertarian method, from which he draws conclusions favouring radical redistribution which sharply contrast with the more familiar libertarian work of theorists such as Robert Nozick. In this article Steiner tackles the perennial problems of reconciling liberty and equality by defending a particular conception of equal rights. His style is characteristically accessible and playful, with the article centring on four parables, only the last two of which are reproduced here.

This article is concerned with the perennial claim that liberty and equality are incompatible and, hence, that any attempt to reduce substantive inequality promises to diminish individual liberty in society. Agreement on this familiar proposition is widespread among social and political philosophers, and is by no means confined to the ranks of those with classical liberal or libertarian commitments. I shall presume that a person is unfree to do an action if, and only if, someone else would prevent his doing it. It is this conception of liberty with which those who have libertarian commitments, of one sort or another, have been concerned. And it is the essence of such a commitment that most, if not all, of the restrictions on his liberty to which an individual is subject, should be restrictions which he has contractually incurred. This requirement is held to be incompatible – or at least very unlikely to be compatible – with what would be necessary to secure any sort of substantive equality among all individuals in a society. I shall argue that this contention is mistaken and that one sort of substantive equality is not only compatible with, but is necessary for, the satisfaction of this libertarian requirement.

[Steiner next considers two 'parables' which are ommitted here]

Third Parable

Text

Red, White, and Blue sit down to play a game of Monopoly. Within a short space of time every property on the board has been acquired by one or another of the three players. At this point, Black appears on the scene and is invited to join in the game. He agrees and is promptly supplied with the same amount of cash as was originally assigned to each of the others. However, being a somewhat litigious fellow, Black immediately protests that the terms of this arrangement are inequitable. He contends that he will be unfairly disadvantaged in having to make the required rental payment whenever he lands on another's property. To this, the others politely reply that they too are subject to the same obligation, and that no greater payment will be demanded of him for occupying any property than is extracted from each of them in similar circumstances. But Black impatiently rejoins that nearly every move he can make will result in his having to pay rent to either Red, White, or Blue,[1] whereas this is not the case for each of them. Moreover, he complains, in the initial stage of the game and prior to his arrival, they were each frequently at liberty to 'squat' on these properties without paying any rent at all, since many of them were as yet unowned.

At this juncture, Red, White, and Blue begin to become somewhat annoyed with Black's churlish attitude and proceed to point out to him, in no uncertain terms, that the rents he will owe them represent nothing less than well-deserved compensation for the services they are providing him and the sacrifices they have hitherto made. Blue reminds him that they only acquired these properties through purchase. And White and Red hasten to add that rents reflect the cost to them – and the convenience to him – of having houses and hotels to stay in while occupying these delightful spots.

Black peevishly acknowledges that some payment for the use of these facilities, where they have been installed, would be justified. But he grumbles that he cannot see why he should have to pay Blue as much as £35 to occupy Park Lane while paying White a mere £4 to stay in Whitechapel Road, when both of these unimproved sites offer no such amenities. Predictably, White's facetious offer to raise his rent to parity with Blue's succeeds only in evoking a murderous glare from Black, who humourlessly denounces the differential as entirely unjustified. Whereupon Blue, on a more conciliatory note, suggests that the difference in rents can be entirely explained – and justified – by reference to the difference (£145) between the original purchase prices of the two properties: 'If I were to charge only the same rent as White', he ruefully confides, 'I should soon be had up before the Bankruptcy Court'. But Black is unmoved. He gracelessly retorts that he, unlike the rest of them, never even had a chance to purchase Park Lane – or any other property for that matter – and cannot accept that he should now be obliged to respect Blue's title and pay him rent.

Red, who had lapsed into a reflective silence during this exchange, now ventures a suggestion. 'Suppose we were to amend the rules of the game in such a way as to deprive the three of us who started it of any advantage we thereby enjoy over Black. Blue reasonably feels that the price he paid for Park Lane entitles him to charge a high rent on its occupancy. Suppose that Blue, and White and myself as well, were to be reimbursed with the purchase prices of all our properties. This would deprive us of any justifiable grounds for charging rent on our unimproved sites. But it would be entirely justified to demand payment from anyone occupying a property to which we, through sacrifice and effort, had made some improvement.'

'Not good enough', replies Black, sensing that he is getting the upper hand and being by nature disinclined to demur from pressing a possible advantage to the full. 'For it would still be the case that you three had and have a chance, denied to me, to make profitable improvements to the unimproved sites you had completely acquired before I came on the scene. Blue could continue to extort £190 more for the rent of his Mayfair house than White can get for exactly similar accommodation in the Old Kent Road. That may have to be acceptable to Red and White, since they originally had some chance of acquiring Mayfair themselves. But I didn't. Hence Red's proposal fails to eliminate the disadvantage of a later start, and no late starter could rationally consent to this distribution of property.'

Faced with the loutish obstinacy of this barrack-room lawyer, Red, White, and Blue hold a quick conference and come up with what is to be their final offer. They suggest that the saleable value of each property (including its improvements) be determined by a mock auction; that a similar valuation be made of its improvements alone; that the latter figure be subtracted from the former; that this difference be calculated as a proportion of the former; and that this proportion be deducted from all rents paid, and divided equally among all the players. This procedure, it is claimed, would eliminate the alleged advantage enjoyed by the original three, inasmuch as it would 'nationalize' the *pure rent* element of their property incomes and leave them with only those revenues which are due compensation for their productive efforts. (Thus the rate of tax on rents for unimproved sites would be 100 per cent.) Since compensation commensurate with the value of one's services to others is the most that any person can reasonably expect from them, and since this procedure would satisfy that expectation, there could be no reason for claiming that the original acquisition of property rights – when they have been thus encumbered – would confer any unfair advantage on their owners. 'Hence', Red, White, and Blue conclude, 'you should respect our property rights, and pay our rents, under these conditions.' Black, surly as ever, ponders this proposal, grudgingly concedes its merit, and joins in the game.

Commentary

Red, White, and Blue are wise and just men. They have studied the teachings not only of John Locke, but also of Henry George and the early Herbert Spencer. Like many turn-of-the-century Liberal members of Parliament, as well as some of their socialist colleagues (a preponderant number of whom reportedly claimed to have been influenced more by George than by Marx), they locate the source of contemporary social injustice not in the dire poverty which the current allocation of property permits, nor even particularly in the rigours of a competitive economy. Rather, it is to be found in the cumulatively compounded effects of an inequitable distribution of original property rights, that is, rights to natural resources. According to George, it is the historical transmission of these rights to finite and non-reproducible objects, and their correlative obligations – as ramified through the price system – that both accounts for the greater proportion of prevailing social inequality and retards economic growth, by conferring monopolistic power on resource owners who are insulated against competitive pressures to put their resources to more productive use. Nor, however, would he have allowed that a contractual distribution of original property rights, along the lines indicated in the second parable, could overcome this difficulty – for the reasons set out in the preceding commentary. Advancing what he considered to be the logical conclusion of Lockean natural rights premises, George argued that a distribution which is just (as well as efficient) must be one which rewards people proportionately to their productive contribution, and that this is only possible within a structure of property rights which are entirely contractually derived. The remedy for distributive in-justice is not to restrict freedom of contract and the consequent scope of eco-nomic competition. On the contrary, it is to extend them and, in particular, to establish the obligations correlative to property rights in natural resources – from which all other property rights ought contractually to derive – upon a contractual foundation.

George was thus led to confront the problem: how to constitute a set of property rights and obligations upon a foundation that could be construed as contractually underwritten by members of later generations as well as initial appropriators. Given the non-contemporaneity of all these persons, such a contractual construct might have to be only hypothetical in character. But, for the reasons offered to Black by Red, White, and Blue, this would not detract from its status as a remedy for injustice, in so far as injustice is held to consist (among other things) in forcibly depriving a person of any of the value of his services to others. The early Herbert Spencer, strongly influenced by Thomas Hodgskin and indirectly by the writings of the land reform radicals, of Ricardo on rent and of John Stuart Mill on what came to be known as the 'land question', had previously been exercised by this same problem and had proposed land nationalization as its solution.[2] Indeed, one of the clearest statements of the problem in terms of natural rights theory is to be found in George's telling attack on Spencer's later recantation of this proposal.[3]

Yet, as the parable suggests, George himself did not favour nationalization of natural resources as the appropriate remedy. A hypothetically contractual basis for resource ownership seemed to him an equally just, administratively simpler, and substantially less disruptive means of securing what Spencer had sought to achieve by actual contract (in the form of state leasing of natural resources). The 'Single Tax' would extract the pure rent element from resource owners' property and return it equally to each member of society (i.e. inasmuch as it would be mediated through democratic political institutions), who could thereby have no reason to believe his lot to be prejudiced by original appropriation or the set of property rights contractually derived from it.

The Georgist diagnosis and prescription are interesting, and not only to anti-quarians. In the first place, his analysis constitutes the culmination of an important and unduly neglected theme in political and intellectual history that has its roots in at least the eighteenth century and arguably much earlier. But second, it represents an approach to the problem of social injustice that has much in common with Marxist and other socialist accounts. (George was often accused of being a socialist.) For it seeks to show that the specific form of injustice which we call *exploitation* can exist even in a society in which – unlike those sustaining slavery or serfdom – individuals' economic interactions appear to be entirely governed by their own contractual undertakings. George's point, of course, is that this appear-ance is misleading. Persons do not receive the full value of their services because the property rights framework, within which they strike their bargains, possesses significant non-contractual elements emanating from the unencumbered (or inappropriately encumbered) character of natural resource ownership. Like Marx, but in a considerably more perspicuous fashion, George reaches his conclusions through a synthesis of ethical and economic reasoning.[4] And his prescription, when compared to other proposals for the elimination of exploitation, is a thing of such elegant simplicity as to be intellectually beautiful.

And yet, it is ultimately flawed. Its inadequacy as a just corrective of the prevailing set of property rights, lies in the fact that the resource valuation it requires, being based on market prices, renders the remedial tax a mathematical function of that prevailing set of rights. Since market prices are *distribution-relative*, they cannot consistently be treated as parametric for determining the extent to which that distribution is unjust. In the case of the present parable, the respective preference schedules of Red, White, and Blue would exert greater determinative influence on the mock auction valuations than would Black's, because they already possess property and he does not. The Georgist theory thus displays both the attractions and the limitations of using a *valuationally-based* concept of exploitation and, by implication, of hypothetically contractual rights and obligations. Hence, the terms on which Black has agreed to join the game of Monopoly are not ones which represent an unambiguous advance in satisfying the libertarian requirement.

Fourth Parable

Text

Following a shipwreck, ten persons find themselves on an otherwise deserted island from which escape is physically impossible. Their natural captivity is, however, somewhat alleviated by the fact that the island is endowed with fresh running water, some animal life, a sandy beach, some vegetation and reasonably fertile soil. Nevertheless, difficulties soon arise. One of the group is, it seems, a dedicated nudist who loses no time in taking advantage of the sunny weather and sandy beach to pursue his avocation. When reproached by several of his more scandalized companions, he is quick to point out that they have no authority to require him to do otherwise – to which they rejoin that the beach is not his personal property to use as he pleases. His reply to them is, of course, to precisely the same effect. In the meantime, three other members of the group set about to cut down some of the island's larger trees in order to build a shelter for themselves. To this, all the remaining members take great exception, variously arguing that such a move would severely detract from the island's beauty, contribute to the erosion of fertile soil, and critically reduce the amount of natural shade available to all. Again, their arguments soon become ones about property rights. Even a proposal, that the island's fruit be rationed in proportion to the size of individuals' appetites, fails to command the universal agreement confidently expected by its proponents. For it appears that, while none wish entirely to forgo eating fruit, some members prefer to employ at least a portion of the available fruit as fodder for the animals they hope to domesticate, while one or two others profess to find the sight of naturally decaying fruit aesthetically attractive. So, as in the other cases, arguments gradually turn from the relative desirability of alternative uses of available resources – about which agreement is difficult – to questions of property rights.

It is at this point that one of the group's members – a lawyer by training or, perhaps, a political philosopher – volunteers the following insight into the vexing issues confronting them. He observes that, while each person has views about what sorts of conduct should or should not be permitted in this society, none possesses the authority to impose those views on the rest. Furthermore, it is clear that issues about permissible conduct invariably resolve themselves into issues about who may use what without suffering interference from others. But no one is immediately prepared to assign the unencumbered use of anything to anyone else.

'We are', the lawyer observes, 'each treating one another as though the island were our own personal property. It would therefore appear that a correct description of our situation is that we are each shareholders in the island which is thus a jointly owned asset *and* that we each consider our shares to entitle us to exercise a veto against any assignment of our assets of which we do not approve.' The members of the group immediately recognize this characterization of their situation as an accurate one, but are at a loss to see how it can in any way assist them in getting on with the various things they each want to do. Again the lawyer: 'I suggest that we formally constitute ourselves as a decision-making body, and entertain proposals from those of our members who wish – either individually or in some combination – to make some use of the island's resources. Since each of us is armed with a veto, the various assignments eventually decided upon by this body must be presumed to command the assent of all and, therefore, any interference by anyone with what has been assigned to another would have to be viewed as a violation of contract. Of course, we must expect a lot of hard bargaining to occur before any such allocation can be made. But this way of looking at our situation, and this way of proceeding, appear to be the only ones which promise protection of each person's liberty inasmuch as no one will be obliged to submit to restrictions which he has not contracted.'

The members of the group ponder this suggestion and eventually, though perhaps with some reluctance, come to accept it. But just as negotiations are about to commence, one of them speaks out. 'Haven't we overlooked a rather important consideration?' he asks. 'Surely we are forgetting the lesson of the second and third parables. Suppose that, in twenty years' time, we have amongst us several new members who are the offspring of present members and who have attained adulthood in the interval. Will they not consider that any obligation they might have to respect the property of others could only arise, as in our own cases, from its having been contractually undertaken? If we, as shareholders, now proceed to make permanent private allocations to each of ourselves, then presumably this has the effect of dissolving our joint ownership and there will be nothing for our children to be shareholders of. I do not think it will do to say that an offspring's property rights are a matter of concern only to his parents. For this in no way implies an obligation on his part to respect the property of others. And in any case, there is no reason why the rights of these offspring – who will, as it were, be persons in their own right – should be determined by what their parents (who may have been utterly profligate) may or may not have done with what was originally assigned to them.'

This intervention in the proceedings immediately throws the group into complete consternation. But once again, the lawyer comes to the rescue. 'It is true', he concedes, 'that my proposal in its initial form fails to take account of the problem posed by later arrivals in our midst. I therefore recommend the following modification.

The shareholders' body will *not* dissolve after making its set of allocations. Later arrivals, when and if there are any, will become shareholders as they reach the age of majority when they would normally assume the burdens and benefits of full legal responsibility. Since any prevailing set of allocations is contractually entitled to the respect of all – and only – those who were shareholders when that allocation was made, it follows that the only way in which the obligation to respect others' property can be said to be contractually incurred by more recent shareholders who were not parties to that earlier allocative decision, is if prevailing allocations are subject to their approval. Current shareholders would thus be well-advised, though by no means obliged, to take this consideration into account when making their decisions about who should get what and what should be done with it. The contracts into which the shareholding body enters would thereby assume the character of a lease for an unspecified term. And all shareholders would thereby be bound to respect the agreed rights of leaseholders and to impose upon them no restrictions other than those contractually agreed to.' The members of the group grimly contemplate this new proposal, which they finally accept, and then sit down to engage in some very hard bargaining.

Commentary

The lawyer succeeds where Henry George failed. He devises a formula for the universal and perpetual reduction – to two – in the number of non-contractually prohibited activities: violations of personal (bodily) integrity and violations of contract. And he achieves this theoretical result by providing all property rights with a foundation in the contractual undertakings of all existing persons. Once an individual becomes contractually entitled to an object, he may do with it – and only with it – what he pleases, subject to the terms of the contract. He is at liberty (a forcibly protected liberty) to transform it, exchange it, invest it, consume it, give it away, etc. The different distributions which may eventuate from persons exercising their liberties and using their contractual allocations in these ways are themselves contractually underwritten. It is true that later shareholders can revoke the set of titles prevailing when they first appear on the scene. Indeed, it is their having such a right that ensures the contractual status of their obligations to respect those allocations which are not revoked, as well as those re-allocations which may be (unanimously) agreed upon. For although revocation is a prerogative solely of new arrivals, allocation is the right of each and every person. That is, and as the lawyer says, each shareholder's right includes the power to veto.

Is this implausible? Arguments in political philosophy characteristically contain some premises which are normative propositions and some which state con- ceptual truths. The lawyer's case rests not only on the libertarian normative view that violations of personal integrity and of contract should be the only activities which are non-contractually prohibited. It also relies upon the conceptual truth that a property right is a right *in rem*, that is, a right against the world. As such, it entails enforcible obligations on the part of all persons who are not the holder of that right. This necessary truth, taken in conjunction with the normative pro- position just stated, implies that such obligations must be contractually incurred by all those to whom they are ascribed, i.e. everyone.

Even if theoretically plausible, is not the lawyer's proposal highly impracticable? Such questions invariably trade on a pivotal ambiguity. Impracticable *for whom*? If revocation of some or all prevailing titles were universally disadvantageous, it would presumably not be undertaken. In this respect the lawyer's remark, that current shareholders would be well-advised (though not obliged) to consider later shareholders' interests in making their current contractual arrangements, is highly apposite. There is no reason to suppose that later shareholders would enjoy greater immunity from the disruptive and destabilizing effects of revocation. Nor would they be unaware of the fact that any subsequent re-allocation must enjoy the consent of all, including those whom they have dispossessed. But if, on balance, some – or even one – of the later shareholders considered revocation to be less disadvantageous, upon what grounds could it nevertheless be pronounced impracticable? If, 'rights are trumps', and if trumps override all other kinds of practical consideration, the grounds for judging as impracticable someone's exercise of his right of revocation can ultimately only lie in an ethical commitment which asserts the normative superiority of other practical considerations (for example, maximizing social utility) over the demands of respecting individuals' rights. Such a commitment is, of course, plausible enough, though not itself entirely free from theoretical ambiguities and counter-intuitive consequences. But it is, in any event, a distinctly different kind of commitment from the libertarian one explored in this paper. And its connection with the requirement of minimizing uncontracted enforcible obligations is, at most, a contingent and largely historical one, as the first parable indicates.

Review and Conclusion

Libertarians characteristically think of themselves as favouring a free society, a society in which individual liberty is maximized. But understandable as this characterization may seem, it is not quite accurate. For state officials in our society enjoy a considerable amount of individual liberty – as do legislators – and their liberty increases every time the government takes on a new function or nationalizes another industry. Each such move – as libertarians have not failed to point out – increases the scope for such officials to exercise *their* personal choice and to give effect to *their* preferences. Libertarianism is, therefore, not a demand for *greater* individual liberty in society: such a demand, I would contend, is without meaning. It is, rather, a demand for *equal* liberty amongst all members of society. The libertarian injunction is not properly understood as one to maximize individual liberty. What it prescribes is the minimization of uncontracted enforcible restrictions on individual conduct. *And this prescription is not translatable into one enjoining the maximization of anything.*

There is another way of putting this same point. The libertarian is vitally concerned to secure a society in which the enforcible obligations to which any individual is subject – apart from his obligation to refrain from overt violence against the persons of others – are all obligations which he has personally contracted. And they correctly see the vast structure of regulations and prohibitions to be found in most modern societies, and many earlier ones, as entailing obligations and liabilities which are in no sense consistent with this requirement. But for reasons which are

not at all obvious, they have often paid insufficient attention to the fact that each
and every property title imposes obligations on all persons who are not the holders
of that title – obligations which can be said to have been contractually incurred, at
most, only by previous holders of that title or of the titles from which it derives.
For the rest, these ubiquitous obligations are uncontracted but none the less
enforcible restrictions on their conduct.

None of you sold me my house. All of you are enforcibly obligated to refrain from
setting up a betting-shop in my front parlour. Of course, if one of you had sold me
my house, or if one of you had sold the house to the person who sold it to me, or
if one of you had sold him the materials for constructing the house, your obligation
would indeed be a contractual one. But it is quite clear that the overwhelming
majority of enforcible obligations, to which each of us is subject in respect of others'
property, was never incurred in this way. Such obligations are as inconsistent with
the aforesaid libertarian requirement as are those imposed by Keynesian or welfare
or mercantilist or any other form of meddlesome state.

Historical entitlement conceptions of property rights avoid the error correctly
attributed to competing conceptions which 'treat objects as if they appeared from
nowhere and out of nothing' and were not the products of personally owned
labour. But historical entitlement conceptions attend insufficiently to the fact that
natural resources are, precisely, objects which appeared from nowhere and out of
nothing. And it is thus not surprising that the Achilles' heel of such conceptions
can almost invariably (George is the exception) be located in their accounts of the
right to initial appropriation, from which all other historical entitlement-based
property rights logically derive. Notoriously, such accounts ignore the fact that
appropriative rights cannot be constituted by historical principles and must necessarily derive from end-state ones and, moreover, end-state principles the validity
of which can logically extend to an indefinite number of human generations.

Let me conclude with the following observations. Libertarians are surely on the
right track in holding that the principles of distributive justice must contain
significant historical (and unpatterned) elements. We *do* think that the depriva-
tions forcibly imposed upon individuals should bear some close relation to what
they have done. And it would therefore be peculiar and inconsistent were we to
claim that the same criterion should have no application to their forcibly protected
gains – that there can be a thorough-going asymmetry between the demands of
distributive and retributive justice. Nozick rightly notes that, as against distributive
theories which embody only end-state principles,

> One traditional socialist view is that workers are entitled to the product
> and full fruits of their labour; they have earned it; a distribution is unjust
> if it does not give the workers what they are entitled to. Such entitle-
> ments are based upon some past history … This socialist rightly, in my
> view, holds onto the notions of earning, producing, entitlement, desert,
> and so forth, and he rejects current time-slice principles that look only to
> the structure of the resulting set of holdings.[5]

As was previously remarked, socialists and non-socialists share the same general
conception of exploitation, which is held to consist in individuals not receiving the
full value of their services to others because their economic interactions are not

entirely governed by their own contractual undertakings. This is clearly true of slavery. What is more, non-socialists (as well as socialists) believe it to be also true of serfdom, and this despite the fact that the exchange of services between lord and vassal was contractually constituted. The basis for the charge of exploitation even in these circumstances lies in the fact that such contractual undertakings occurred within a wider structure of enforcible obligations which were not themselves contractually agreed by lords and vassals. That these arrangements embody an historical entitlement principle is a necessary, but not sufficient, condition for withdrawing this indictment.

The programme of *laissez-faire* and the free market is to secure the widest possible dispersal of economic decision making. And the object of natural rights doctrine, with its associated historical entitlement principle, is the widest possible dispersal of individual liberty. It is a statistical axiom that the widest possible dispersal of a variable over a population is its equal incidence in every member of that population. The lawyer's insight – and that of some conceptions of socialism – is that, in a normative social order, economic decision making and individual liberty are indissolubly linked through the institution of property rights. Each person's possession of a veto on the initial allocation of property eliminates the possibility of his being exploited, by minimizing the number of non-contractual enforcible obligations to which he is subject. Such an arrangement is, recognizably, a form of socialism. But it is also one which, from a libertarian perspective, incorporates the virtues of the first three parabolical societies while discarding their defects.

Notes

1 Except those which involve the good or ill fortune of landing on Go, Chance, Community Chest, Free Parking, Go to Jail, and Tax.

2 H. Spencer, *Social Statics*. London: John Chapman, 1851.

3 H. George, *A Perplexed Philosopher*. London: Henry George Foundation, 1937, originally published 1892.

4 H. George, *Progress and Poverty*. London: William Reeves, 1884.

5 R. Nozick, *Anarchy, State and Utopia*. Oxford: Basil Blackwell, 1974.

Constructing and Deconstructing Liberty: a Feminist and Poststructuralist Analysis

Diana Coole

Queen Mary and Westfield College, University of London

For much of the late twentieth century British political scientists were an overwhelmingly male occupational group, and like any other form of intellectual or practical enterprise political theory ran the risk of an accumulation of implicit biases and explicit silences reflecting this limitation. Coole's article illustrates her view of the scale of this problem by dissecting Isaiah Berlin's classic discussion of negative and positive liberty (taken as expressing the dominant mainstream in political theory) from the viewpoint of feminist authors and post-structuralists such as Foucault and Derrida. Her argument starts from the different male and female experiences of 'private' and 'public' spheres, arguing that privileging negative liberty reflects multiple male biases. But Coole also goes on to raise important caveats about feminists' normal enthusiasm for positive liberty.

The voluminous debates concerning the relationship between negative and positive concepts of liberty, themselves act as internal impediments to free discussion of the term. They fail to question the foundations on which these concepts rest: foundations which, I shall suggest, operate as constraints on what we conceive as free subjects. Worse, by perpetuating those constraints, they themselves exercise a quiet power that limits our visions and aspirations of liberty, helping to construct us as unfree selves. To develop this theme I shall draw on feminist and post-structuralist approaches. I have also used Isaiah Berlin's classic account of 'Two Concepts of Liberty' as an elegant summary of the dominant themes of liberty to be found in modern political thought.

In order to advance my critique, I have focused on gender. Protagonists in the 'two concepts' debate have generally preferred to use class distinctions, insofar as they have interpreted the positive 'freedom to' in a materialist sense, to argue that the negative liberty which abstractly promotes freedom in the market, also robs many of the opportunity to exercise their freedom in any meaningful or egalitarian way. The absence of external impediments must then be supplemented by the presence of external resources. Although this sort of critique might usefully be made on women's behalf, my intention is rather to use gender in order to question the internal structures and problematics of both concepts of liberty.

This perspective nevertheless carries important political implications for feminism, which has implicitly made extensive use of both versions of liberty. In the negative case, it is often suggested that women will only be free when they are liberated *from* something. A considerable amount of feminist analysis has accordingly focused on discovering what it is that oppresses women, in order for them to concentrate their political demands on the negation of such phenomena. Yet as the pursuit of sexual equality has yielded to more self-conscious assertions of difference, doubts have arisen as to the adequacy of concentrating on impediments, for this defines women's freedom only in terms of their opposition to patriarchy. Accordingly, feminists have been drawn towards a more positive conception, not only because this more adequately allows consideration of internal (psycho-cultural) impediments to freedom but also because it addresses questions such as 'who are we?' What is it that women want to be free *to* do or be? Some notion of identity, of what it would mean to be a free and authentic feminine/female subject, has thus become an attractive alternative to leaving the free woman as an empty space defined only by what she opposes. Post-structuralist reappraisals of subjectivity nevertheless suggest that both conceptions of liberty are problematic for feminists. I will discuss this by exploring a series of spatial metaphors found in both negative and positive concepts.

The Spaces of Negative Liberty

In 'Two Concepts of Liberty', Berlin equates negative liberty with a right to privacy, which is, in turn, associated with 'a high mark of civilization' that he dates from the Renaissance or Reformation. In other words, this is a specifically modern concept and arises, he contends, from addressing the question 'what is the area within which the subject – a person or group of persons – is or should be left to do *or be* what he is able to do *or be*, without interference from other persons?'[1] In attempting to define the boundaries of this personal liberty, Berlin utilises a series of spatial metaphors: 'the wider the area of non-interference the wider my freedom'; a 'frontier' must be drawn between private and public life. Negative liberty is concerned not with the source of authority but with 'the area of control'; with a 'vacuum in which nothing obstructs me'.[2] Around each private and isolated unit, a *cordon sanitaire* is thus constructed. These metaphors of separate and divided spaces work by invoking certain oppositions: between inside and outside, self and other, individual and state, private and public, liberty and coercion.

Coercion marks for Berlin the antithesis and limit point of freedom. It is a term he defines as deliberate interference with other persons, such that freedom declines as coercion increases. Like liberty itself, coercion is both an intentional act and a capacity possessed by identifiable agents. Although it is ultimately the law that protects us from coercion, Berlin also emphasises the protective value of a culture centred around criteria of normality: 'rules so long and widely accepted that their observance has entered into the very conception of what it is to be a normal human being and, therefore, also of what it is to act inhumanly or insanely'.[3] A 'normal' person, he believes, will spontaneously recognise and honour the personal frontiers of liberty. Berlin himself apparently pays homage to the sanctity of these frontiers of non-interference, by refraining from any explicit suggestion as to what free persons are like or what they might choose to do with their liberty. In principle, they remain within the vacuum to which he has consigned them, merely empty spaces.

A poststructuralist approach raises even more serious problems for negative liberty, for its suggestion is that far from being possible sites of liberty, the bodies and subjectivities which make up the individual and its sense of self, are *already* the effects of power. From this perspective, there is no moral, rational or natural individual who forms the bedrock of human society and its values; there is no essentially free subject whose project of liberation would be to throw off the shackles of power that constrain it. Subjectivity, of which our sense of ourselves as discrete and autonomous individuals forms a part, is for it an effect of discourses in which knowledge and power are inextricably interwoven. In speaking and being spoken about, subjects are in a constant ferment of (self) construction, such that their sense of who they are is always unstable and a site of struggle. Discourses are never innocent then, but shot through with power relations. This applies also to political theory and its conceptualisations of liberty. The subject they describe as the origin and *telos* of freedom, as natural and ideal, would already be part of a strategy of power which incites the subjectivities of which it speaks. In principle there is nothing to encircle and protect, because power goes all the way down.

With this in mind, we might now ask further questions about Berlin's formal geography of freedom. Might it not already contain a particular image of free subjectivity which both reflects and encourages our subjection? Berlin himself acknowledges that his sense of 'freedom from' involves an 'individualistic ... conception of man' [sic].[4] But it must also imply a number of things about these individuals. They must experience themselves as different from others as well as opposed to them: the self is constituted as not-other, as possessor of its own personal qualities and desires, unique in its self-identity. It is an autonomous self in that it is responsible for recognising and pursuing its own interests and needs: to be free, it requires knowledge and self-knowledge. It is also therefore a rational self, able to conceive its own goals as well as calculating the best means of achieving them. Although negative liberty is, *prima facie*, about empty spaces and unprescribed subjectivities, it emerges on closer inspection as dependent upon a rather specific, liberal, Enlightenment view of the self, predicated on a particularly modern and constraining distinction between rational and irrational. Those who are not, or cannot become, rational, are then excluded as candidates for freedom. Or, to put it rather differently, the freedom they might claim does not count because it is not considered to be rational choice. This is not simply to repeat the familiar claim that women (among others) have been defined as too irrational to count as free and autonomous persons in political thought and law (although the public/private dichotomy intrinsic to negative liberty has been used in precisely this way to exclude women); but excluded in general are those who cannot offer a rational account of their acts; who cannot justify their goals according to acceptable criteria of normality; who cannot discover efficient and logically commensurable means for attaining their ends. In short, those who are not acquitted before the court of instrumental-purposive reason are vulnerable to sanctions and exclusion from the ranks of the potentially free, while we are all invited to construct ourselves according to its prevailing norms as a precondition of our freedom.

Although Berlin alludes to the importance of normality, he presents this not as a constraint but, tautologically, as an uncontestable code all humanists (that is all normal people) would accept. Although he acknowledges the historical credentials of negative liberty's view of self, the claims made on its behalf rely on the assumption that a true account of some natural, rational individual, which has finally achieved self-consciousness regarding its own nature and needs, but which was previously buried beneath the obfuscations of tradition, has now been excavated. In other words, while accepting that the ideas of negative liberty are historically modern, their foundation rests on assumptions about an ahistorical and universal individual whom modernity can finally set free. There is no recognition that this deep and natural self might also be a product of modernity, with its particular (and exclusionary, constraining) understanding of the relation between reason and liberty.

Nevertheless, I suggest that this particular view of the self is uncontestable within this frame of reference, because this negative account of freedom, and its assumptions regarding the subject, so intimately and irremediably correspond. It is unthinkable that such freedom would be demanded for a different type of subject or that the subjects it describes could aspire to a different sort of freedom. Inversely, if they are to claim this sort of liberty at all, they must themselves become the sort of subject which it presupposes. In this way, the discourses of liberty function as a form of power, constraining us to satisfy those conditions under which we might be defined as free. It would then seem that the liberal commitment to value-pluralism is undermined by a subject-monism, insofar as subjects are defined in such a way that their opportunities and choices are already logically circumscribed. Negative liberty then tries to offer a formula for protecting certain individual practices but it has nothing to say about freeing our identities from the constraints it takes for granted and even advances.

A poststructuralist approach thus helps to advance feminist critique. The latter's position has been that political thought privileges men and masculinity, and that women's different subjectivity has been silenced and devalued by patriarchal ideology. But for poststructuralism, there is nothing behind the mask or the veil to which appeal might be made. Ideology/knowledge does not mystify truth but engenders it; power does not suppress or distort subjectivity but produces it. Foucault is especially explicit here, insisting that there is no private domain of everyday life or of the self that is not traversed, inscribed, constituted, by power. Freedom cannot exist in an undefined and undefiled vacuum, as Berlin claims. Indeed, the illusion that it can is part of the strategy of a power that both blinds us to our subjection and requires that we operate with a certain degree of autonomy and self-discipline.

Rather than explicit or deliberate coercion, where power is empirically obvious and possessed by identifiable agents who act with intent, Foucault locates a fragmented, multiple, circulatory power of which we are all both vehicles and victims. It is impossible to formulate a notion of liberty as freedom *from* such power, because its 'capillary form' is anonymous and ubiquitous, reaching into 'the very grain of individuals', where it 'touches their bodies and inserts itself into their actions and attitudes, their discourses, learning processes and everyday lives'.[5] To suggest that a private domain might exist without power is thus a dangerous distraction and draws, Foucault suggests, on an anachronistic theory of the juridical subject supported by an obsolete (and again, spatial) distinction between legitimate and illegitimate spheres of power. Although political theory still clings to this view, it has had little purchase since the Enlightenment, when new forms of disciplinary micro-power emerged quietly, haphazardly, contingently, to subvert the rights and liberties on which political theory insists. Its instruments are seemingly banal or benign: complex arrangements of bodies in time and space (which discipline them); the discourses of the human sciences (with their criteria of normality and encouragement of surveillance); self-confession (with its self-creating, self-disciplining imperative).

The body is not therefore a natural repository of insatiable appetites, negatively free when it is unimpeded in their satisfaction, as a Hobbes or Bentham insist; it is not a material foundation in which true, authentic needs might be discerned, as Marxists, feminists and exponents of positive liberty sometimes contend; nor, finally, is it a reservoir of libidinous desire awaiting release from repression, as Freudians and some feminists suggest. The way we experience our body and its imperatives is a positive effect of power and not a 'vacuum' or natural substratum to be satisfied in the absence of constraint. For once the body was objectified and analysed in its constituent parts, it could become a target of a disciplinary power that pays meticulous attention to its functions in order to rearrange and control them. Foucault's point here, is not that natural bodies were subjected to greater regulation but that this new anatomy of power literally created a useful and docile modern body out of disparate parts. Moreover, knowledge derived from its object-ification was used to rank and thus individualise subjects by means of new and exclusionary oppositions, such as those between normality and abnormality, health and sickness, sanity and madness:

> The individual is not to be conceived as a sort of elementary nucleus, a primitive atom, a multiple and inert material on which power comes to fasten or against which it happens to strike, and in so doing subdues or crushes individuals. In fact, it is already one of the prime effects of power that certain bodies, certain gestures, certain discourses, certain desires, can be identified and constituted as individuals.[6]

As an example of this process, feminists have made use of Foucault's approach to show that disciplinary power produces not just obedient subjects but gendered ones, too, where women are subjugated according to gendered criteria of normality producing both the female body and a feminine identity. Accordingly, women's bodies are continuously deconstructed and reassembled in terms of their various reproductive organs and sexual parts, as different discourses evolve. Each part is subjected to a complex moral, medical, aesthetic, pornographic, even feminist, pathology. In modernity, female bodies are 'hystericised', a term Foucault used to convey the way they are conceived as saturated with sexuality; with reproduction and eroticism. 'Experts' can then pronounce on normal and abnormal sexual pleasure and reproductive health. Gestures, comportment and presentation also fall under detailed scrutiny and prescription. In short, there is no natural female body, foundation or feminine desire or liberty, but a jigsaw of pieces ordered in a specific way. Female flesh is (re)created as an effect of discursive practices in terms of its size, shape, expressions, habits, pleasures and general appearance. From dieting and exercise, cosmetics and fashion, to ways of walking and sitting, it is subjected to a series of complex yet invisible norms in its most minute and intimate presentations. These material effects of power then succeed so well precisely because of the complicity they inspire. To obey is to experience an illusion of self-expression, autonomy and free choice. For as Rousseau recognized, obedience is experienced as liberty once it is willed, habitual and conflict-free. Every woman falls under an absent yet ever-present patriarchal gaze – a 'panoptical male connoisseur' as one critic puts it – which is profoundly and inextricably enmeshed in her sense of self-identity. There are no obvious institutions or illegitimate sanctions from which freedom might be demanded, even where this insidious form of power is glimpsed. If we determine to shrug off its effects, to achieve autonomy and escape false consciousness, then poststructuralism would suggest that we only ensnare ourselves once more in the labyrinths of a power that has no outside but which catches us in a new place when we would speak of our liberty and construct ourselves as potentially free subjects.

Insofar as we accept such an analysis, the nature of the *externality* of impediments thus becomes highly problematic; power appears to operate far more intimately and to leave intact no preserve within which any free individual might be protected. Perhaps we might call such illusory spaces 'reservations', with all the connotations that term carries. While feminists might question where the boundaries between freedom's spaces should be drawn; poststructuralist accounts strengthen their more radical beliefs that those boundaries serve only to foster an illusion of possible liberty and a process of exclusion, thereby serving the interest of power.

The Spaces of Positive Liberty

To what extent might such criticisms of a negative conception of liberty be addressed to its positive counterpart? Or, on the contrary, does the latter avoid such problems and offer a more adequate or beguiling idea of freedom, especially perhaps for women? Positive liberty originated in classical (Socratic–Stoic) thought and its modern usage is generally associated with Rousseau, himself a critic of post-Hobbesian conceptions of freedom, rationality and subjectivity. We would therefore expect quite different foundations for it. In fact, Berlin finds this sense of freedom not only antithetical to its negative formulation but ultimately to liberty itself. Although many of his critics have subsequently unravelled Berlin's clear analytic dichotomy, they have tended to concentrate on formal confusions at a semantic level, rather than interrogating the underlying foundations of the two concepts. My contention is that despite obvious differences, the positive version also rests on exclusionary oppositions conveyed by spatial metaphors and that it, too, is guilty of helping to construct the subjects it prescribes as quintessentially free.

Positive liberty is explicitly concerned with subjectivity and the empowerment which certain of its forms bring. It is about an enabling freedom; about capacities and self development. It implies a process rather than a state and is dynamic in its presentation of the self. At the basis of this idealist account of 'freedom to' lies a concern with self-mastery; as such, the self is problematised as a goal and ethical imperative, not treated as a mere given or empty unit. Self-mastery or self-discipline is explicitly associated with rationality and autonomy, but these are no longer presented as synonymous with the human state. Instead they are to be realised in the process of an ongoing struggle within the self.

This concept does not then use negative liberty's image of separate spheres, because it is concerned with internal impediments and the evolution of an inner self vulnerable to dark forces and (self-) enslavement. Yet it does still rely upon spatial metaphors, most obviously to depict a divided self (rather than a self opposed to others). For what is in question, is the relation of the self to itself, where the 'lower' self of passion and appetite threatens to keep the 'higher', rational self in subjection to an insatiable and capricious desire. Horizontally differentiated and material spaces are thus replaced by a vertical and more obviously hierarchical model of the subject's topography, which is underpinned by more fundamental oppositions between mind and body, reason and non-reason. I shall suggest later on that these latter oppositions also invoke metaphorical notions of space, which are coded in gendered terms.

The qualities of rationality and autonomy to which this free self aspires are apparently similar to those I found implicit in the negative view. However, the rationality that is sought as integral to freedom is now more obviously related to objective notions of authenticity, personal integrity and self-identity. It is less fixated on, and even hostile to, modern credentials of reason as instrumentality, calculation and rational choice. Liberty no longer means being left alone to define and pursue just any interest but an ability to frame a coherent life-plan; to transcend internal impediments to freedom, such as uncontrollable desire or a heteronomous self-identity and 'false' need, shaped by persons or processes outside one's control or knowledge. Its concern is less with being a free *individual* (in possession of opportunities and options which might be redistributed, measured or patterned) than with being a free *subject* (where it is the constitution of subjectivity itself that defines freedom).

From this perspective, exponents of positive liberty might make a similar criticism of its negative formulation to that implied by poststructuralism: namely, that it pays insufficient attention to the self who would be free. Indeed, it is possible to define positive liberty in such a way that it becomes quite compatible with the spirit of poststructuralism, where self-constitution is a creative (aesthetic) process in which the configurations of subjectivity remain plural and open-ended. However, this openness is not (as Berlin et al. rightly see) what positive liberty has advocated: rather it holds a closed, rationalistic and teleological view of what a free subject is like. It may be enslaved by the otherness within itself but we know in advance what its successful resolution would look like. A free subject is one who achieves rational integrity; who is transparent to itself; who becomes a unified subject; who is normal insofar as it subdues its otherness and abnormalities (i.e. its nonrational and irrational powers); who has a single identity. Unlike negative liberty, this positive version does not assume a given rational and self-knowing subject which merely awaits its release. That self must be forged, through (as Hegel says of masculinity,) 'the stress of thought and much technical exertion'.[7] However, it does preconceive what that free self will be like at the end of its struggles and is therefore heavily prescriptive.

For more recent exponents of positive liberty, it is true that internal impediments are more likely to originate in external, ideological forces and a less closed and teleological prescription of authenticity is at work. Yet there remains the ideal of the free subject as one who is finally rational; who exercises reflective judgement and moral discrimination as an ongoing process of liberation, even if these cannot now win an ultimate victory in a finished state of liberty. Indeed, it is this contention of some core of rational subjectivity which would lay claim to freedom and thereby ground resistances to, and normative critiques of, its constraints, that most fundamentally distinguishes critical modernists like Habermas or Taylor, from postmodernists like Foucault or Derrida. The former taunt the postmoderns with lacking both counterfactual liberties that would give meaning to a problematically ubiquitous power and any normative position from which such power might be criticised. Their way of construing power as a negative and oppressive force, most insidiously exercised via ideology, does seem necessarily to imply something which is corrupted or suppressed but which might yet reveal itself. If however we accept Foucault's contention that power is also positive and productive (if, that is, we recognise that power is *also* conceived in negative and positive terms), then we are at least obliged to look more suspiciously at the sacrifices and exclusions such subjectivity might entail and more sceptically at its innocence. In any case, a certain paradox emerges at this point: if for the critical modernists rational subjectivity is real but (irremediably?) suppressed, for the postmodernists it is only too evident but contingent and illusory. In neither case is it obvious how it might provide a foundation for any meaningful force for liberty or resistance.

These questions are important for feminists insofar as they have understandably been attracted by a conception of liberty which engages internal impediments and anticipates free identities. In conformity with their own emphasis on the constraints that operate on a psycho-cultural level, positive liberty opens up questions about the sort of self a woman might struggle to become. Would this self then be some (universal? unique? contingent?) previously suppressed feminine self, or the (apparently ungendered) discriminating and critical self whom critical theorists would galvanise against ideology?

On the basis of my preceding discussion of poststructuralism, I think three caveats should at least be aired regarding feminist enthusiasm for positive liberty. First, how could we be sure that any ideal of the self avoids power, rather than issuing in a new set of constraints? It is important that even if it does not (that is, even if our sense of ourselves as discriminating and critical *is* an effect of certain discourses rather than an intuitive expression of some stubborn inner freedom) it might still intervene in the circuits of power to shift and perhaps lessen the burden of particular constraints. Such a possibility seems to be left open by the later Foucault, for whom power entails strategy and negotiation within a ubiquitous yet loosely-textured web of reciprocal relations. However, this would require us never to confuse such processes of resistance and liberation with some final goal of (individual or collective) realised freedom. For *any* attempt at equating liberty with a particular identity risks closure, homogeneity and constraint via its renewed standards of normality and exclusion.

At the very least then, we should be wary of uncritically accepting equations between autonomy, identity and liberty. Yet on the other hand, we cannot simply dismiss them. For many feminists are equally concerned lest a postmodern strategy of abandoning the quest for identity and autonomy should be uncritically pursued, since this can also be interpreted as a strategy of power that would silence women just as they were acceding to subjectivity and claiming autonomy for themselves.

The implication of Foucault's work is that our concern with self-discipline and autonomy arises from the imperatives of a disciplinary regime which engenders such subjects as conducive to an economical expenditure of power, rather than from a vocation for positive liberty. Yet feminist concerns suggest that we would wish nevertheless to retain these forms of relative empowerment as at least a strategy and facet of the self, even if it is a constructed and contingent, not foundational, facet.

Secondly, as Mary Lyndon succinctly warns: 'To claim essential womanhood, to assert oneself as subject, to demand the freedom to write "like a woman", to reclaim women's history, to speak their sexuality is a powerful temptation. Yet if we would excavate an allegedly repressed identity, we risk reinvoking images secreted by patriarchal discourses; if we would invent an authentic identity for ourselves, we risk imposing new, feminist, criteria of normality and exclusion once we are tempted to "name the rose"'.[8]

Finally, a third caution returns us to the spatial structurings on which positive liberty relies. We must look carefully at the language of (self-) control on which conceptions of positive liberty depend. We need to ask about what is controlled, as well as considering the relationship between controlled and controlling elements. It is in this context that I shall suggest a second and more foundational, spatial metaphor that underlies conceptions of positive liberty and embeds it in a deep structure of sexual difference.

To explicate this, it will be useful briefly to return to my criticism of negative liberty. I argued that this implicitly relied on an assumption about capacities for free subjecthood which rested on a rational/irrational opposition. Its tacit under-standing of rationality is a narrow one which circumscribes the freedom to which subjects might aspire. Because this opposition is also mapped by liberal thought onto the spatial distinction between public and private, women in particular have been excluded from definitions of free agency. My point about positive liberty is that it draws on an apparently similar opposition of rational/nonrational. This in turn maps onto the vertical spaces of the divided self, which would subdue its passions, emotions, body and dreams; its madness, instincts, intuition and fantasies in the name of self-mastery. In other words, the free self is construed as one who suppresses its own opacity and 'otherness'; that which is nonrational within itself. This nonrational element may vary according to current definitions of normality and deviance but my point is rather that its content has been remarkably stable within western culture since the Greeks. In fact the will to individual self-mastery here is strictly analogous to the project of western metaphysics generally, which would suppress a wild region of chaos, heterogeneity and difference in order to achieve a transparent language and self-expression that might fully and adequately represent the world and so master meaning.

The route taken by this argument thus brings us back to poststructuralism, although to that of Derrida rather than Foucault. The contention here is that western culture relies on binary yet hierarchical oppositions in order to express meaning at all but that the lesser term is suppressed and excluded despite its necessity in supporting the privileged and explicit term. Deconstruction then alerts us to what is silenced yet present through its absence and this is what I have been attempting, in a rather non-technical way, in my discussion of liberty. The positive conception of liberty then invokes foundational oppositions and these, as feminists (as well as Derrida) have shown, have been consistently aligned with masculine/feminine, where it is the latter that is associated with those nonrational forces whose suppression is necessary if the illusion of rational and linguistic mastery is to endure (and conversely, whose invocation is needed if that illusion is to be subverted). Thus madness, nature, flesh, subversion, nonsense, multiplicity have been consistently coded as feminine. For western culture generally, that which is defined as feminine must thus be silenced, as reason's other. Similarly, for the self who would achieve positive liberty, what is defined as the feminine part of oneself must be repressed. Thus while negative liberty would exclude a femininity which it associates with irrationality and constructs as a characteristic of women located in the private sphere, positive liberty would exclude the feminine as a metaphorical and psychological sign of reason's other. In both cases, femininity might be associated with actual women only contingently, but in practice patriarchy conflates them such that it is difficult to see how women (or indeed, men) might be free to pursue liberty, whatever that might mean, as long as western culture's founding oppositions remain intact. In other words, if we are serious about liberty, we need to look more deeply into the related constructions of meaning and subjectivity and this is what poststructuralism and feminism invite us to do.

Conclusion

To end with a new definition or project of liberty would clearly be antithetical to my argument. Feminist and poststructuralist analyses of the 'two concepts' nevertheless suggest some important concluding points.

To begin on a meta-level, they direct us to the language of political theory. They show that spatial metaphors are not used neutrally or innocently but carry prescriptive and exclusionary codings about material and cultural spaces. Allusions to private/public or lower/higher, invoke further distinctions between inner/outer, centre/margin. These in turn suggest relations of power regarding privilege and exclusion, which build on profound cultural meanings about gender and about normal or deviant forms of subjectivity.

This leads to my second point which is, that any discussion of freedom must pay attention to the subject who would be free, recognising both that constraining assumptions are often operative on this level and that this is a crucial site of struggles for freedom. This is not to propose some ahistorical, decontextualised and even more abstract notion of liberty but rather to insist that we recognise the intrinsic relationship between our assumptions of subjectivity and the type or value of freedom we associate with it. If our assumption about the subject are closed and homogeneous, then our conceptions of its possible freedom will be, too.

A third conclusion must then follow: that any attempt at defining some static state or spectrum of liberty is mistaken. It would be preferable to refer to processes of liberation, where these are in principle non-teleological and ongoing. However I think we should then avoid the usual distinction between liberation (as something positive) and resistance (as something negative); between freedom to and freedom from. For the two are indissolubly intertwined such that we recreate ourselves in the process of resisting constraints (especially those at the level of subjectivity) as they emerge and this complex practice takes place simultaneously on many levels.

Nevertheless, and fourthly, despite the ravages wrought by structuralism and postmodernism, an intuitive sense of oneself as a subject aspiring to freedom does undoubtedly remain strong among modern western individuals. Whether that self is real or illusory, foundational and natural or socially constructed in an environment of power, our fascination with discourses about liberty is motivated by a sense that modern conceptions of freedom are empowering and address a phenomenon central to our sense of who we are. As such, they are not simply to be rejected; rather the will to freedom we experience (whatever its historical or ontological status) would consistently exhort an ongoing critique of constraints built into our concepts of freedom, such that we engage in a spiralling process of deconstruction and recon-struction. As this proceeds, we might engender different subjectivities with quite different senses of liberation or even perhaps none at all.

Does anything of the two original concepts of liberty then remain? We might retain something of the positive version insofar as it can abandon its teleology of the subject and its metaphor of the vertically divided self. Then it might indicate a process of open exploration and creation of a multi-faceted and complex identity without preconception. Instead of an ideal of self-mastery, it would anticipate a (gender-)complex and heterogeneous self beyond the reason/nonreason oppos-ition. This would not be a free self as such, but one resistant to closed identities and available for (self-)exploration. Of course, this leaves open the question of whether such subjects would themselves associate heterogeneity and plurality with freedom. This process would also be in sympathy with negative freedom's stated quest (and its case against an overly rationalist positive liberty) for a plurality of unprescribed freedoms. It would only push that quest further, into the realm of genuine open-ness and difference, necessarily criticising its modern foundations and throwing liberty into question just where liberal versions have been most constraining.

Notes

1   I. Berlin, *Four Essays on Liberty*, Oxford: Oxford University Press, 1969, p. 121.

2   Berlin, *Four Essays*, p. 144.

3   Berlin, *Four Essays*, p. 165.

4   Berlin, *Four Essays*, p. 128.

5   M. Foucault, *Power/Knowledge, Selected Interviews and Other Writings, 1972–77*. New York: Pantheon Books, 1980, p. 39.

6   Foucault, *Power/Knowledge*, p. 98.

7   G. W. F. Hegel, *The Philosophy of Rights*, trans. T.M. Knox. Oxford: Oxford University Press, 1967, p. 244.

8   M. Lyndon, 'Foucault and Feminism: A Romance of many dimensions' in N. Diamond and L. Quinby (eds) *Feminism and Foucault: Reflections on Resistance*. Boston: North Eastern University Press, 1988.

BRITISH POLITICS

Introduction   *by Patrick Dunleavy*

At the beginning of our period, the study of British politics was carried on primarily by means of political history and institutional analysis of a rather traditional kind. During the 1950s the 'behavioural revolution' in American political science spilled over into British work, radically affecting the analysis of elections and the methods used for assessing the electoral impacts of party politics and political leadership. The behavioural focus also stimulated a lot of early work on interest groups in the later 1950s, their roles and influence then being almost unmapped in any systematic way. During the 1960s these important changes were progressively generalized to raise larger issues about the creation of elites, the operations of the political system as a whole in terms of either state theory, or the overall organization of political power – all of them 'sociological' topics. In the 1970s these developments were consolidated, while the area of major change shifted again towards the study of public policy processes, with new work broadening out from the study of public administration to encompass also a wider range of influences shaping policy outcomes.

One important aspect of professional change in empirical analysis has been the systematization of methods for collecting and analysing evidence. The standards of what counts as a convincing argument in the analysis of British politics have progressively shifted towards a more 'evidence-based' approach. An obvious aspect of this change has been the development of more quantitative analysis approaches, especially clear in the change of electoral studies to become the discipline's one authentic 'big science' area by the 1970s. But in Britain there were considerable barriers to the development of quantitative approaches even in cognate areas, like the study of party politics and interest groups. Government secrecy was very pervasive throughout the period until the early 1990s when controls began to be eased. For example, from 1992 onwards the structure of the cabinet committee system changed from being a state secret to being openly available. But the extent of changes should not be exaggerated – Cabinet papers are still locked away for thirty years. These government restrictions were copied in many minor ways by political parties and interest groups, making the study of political finance in the UK very difficult and fraught for example until the very close of the twentieth century. Since quantitative analysis relies on generating data which are reasonably reliable, comprehensive and well-validated, these restrictions were important limitations.

Yet the slow progress of more systematic work also reflected stylistic preferences amongst many British political scientists for 'soft' approaches, for 'thick' descriptions fitting very closely with the many anomalous features of the UK political system, and for explanations which stress historical continuities and the importance

Published by Blackwell Publishers, 108 Cowley Road, Oxford OX4 1JF, UK and 350 Main Street, Malden, MA 02148, USA

of elite and popular cultures in shaping how the polity works. Only in electoral studies did reliance on quantitative data become a *sine qua non* for professional debates, and then within a framework for analysis which seemed quite limiting to some critics. However, the converse effect has been that most analysis of British politics remain quite 'joined up' and open to wider theoretical interventions and movements. The nature of the UK state, for example, has been debated intensively in every decade since the late 1960s, along with the characteristics of British political culture and the origins of the multiple behavioural constraints which seemed to have kept liberal democratic processes vigorous despite a prima facie under-developed set of political and constitutional arrangements.

Our selection of papers on British politics reflect these multiple influences across different field of study – the core executive; the analysis of interest group influence and its import for the political system as a whole; electoral analysis; and the study of party systems. (In addition two more theoretical pieces included in the next section extend the analysis to include political economy aspects – how governments are affected by the business cycle; and public policy processes, as reflected in the extensive policy networks literature.)

The Routes of Entry of New Members of the British Cabinet, 1868–1958

F. M. G. WILLSON

Nuffield College, Oxford

The most obvious, but perhaps the hardest, step in developing quantitative approaches is to start counting things – at its simplest to transform information usually presented in a literary form into lists with numbers. D. N. Chester and F. M. G. Willson pioneered the introduction of more systematic counting practices into British public administration studies in the late 1950s. Their approach emphasized that analysts must form conclusions from the whole of the evidence available, rather than just selectively highlighting those elements which might be most convenient for their particular line of argument, as historical accounts can often do. Allied with this effort is an enlargement of the amount of simplified material that can now be covered in one pass. Willson's focus here is on how men (and a very few women) came to reach cabinet rank over almost the whole of the century up to the time he wrote. As well as pioneering a more behavioural approach to a field that we would now call 'core executive studies', this paper created an important bridge between studying the heart of the government machine and the wider debates about the sociological features of British elites.

I am inclined to think that Ministers of Government require almost as much education in their trade as shoe-makers or tallow chandlers. I doubt whether you can make a good public servant of a man simply because he has got the ear of the House of Commons.... Look at the men who have been leading statesmen since our present mode of government was formed – from the days in which it was forming itself, say from Walpole down, and you will find that all who have been of real use had early training as public servants.... Those who have been efficient as ministers sucked in their efficacy with their mother's milk.... They seated themselves in office chairs the moment they left college.

Anthony Trollope: *Phineaus Finn*

One of the most familiar generalizations about the British Cabinet is that its members are nearly always men (and, very occasionally, women) whose high standing in political life has been earned through years of service to Parliament and Party, and who have usually collected a good deal of ministerial experience of one sort or another before being invited to sit regularly in the Cabinet room. As a brief general statement this is unexceptionable, but the details are worth filling in, both because of their intrinsic interest and because they reveal some modern changes in constitutional practice.

Politics is one of the most unpredictable of careers even in so stable a political society as ours. Disraeli's analogy of the greasy pole was accurate as well as colourful. The swing of the political pendulum follows no rigid time scale: the electoral system often gives a disproportionately large number of seats to the majority party. These are but two of several institutional factors which, together with the immense variety of individual experience, make any attempt to produce generalizations about politicians' progress up the ministerial hierarchy very risky indeed. It behoves one, therefore, to use only material defined strictly enough to offset, as far as possible, the dangers of quantitative assessment based on small numbers.

The data used here is the parliamentary and ministerial service of all those who joined the Cabinet during the ninety years since Gladstone formed his first Liberal Administration in December 1868. The tendencies to change are brought out by comparing figures for the period from December 1868 to December 1916 with figures for the years since December 1916 – the date which marks off the old, informal nineteenth-century Cabinet from the modern highly 'institutionalized' body.

Unorthodox Recruits

Comparisons of Cabinet Ministers must, of course, be of like to like if they are to have any validity, and in the context of the last ninety years this raises an immediate problem and pinpoints the first tendency to change in constitutional practice. Before 1914 it was an overriding assumption that the Cabinet should be composed exclusively of parliamentarians – not just persons who on being chosen for the Cabinet would be found places in one House or the other, but persons who had solid practical experience as MPs or in the upper Chamber, or both; and this, in turn, implied long active participation in party politics. An unorthodox background might, on the other hand, be expressed as involving non-membership of the *genus* 'British career politician'.

Between Gladstone's first acceptance of office as Prime Minister and Asquith's resignation of that post, there were 109 new entrants to the Cabinet. Only one of them failed to meet the criteria of orthodoxy and, significantly, Lord Kitchener appeared in the Cabinet only as a result of the great emergency of August 1914. He had been ennobled as long before as 1898, but was in no sense a party politician.

Since December 1916, however, the practical monopoly of Cabinet membership which the orthodox career politicians had hitherto enjoyed has been broken – not drastically but quite notably. Of the 173 new entrants, no less than 28 have been sufficiently unorthodox to make it necessary to group them separately. Two – General Smuts in 1917 and Mr R. G. Casey in 1942 – were Commonwealth statesmen who never sat in our Parliament. Most of the other 26 entered the Cabinet with some parliamentary and ministerial qualifications, but these were either nominal (such as membership of but non-attendance at the House of Lords) or were gained over a very short time and/or in highly abnormal political circumstances. No precise criteria of unorthodoxy can be laid down, and in drawing up a list of the unorthodox an element of personal choice is inevitable. Some people might argue over the inclusion or omission of a few names, but nobody is likely to dispute the existence of a sizeable group of ministers who cannot by any stretch of the imagination come within the generally understood category of career politicians.

Five of the twenty-six were soldiers or sailors. Lord French, when Lord Lieutenant of Ireland, shared a seat in the Cabinet with his Chief Secretary. C. B. Thomson, who retired from the Army in 1919, accepted a peerage and became Secretary of State for Air in 1924 and 1929. Lord Chatfield, ennobled in 1928 at the end of a distinguished naval career, succeeded Sir Thomas Inskip (Viscount Caldecote) as Minister for the Co-ordination of Defence. Lords Ismay and Alexander of Tunis were both called to the Cabinet by Mr Churchill (as he then was) in the winter of 1951–52.

Another five were ex-officials. Lord Chelmsford, who succeeded to his title in 1905, spent almost the whole of the years from then until 1921 in Australia and India, and was not politically active after that until he joined the first Labour Government. Lord Olivier and Sir John Anderson (1st Viscount Waverley) had each completed a career as a civil servant and as a colonial governor before being pressed into service by MacDonald and Chamberlain respectively. Thirty years as Secretary of the Committee of Imperial Defence and of the Cabinet preceded Lord Hankey's time as a Minister. Sir James Grigg combined home civil service and overseas experience before becoming Secretary of State for War in 1942 and entering the 'Caretaker' Cabinet of 1945.

Three eminent lawyers – Lords Sankey, Maugham, and Simonds – all reached the Woolsack and the Cabinet without the usual preliminary of being a Law Officer or even of sitting in the Commons. Sir Robert (later Viscount) Horne, a prominent Scottish advocate, did distinguished work at the Admiralty in the First World War as a temporary civil servant, entered Parliament at the 'Coupon' Election, and was immediately made Minister of Labour, becoming a member of the supreme executive a few months later. Lord Amulree, a barrister with a long record of service as Chairman of Government committees, took over the Air Ministry after Lord Thomson had lost his life in the disaster of the R101. Sir Walter (now Viscount) Monckton was Solicitor-General in the 'Caretaker' Administration but only entered the House of Commons a few months before the fall of the Labour Government in 1951, and was given Cabinet office by Mr Churchill as Minister of Labour.

An historian, a doctor, and a physicist owed their Cabinet places to Lloyd George and Mr Churchill. H. A. L. Fisher came to the Board of Education in 1916, and joined the Cabinet in November 1919. Sir Auckland (later Lord) Geddes, was in the Cabinet for a few months in 1919–20 after serving in one or two ministerial capacities since 1917. Lord Cherwell was a Minister without a seat in the Cabinet during the Second World War, and entered the Cabinet of Mr Churchill in 1951.

Recruits from business, industry, and trade unions begin with Sir Eric Geddes, one of Lloyd George's men of 'push and go', brought into the war machine to become simultaneously an MP and First Lord of the Admiralty in 1917, graduating to the Cabinet as the first Minister of Transport in 1919. Ernest Bevin came straight to Parliament and the Ministry of Labour and National Service in May 1940, and was invited to join the War Cabinet a few months later. Mr Oliver Lyttelton (Viscount Chandos) and Lord Woolton were later war-time additions. Mr Attlee (as he then was) brought Lord Inman to the Cabinet: Mr Churchill introduced Lord Leashers, who had been ennobled and appointed Minister of War Transport in 1941 but had not sat in the War Cabinet. The most recent unorthodox appointment [in 1959] was that of Lord Mills, as Minister of Power, by Mr Macmillan.

Many of these appointments can be attributed to one or other of three particular causes – the special administrative demands of two World Wars, the need to make up for the weaknesses in the personnel of the Parliamentary Labour Party during the first two minority Labour Governments, and the desire of Mr Churchill in his last spell as Prime Minister to have around him some of the trusted colleagues of his war-time Administration. But these factors do not explain every unorthodox appointment. Moreover, once an 'unorthodox' Minister enters the Cabinet he may well stay on the stage of high politics for future spells of office – indeed since 1914 only Bonar Law's and Baldwin's three Cabinets (less than eight years out of forty-four) were without one or more of them.

The extent of these unorthodox appointments has not been noticed or assessed hitherto. In the third edition of *Cabinet Government*, [1958], Sir Ivor Jennings still restricts his attention in the relevant context, as in his first edition in 1936, to the unorthodoxy of Ministers holding office for short periods without being peers or M.P.s, and quotes the appointment of Brigadier-General Thomson in 1924 only as an example of the Prime Minister's freedom of choice.[1] Nor does any other authority do more than note the infrequent recruitment of an 'outsider': thus Professor Mackenzie and Mr Grove merely remark that 'There are exceptional cases in which an eminent person (very occasionally a civil servant) is brought into Parliament and into the Cabinet to give an impetus to the work of some Department which he knows very well.'[2] While it would be ridiculous to make too much of a development stimulated largely by emergency conditions, it is none the less worthy of note that at least one in every seven recruits to the Cabinet since December 1916 has not been an orthodox career politician. The presence of Lord Mills in the Cabinet today [1959] is a reminder that a constitutional practice has arisen which, if not yet normal, is certainly sufficiently usual not to demand any special explanation or defence when it is invoked. And, as will be seen, this sporadic unorthodoxy may be contrasted with at least as striking a growth of conformity in the official qualifications of the more usual recruits. It is to these latter that we may now turn.

The Professionals – Years in House and Office

When allowance is made for the 29 unorthodox recruits, we are left with 253 career politicians who entered the Cabinet between December 1868 and the present day. How long had these people served in Parliament before coming to their tasks as members of the Supreme Court of State? The answer cannot be given easily: the whole question is complicated by the existence of the House of Lords. A politician's service as an MP is unequivocally measurable: the political service of a peer is often difficult if not impossible to measure in terms of years and months.

Orthodox Cabinet Ministers fall into three categories in this context. First, those whose parliamentary experience before reaching the Cabinet was wholly acquired in the House of Commons. This is by far the largest group, comprising 214 Ministers – 87 before 1916, 124 since then. Secondly, at the other extreme, are those who never sat in the Commons, but gained all their political experience as peers: there were 10 of these between 1868 and 1916 and only five thereafter – Lords Listowel and Selkirk are the only two since the Second World War who belong to this class. The third group is made up of men who had experience as MPs and then either succeeded to titles or were raised to the peerage and served for some time in the Lords before entering the Cabinet. These latter number 11 before 1916 and 13 since.

Most of the 24 peers who had previously sat in the Commons continued their active political careers in the Lords until they reached the Cabinet, and their service in the upper House can be properly counted as parliamentary experience. This would apply, for instance, in the cases of the two contemporary representatives of the group – Lords Hailsham and Home. But some did not have these consecutive careers in the two Houses. Several men, having done a spell in the Commons and then gone to the Lords, were removed subsequently – sometimes for long periods – from the domestic political scene, either for private reasons or because their political careers took a different turn. Thus, for example, the 9th Duke of Devonshire spent five of the fourteen years between his succession to the title and his appointment as a Cabinet Minister in the office of Governor General of Canada. The 7th Marquess of Londonderry was for six of the thirteen years which passed between his succession and his entry to the Cabinet, a Minister in the Government of Northern Ireland. Because of this sort of factor, it is safer not to attempt to calculate what periods in the careers of this group of peers can be classified unequivocally as parliamentary. And this conclusion must apply even more definitely in the case of peers who entered the Cabinet without having served at all in the House of Commons. A man may succeed to a title before even reaching his majority, may take his seat in the House of Lords at twenty-one, and may become a Cabinet Minister at sixty-five. It could be that in the intervening forty-four years he has been, continuously, a career party politician, but equally he may not have taken any active part in party or parliamentary affairs for the first twenty or thirty of those years.

House of Lords experience, therefore, cannot be used safely in any quantitative assessment of pre-Cabinet parliamentary service, and we must confine analysis to service in the Commons. If we count in the peers who previously served as M.P.s, then the relevant arithmetic shows that, on average, each Cabinet Minister on taking office could look back on nearly fourteen years spent in the Commons. Before 1916 the average rises by about a year, and since 1916 it drops by the same amount. If the calculation is restricted to those whose pre-Cabinet service was exclusively in the House of Commons, the averages all fall by roughly six months. If exception be taken to averages, the breakdown in Table 1 may be more acceptable.

Table 1: Years in House of Commons before taking Cabinet Office

	5 or less	6–10	11–15	16–20	21–25	26 and over	Total
1868–1916	7 (4)	23 (21)	39 (35)	13 (12)	13 (12)	3 (3)	98 (87)
1916–1958	12 (12)	33 (33)	43 (40)	28 (23)	16 (14)	8 (5)	140 (127)
Total	19 (16)	56 (54)	82 (75)	41 (35)	29 (26)	11 (8)	238 (214)

The figures in brackets refer to ministers whose pre-Cabinet service was exclusively as M.P.s.

It is clear that the chance of a career politician entering the Cabinet without being thoroughly versed in the life of the House of Commons is very slight. Of the 19 who had five or fewer years experience, four later served in the Lords before reaching the Cabinet. None of the others had less than two years in the Commons: the only ministers in this category since 1945 are Mr Harold Wilson with two years and Mr Gordon Walker and Mr Gaitskell with five each.

We can now turn to the length of service in a ministerial capacity which makes up a second side of most Cabinet Ministers' apprenticeship. 'Ministerial capacity' covers service as Government Whips, Officers of the Royal Household whose appointments are 'political', Law Officers, Parliamentary Secretaries, etc., Ministers of State, and 'full' Ministers without seats in the Cabinet. For this experience – as easily measurable as membership of the House of Commons – we do not need to exclude any orthodox Minister.

Each one of the 108 orthodox entrants to the Cabinet between 1868 and 1916 had served on average before joining the Cabinet for about 3½ of his years in Parliament in some ministerial capacity or other. Since 1916 the average for the 145 entrants was 4½ years. Again the figures may be broken down further:

Table 2: Months Spent in Office before Entering the Cabinet

	Nil	1–12	13–24	25–36	37–48	49–60	61–72	73–84	85–96	97 and over	Total
1868–1916	20	12	11	14	11	17	9	2	3	9	108
1916–1958	20	18	14	18	12	20	15	6	9	13	145
Total	40	30	25	32	23	37	24	8	12	22	253

Perhaps the most interesting single figure in this table is the 40 men (no women) who reached the Cabinet without any previous ministerial experience. The two figures of 20 before 1916 and 20 since then give a misleading impression, however. Of the 20 who came to the Cabinet in the later period, no less than 13 were Labour Ministers brought from back-bench to office and Cabinet simultaneously in the two minority governments of James Ramsay MacDonald – the latter himself being one of them. The remainder – seven – is a fairer measure of the rareness of such rapid transitions since 1916 – a rareness which has become more intense over the years. No such appointment has been made, in fact, since Mr Aneurin Bevan and Mr George Isaacs were brought into the Cabinet by Mr Attlee in 1945.

There is no significant difference between the pre-Cabinet experience in Parliament and in ministerial office of members of the different parties. Even the Labour Party, a new organization breaking into the system, with very few peers in support and, until 1945, never having as many as 200 seats in the Commons except during the years 1929–31, has surprisingly high figures of average pre-Cabinet service – twelve years in the House of Commons for the orthodox members of all three Labour administrations, and nearly four years in office for the members of Mr Attlee's government. (The ministerial experience of members of the 1924 and 1929 Cabinets was obviously too slight for any valid comparison.)

Orthodox Conservatives and Liberals starting Cabinet careers between the wars first served on average only fractionally longer than Labour MPs in the Commons, but their official apprenticeship increased to 4½ years, partly reflecting the long spell of Conservative dominance. The small coalition Cabinet of the Second World War, followed by six years of Labour rule and then Mr Churchill's introduction of several 'unorthodox' ministers in 1951–52, all reduced severely the number of career Conservative politicians who were included for the first time in the Cabinet between 1939 and 1955. There were, in fact, only 20 of them, and they had served on average over sixteen years as MPs: only three had less than ten years' experience of the House of Commons, and two of these had long years in the Lords behind them as well. Of the 12 new orthodox entrants to Mr Churchill's third Cabinet only Sir David Eccles and Mr Heathcoat Amory entered Parliament after 1939, and the 12 already had on average over six years of ministerial experience behind them. Only under Sir Anthony Eden and Mr Macmillan have the figures been reduced to something nearer those of the Labour Party in 1945–51.

The Professionals – Official Ladders of Promotion

Analysis of the pre-Cabinet ministerial experience of the 213 career politicians who did not step directly from back bench to Cabinet shows one general and two highly specialized channels of approach. Of the latter, one is through the Whip's Office or the Royal Household or both, without any other experience. This has always been a relatively unusual background to a Cabinet career, and it has become steadily more unusual. Only nine entrants between 1868 and 1916, and only six since 1916 passed this way but this does not emphasize the change that took place about forty years ago. No one has jumped directly from a Court Office to the Cabinet since Lord Beauchamp was promoted from the Lord Stewardship (still political at that time) to the Lord Presidency of the Council in 1910; and all but two of the others who had held places in the Royal Household or Junior Lordships of the Treasury had finished their pre-Cabinet spells by 1922. Only two recent Conservative Chief Whips – Mr J. G. Stuart and Mr Patrick Buchan-Hepburn (Lord Hailes) – have succeeded since then in reaching the Cabinet after a ministerial career confined to the Whip's Office.

The second specialized approach to the Cabinet is that taken by lawyers, and here the practice has altered strikingly. The traditional route, through the House of Commons, the Solicitor- and/or Attorney-Generalships, or both, was taken by 14 men between 1868 and 1916. Until 1912 they often entered the Cabinet as Lord Chancellor. All the Lords Chancellors until 1912 had been along this normal route, but then came Haldane, who had never been a Law Officer but came from the War Office. At the same time the Attorney-General – Rufus Isaacs (1st Marquess of Reading) – was brought into the Cabinet, and several of his successors also held the seat until the practice was dropped in 1928. Only seven men have been chosen for the Cabinet after or simultaneously with holding a Law Officership alone, since 1916; two came in as Attorney-General and the other five joined the Cabinet in administrative posts. It is interesting to find that, although three 'unorthodox' appointments were made direct from the Bench (Lords Sankey, Maugham, and Simonds) no orthodox lawyer-politician has become Lord Chancellor without first holding an administrative portfolio since the 1st Viscount Hailsham accepted the office in 1928.

The remainder of the orthodox politicians who held some ministerial post or posts before entering the Cabinet numbered 66 in 1868–1916 and 113 in 1916–58 – about two-thirds of the total in each case. They had all served previously in one or more 'administrative' offices – i.e. to define them negatively, posts other than those of government Whips, places in the Royal Household, or Law Officerships. Seven in the earlier and 10 in the more recent period held Household Offices or posts as government Whips in addition to holding administrative jobs. But any official experience at Court or in the Whips' Office has become steadily rarer in the early career of a Cabinet minister. Since 1939 only Sir Thomas Dugdale has entered the Cabinet after beginning his ministerial life as a Junior Lord of the Treasury, and only Lord Selkirk has done so after starting as a Lord-in-Waiting. None in the first period, and three in the second, combined experience as Law Officers with administrative posts before entering the Cabinet. This leaves 59 out of a total of 108 orthodox entrants in the earlier years and 99 out of 145 in the second period whose apprenticeship was served exclusively in one or more of the non-Cabinet administrative places. Nine of those in the first and 15 in the second period jumped all the junior posts and started their ministerial careers as heads of departments or in equivalent non-departmental jobs such as Lord Privy Seal. Another 12 in the first period and 39 in the second began as Parliamentary Secretaries, Ministers of State, etc., and then served as 'full' ministers outside, before being invited inside the Cabinet. The rest – 38 in the earlier period and 47 in the later – after filling one or more junior posts, collected portfolios and places at the Cabinet table simultaneously.

Within this whole area of 'administrative' apprenticeship there are no significant patterns of promotion, whether the group be taken as one unit or split up according to period or party. The one exception to this is the much larger proportion of ministers who have served as 'full' ministers outside the Cabinet before entering it since 1939 than before that year. This is readily explained in terms of the larger number of ministries and the practice which has grown up of leaving several of their political chiefs out of the Cabinet. Of the 26 orthodox recruits to the Conservative Cabinet since 1951, no less than 18 had previous experience as a head of department or held office of equivalent status. Another point of some interest concerns holders of the office of Financial Secretary to the Treasury who, traditionally, have been regarded as being well on the road to the Cabinet. Since 1868 there have been 52 holders of that office, of whom 33 subsequently became Cabinet ministers. Of the 19 who were not (or have not yet been) so promoted, one was a non-parliamentarian appointed for special administrative duties during the First World War (Sir Hardman Lever) and four who are now in mid-political career probably still have many chances of achieving Cabinet status. If these five are discounted then one can say that three out of four holders of the Financial Secretaryship to the Treasury since 1868 have become members of the Cabinet; and the proportion reaching the Cabinet has been almost exactly the same before and after 1916.

Some Conclusions

There has been little difference over the last century in the time a career politician must expect to spend in Parliament before he reaches the Cabinet. If anything the overall period is now a little shorter, no doubt because of the reduced size of the House of Commons, the decline in the importance – and therefore in the propriety – of choosing many ministers from the Lords, and the sheer increase in the number of offices to fill. The amount of experience of office demanded has grown noticeably, however; and even if due allowance is made for the effects of the two World Wars in reducing the intake of ministers to the Cabinet, the permanently increased number of non-Cabinet offices to fill will doubtless ensure the continuation of the longer spell as a journeyman minister, at any rate if the balance of power changes often enough at the hands of the electorate.

The ambitious office-seeker of the present day must recognize, therefore, perhaps with some sorrow, that his chances of avoiding a thorough ministerial grooming are much slighter than formerly. The possibility of his making a dramatic jump from back-bench to Cabinet is increasingly rare. He must reconcile himself to a rather longer spell of apprenticeship in office than did his earlier counterparts; and unlike them, he must take care to ensure that his official experience is predominantly administrative. He must avoid the Whips' Office and shun the dignities of the Court. Even if he is a lawyer-politician with his eye firmly on the Lord Chancellorship, he must broaden himself before or after service as a Law Officer by finding a departmental home for a while: otherwise his call to the Woolsack may never come. In short, the orthodox career politician must nowadays be, in a parliamentary and ministerial context, more orthodox than ever if he wishes to reach the Cabinet. The variations once indulged within the greater orthodoxy of parliamentary membership are apparently now much less acceptable to the makers of Cabinets. The professional politician must have kept to a straight and narrow path: the modern tendency is for variety of background to be added to the membership of Cabinets only by the appointment of people from right outside the parliamentary ranks. This brings us back to the unorthodox recruits.

From one point of view it might be claimed that the appearance of so few 'outsiders' in the Cabinet during a period when the tasks of government have multiplied enormously and when the pressure of total war has twice exerted its distorting influence, is a testimony to the strength and comprehensiveness of the parliamentary tradition and to the high calibre of those who tread the normal party-political and parliamentary path. At the same time a student of parliamentary government might draw less comforting conclusions, even while admitting all the difficulties and peculiarities of the last fifty years and while admiring the outstanding qualities of many of the unorthodox recruits and their enrichment of public life. Is there not room for some wonder whether – even allowing for the basic factors of more and bigger jobs, not so many MPs, and fewer available peers – a career politician who combines the qualities required to be a sound parliamentarian with sufficient administrative ability to hold down a Cabinet office is a rarer bird in the conditions of the twentieth than in those of the nineteenth century? And if there is any semblance of a positive answer to that question, may it not be significant that recourse to the non-party and non-parliamentary specialist administrator has gone along with an increasing rigidity in the attitude of parties towards their members and a growing tendency for Parliament to become an overwhelmingly full-time job? In fact, is there a chance that some men who would be potentially first-class ministers do not take part in public affairs because they are repelled by the character of modern political life? Or is it possible that years of experience of a contemporary party and parliamentary career inhibit rather than stimulate the development of a capacity for dealing with the ever-widening scope of a Cabinet post?

Notes

1   In both editions see chaps. 3 and 5

2   W. J. M. Mackenzie and J. W. Grove, *Central Administration in Britain*, Longmans Green, 1957, p. 336.

Consensus or Elite Domination: the Case of Business

J. P. Nettl

Writing at the end of a period of extensive work on interest groups and pressure groups, Nettl sought to use the literature to address broader questions of characterizing the British state as a whole. His chosen focus on the role of business was an important area for pluralist theory, a key front on which to combat views of business elites as dominant. Unusually for an academic political scientist, Nettl had previously had a successful business career, and his analysis combines a degree of 'insider' knowledge with a theoretical concern that was unusual at this period. Our selection here is confined to Nettl's account of what he saw as a distinctive feature of UK policy-making, the role of a carefully constructed, maintained and nuanced consensus and of actors' role-playing, in sustaining co-operative behaviour. But his full paper includes a more extensive discussion of the precise mechanisms by which Whitehall and British business elites achieve concertation of decisions.

This article attempts to demonstrate a general thesis from a particular segment of society. The general thesis is that the famous British consensus is not a sort of social or political ectoplasm which emanates from, and hovers over, the consentient, but a social institution with its own structure, procedures, attitudes, beliefs. Nor is it equally shared. Instead, like a magnet, it sucks in members (or servants) from the periphery – away from their own self interested groupings. In doing so it emasculates these groups, while preserving their outward shell of autonomy and independence. Pressure group politics are therefore less 'real' than they seem – their very success in Britain, which has thrilled (American) political commentators searching for limited and orderly struggle as the highest form of organized democracy, may indeed depend on this element of shadow-boxing.[1] It will be argued moreover that the consensus has its peculiar and particular exponent, both vehicles of consensus attitudes and ideal type – the higher civil service. It does not create the consensus, nor is it created by it; nonetheless it is the centre of its magnetic field, its institutional expression.

This general thesis is examined in the particular context of the business community in its relations with Whitehall. The relationship is discussed in its various aspects – social, procedural, structural, legal, and from the point of view of policy, public and sectional. The usual practice in such cases is to use the tunnel method: broad general proposition – particular and 'narrow' application including 'proof' – restatement of broad general proposition with 'proof' of the validity of the connexion between the particular and the general. I shall be less orderly, shuttling back and forth from the general to the particular all the time. I believe the one makes no sense if divorced from the other, even for a short space of time.

It is a large subject and I can only sketch the problem in an article, ask more questions than I can answer and, even where an answer is attempted, indicate the manner of answering rather than provide the substantive answer itself. But perhaps this manner of approach will, if found valid, enable others to screw out answers from the intractable plethora of social relations in England.

Before we get down to any *relationship*, we must briefly examine the state of the related. I hope to show that as far as the business community is concerned, it is a state of remarkable weakness and diffuseness – compared, say, to organized labour or the professions. Lacking firm sense of their distinct identity, and belief in their distinct purpose, businessmen have been particularly vulnerable to the pressure of the consensus as emanating from Whitehall. (I have of course to show, and not merely to assume, the latter's strength and cohesiveness – indeed its very existence.) The whole problem is largely virgin soil. There is a certain amount of factual material concerned with the structure and methods of government in order to be able to study its relations with the structure and methods of business. The new (in Britain) subject of pressure groups has again opened up certain aspects of business-government relations, but not in an exclusive sense; pressure groups are part of the political input process (in the broadest sense of 'political') in which business is an also-ran. Significantly the best detailed studies of pressure groups in Britain do not relate to business at all, but to professional organizations. Then there is the amorphous field known as 'economics', particularly policy and planning, in which government action on the economy has been discussed – the economy being a nameless, faceless, passive honeycomb of 'firms'. Finally business has been studied *per se* – with the government now in the role of faceless though active juggler of the parameters. Thus there is much incidental information on the relationship between government and business, but usually with the one serving as a vaguely limiting or activating factor of the other. No specific study of the dynamic, exclusive and precise relationship exists. Nor, of course, has this relationship been used as evidence of wider social problems.[2]

The Image of Business

Let us start with that mythical beast, the rugged entrepreneur: individualistic, non-conformist, aggressive, anti-social – the spider who sits at the centre of all the symmetrical webs of economists' models relating to perfect competition or the market economy. Historically, he is the product of ignorance and neglect; the government and the social forces behind it were hardly aware of his social or political existence until he had created his revolution – in the North, at the far end of the kingdom. For a long time, most of the legislation which took note of his existence was designed to inhibit him rather than positively to help those who worked for him, not to speak of helping him. The significant difference between the industrial revolution in England and elsewhere in Europe was the indifference of the central government, its failure for a long time to see any but undesirable consequences in what was happening – the ruin of agriculture. It seems to be a valid generalization in Europe that the later industrial take-off and drive to maturity took place, the greater the extent to which governments got in on the act. And, just as many of our constitutional forms relate to the eighteenth century – a gap bridged by myth – so does the popular picture of the businessman still portray the rugged individual with the Yorkshire accent, with his aggressive contempt for the bewildering allurements of wicked London. We still find him occasionally in the fiction best-sellers of the less sophisticated kind ('Room at the Top'); monotonously he croaks and snaps at us from the television screen and out of the pages of serialized fiction – where, incidentally, we must look primarily for the personalization of our more massive myths, not in the sophisticated novels of Iris Murdoch or C. P. Snow. Curiously enough we also find him deeply embedded in the common-law view of business, which holds that the only possible function of business is to make money – and be very frugal about spending it.[3]

Such a man dislikes and fears government and has as little as possible to do with it. A few real specimens of the type still exist, on sociological parole from Manchester and Bradford. But nowadays the rugged entrepreneur hardly exists any longer, and certainly is typical of nothing but a sentimental attachment to eccentricity. Why then does fiction predominate so grossly over fact? The reason is that this hundred-plus-year-old figure is in fact the only example of a specific business identity that we have. Nothing equally specific or exclusive has ever taken his place. There has, in fact, been a vacuum and he has survived in it. Nor is it an entirely accidental vacuum. The sturdy British businessman to whom successive Presidents of the Board of Trade refer – this is he; Harold Macmillan's reminder that exporting is fun could only have been nostalgically addressed to such as him – he being a man uncouth enough to derive satisfaction out of 'doing' foreigners. As a type the rugged entrepreneur exists largely in the mind of the remoter members of both political parties – and in popular fiction.

This is not an image that businessmen like or even accept, but the point is that try as they might, they have never been able to find a better common image with which to displace it. Literature has not helped. In England, unlike America, business novels are not a recognized literary form; business *characters* in novels do not usually rise above the grotesque antics of John Braine's Brown.[4] 'It is simply that here [in England] we know our audience. Any reading public is a tiny minority of the whole population; with us … the minority shares enough assumptions to be a good audience'.[5] And one of the assumptions shared is expressed by one of C. P. Snow's own fictional characters in *Strangers and Brothers*: 'I'm still convinced that successful business is devastatingly uninteresting'.[6] The pathetic best that advertising has tried to do for business is the figure of the benevolent public benefactor (the bank manager who really looks like a doctor and family solicitor rolled into one, and apparently working for no fee) or the anonymous corporation whose only concern is working for the benefit of the public – and occasionally its employees.

Business in England thus lacks a social identity of its own. The effects are far-reaching. I have, in a different context, previously dealt with the *economic* impact of this problem on profit maximization.[7] In our society there is a general and more particular reason for this lack. The general reason – extending beyond business – is that while we like to think of ourselves as essentially 'individuals', and both admire as well as sustain the articulation of eccentricity – laughing at regimented nations like the Germans – the real social situation is precisely the other way about. It is the Germans who are educated and trained to accept individuality and loneli-ness – hence the Hegelian State as substitute father – while our education is towards group activity, public virtues, team spirit, and the fancy that we are sufficiently cohesive not to need such a state. Having a notion of the public good instilled into us, we do not need to search for it – it emerges. Having group identities *ab ovo* we do not need to create them artificially. Thus there are existing social cohesions which surpass the strength of any specific group identity for businessmen – or teachers or farmers or politicians. One is *either* a rugged individual entrepreneur *or* a public figure, full of public spirit and consensus illumination, who happens to spend working hours in a business firm (but could just as well do so elsewhere).

The more specific reason lies in our attitude to ascription of merit. We do not recognize 'separate but equal' or parallel careers; like the American Supreme Court – though with more success – we enforce integration, at least at the top. Our honours list is a general one, barely divided into civil and military at odd points; businessmen get the same honours as scientists, footballers, professors, politicians – and, most important, civil servants.[8] This applies to an O.B.E. as much as to a peerage. In France, and even more in Germany and Austria, the businessman has, or had, until recently, his own hierarchy of status and honour. The British businessman thus competes for honours designed for entirely different social groups. He is expected, in return, to adopt some of the attitudes that go with, say, membership of the House of Lords – to follow the example of the more regular and 'normal' recipients of honours. The granting of honours – at least higher ones – thus becomes a co-option more than a reward. A well known sub-category of the rugged entrepreneur in literature – charged with special functions of hilarity – is the rugged entrepreneur in ermine. I have always wondered whether the honours scandal under Lloyd George was not so much due to the manner of obtaining the peerages in question as the *continuing* 'rugged' and unreconstructed behaviour of the recipients. Once more we have the well known absorption effect of British society embracing the business world – but at a price of group self effacement.[9]

It is an extraordinary and unique feature of British society that those considered worthy of higher bracket honours – a growing 'safety valve' category – should thereby be promoted to the legislature as well. A title can be a reward – and always was; appointment as royal counsellor was another reward for entirely different services, and one imposing obligations of service; only a special kind of philosophy assumes that both needs can be met with one and the same reward. A philosophy which assumes people – certain people – to be capable of playing a variety of quite different roles with equal distinction, and without conflict between one and the other. This notion necessarily reduces roles to the inferior status of a charade (a typically British game), limited and controlled by that obstinate, pervasive insistence of the common good ('general will' if you like) emerging through all institutional and role disguises by virtue of – what? The public virtues of education, of team spirit, of social cohesion, in short of consensus.[10]

This I believe to be the central mechanism of British society and its sub-function, government. The notion of a division of powers originated in this island, from where it was transported into the practice of the American constitution and the theory of Montesquieu. Here in the last 150 years it has been neither applied nor specifically contradicted, it has simply been gobbled up by the assumption that its positive benefits can somehow always be retained by the unique British capacity for charades. A civil servant can be a judge, a minister of the crown can be a legislator, a businessman can be a civil servant or tax collector, an arts graduate can be a science boss – providing he declares his role and providing he adopts the relevant procedures. Institutional and personal separation, the classical division of powers applied in America and now revived by De Gaulle in France, became an unnecessary (and unspoken) nuisance in Britain and was quietly but effectively emasculated. Today only lawyers and very old fashioned professors of government discuss it as a factor to be reckoned with. What counts are people – flexible, independent, selfless people able to fill any role with unblemished distinction. The only similar notion I have ever discovered elsewhere in the modern world is in the Soviet Union where party members are supposed to be equally able to tackle any assignment with the virtuosity of the allrounder (i.e. Communist).

In C. P. Snow's *The Masters* and again in *The Affair* there is a very pompous and irritating Master of a College, Crawford, who prefaces almost every one of his pontifical, uninteresting and usually obvious remarks with the phrase: 'Speaking now as a scientist' (or 'as a private individual' or 'as Master of the College' or 'as an impartial judge'). None of the characters in the book, or Snow himself, ever for one moment challenge his right to change hats in this fashion – for Crawford only says what others do without saying. A great critic has called *The Masters* 'a paradigm of political life',[11] – and so it is, for the roles and functions of the college officers are – and are intended to be – perfectly capable of transplantation into Government, or for that matter into business. I make, incidentally, no apology for the frequent subpoena of C. P. Snow because he has lived in the stratosphere of the higher consensus and has tried to report it – in all its implications.

This then is the declaration of roles. In practice it operates very much as in literature. Only the English civil service and armed services have developed the special ghost category of 'acting' and 'temporary' positions, in which someone plays a superior role with all the attributes of the acquired rank save one – permanence (and partly pay). The impartial tribunal or commission, indiscriminately composed from among the higher consensus and confronted by the 'expert' (i.e. committed) witness, is another example of role-playing. Of course, experts sit on commission or tribunals too, but those who become deeply committed (i.e. criticize the government too strongly) are often left to cool off in a commissionless tundra for a while. Unpaid magistrates, drawn from a very wide consensus list, are another example. And finally, as we shall see, most extraordinary and least known of all; businessmen 'regulating' their industry on a ministry's behalf.[12]

The other necessary condition is the adoption of the relevant procedure that goes with the role. Examples of this, too, are legion, especially in the adoption of judicial procedures (including representation), by administrative tribunals or local housing inquiries. One of the most piquant examples was the procedure evolved in 1946–47 for assuring the continued internment of dangerous Germans not actually found guilty of specific crimes, a procedure in which amateur judges, prosecution and defence – temporary Control Commission officials and army officers – went through mock trials to deck up a political proceeding in luridly legal colour, to the utter bewilderment of participating German lawyers. And the procedure won; it proved very difficult to 'convict' anybody – because the legal charade required a burden of proof that was simply (and by definition) not available.

In emphasizing role-playing as the structural myth of the British Constitution or polity, I believe that I am close to the central lubricant of British political and social life, for this seems to be the explanation of how the system works, why it works at all. The whole institutional paraphernalia of functional differentiation has been vitiated or scrapped, yet we speak of Executive, Legislature and Judiciary as though they were distinct entities; we speak of business, the professions, government as though these were wholly separate worlds. To see the real potential of our constitution we need only look at daughter versions operated without our myths – Ghana or South Africa. Yet the role playing capacity of the amateur is a myth – unless the British really are a kind of *Herrenvolk*. All roles cannot be equal, one must dominate, for procedural reasons if no other, but more probably because, as Khrushchev has stated, no men are neutral. Just as every conversation between two people is a mild form of tussle for control, so every role played conflicts somewhere with another, played already or yet to be played. As an adequate political system charades, however well acted, are not good enough.

Sociology, though much exercised by the concept and problems of roles, has surprisingly little to offer on this particular problem. The basic concept (an anthropologist's) is one person one role at one time; the problem is how to relate it to the social structure, and how to identify its specific attributes and consequences. In our more sophisticated societies, multiplicity and even conflict of roles has, of course, been recognized. But the accent is still mainly on the role itself (role consensus means agreement about a role, and not different roles within our present type of consensus); on the level of commitment to a single role or to one of several conflicting roles rather than on any multiplicity of sub-roles or, as I have dubbed it, charades.[13] Neither conceptually nor terminologically does role theory cater for a consensus in role expectations that calls for the ability to tackle a host of sub-roles with no more commitment to each than a little stylized and temporary dressing up – adopting procedures and sitting in a chair labelled according to the role. Hence charades, once more.

The consensus I have in mind is not therefore simply an emanation of some unique British quality – though it has some of that too. Nor is it just the product of conscious compromise and group self-denial. I believe that to have a consensus *at all*, you need an ideal type, a model of attitudes, procedures, institutions – an elite. This must not be socially so remote as to make emulation and effective entry impossible. You also need a vehicle that will effectively carry the consensus into society. In Britain this is the higher civil service. It has the access. Its methods, social and functional attitudes, and values are being ever more widely adopted. It allocates honour and rewards much in accordance with its internal scale. It has all the strength of adulation in popular as well as sophisticated literature.[14]

Now from the general to the particular. As I have already stated, the relationship of government and business has not been examined in this context. On the input side (business to government) the student of politics has briefly identified pressure groups. On the output side (government to business) it has been the economists' pigeon. I believe, and will try to show, that in the social relationship between the institutions of government on the one hand and business on the other, the lack of social identity of the latter has been fostered, exploited and pre-empted by government (i.e. the civil service), and that this has led to something like schizophrenia in the world of business.

Though specially strong in Great Britain, the notion of consensus is not uniquely British. It is a feature of all sophisticated societies. But the first problem is: whose consensus? For consensus is not so much the product of compromise as of elite ascendancy and its acceptance. In Britain it is, I maintain, presently a Whitehall consensus. It was not always so. But the political emasculation of the aristocracy as a condition of its survival, together with the remarkable decline of importance of formal politics (House of Commons, party conferences, grass roots) in favour of the executive and its chief, the Prime Minister, have led to the quiet emergence of the Snowmen, the upper civil servants and their mores. Their influence on the professions was socially logical and predestined, their influence over business a more drawn-out and difficult process. Efforts are being made to draw in the trade unions and the arts, though with only limited success as yet.

In America it is just the other way about. There is consensus too (though weaker) and it comes *from* the business community.[15] Top businessmen join the administration – not to be businessmen (like Beeching) but to be administrators (Macnamara). When Americans think of 'organization' or 'administration', they visualize big business as often as government, at least they did until the end of the last war. Significantly the dichotomy individual/organization in American fiction is a business problem, from Theodore Dreiser to John P. Marquand; it was not until the McCarthy era that Merle Miller first used government as the personality-crushing octopus of fiction.[16] Not that the theory of organization meets with universal approval in literature; the optimal view is size and growth *plus* a 'mood of nostalgic reverie for the company town, the home of paternalistic order, domestic virtue and productive work … assumptions – far from being 'capitalistic' or contemporary – are actually Populist and Veblenian'.[17] There is here a view of business as a social philosophy, and both nostalgic 'good' and contemporary 'bad' are more sophisticated – and a much more popular subject for fiction – than the rugged North country millowner of Britain.

In American fiction and in European fact, the choice is between the individual and the corporation – with a happy ending ensuring the triumph of the former (integrity) over the latter (corruption) – or his utter degradation. Only in the English novels of C. P. Snow do the needs of individual and organization have to be reconciled; justice for the former, respectable self-preservation for the latter. The Continent has been fascinated by Snow's proposition, indeed for the whole 'typically English' problem. There the consensus (in so far as it exists) is not concerned either with business or with administration but with questions of political philosophy; business and government are – and are expected to be – in a state of permanent friction, fighting and subverting each other (influence is too polite a word).

I think only Sweden can fairly be compared with Britain. Those, like Gunnar Myrdal, who believe that consensus, self-regulation and widespread charades are the hope of civilized democracy (with perhaps more tolerant public policies in the international 'state of nature') put Sweden first as an example, then Britain. But it seems to me that this system is in many ways a self-denying ordinance, which Switzerland and Sweden has accepted (one might suggestively for once list the things these countries have to do *without*) but for which this country is not yet ready. For Britain, the austere consensus at home is not at all austere in the field of international relations, public policy still demands greatness (at least the equipment that goes with it). Hence the importance of the essentially British make-believe of charades, propagated and best played by Whitehall.

Notes

1 Harry Eckstein, *Pressure Group Politics: The Case of the British Medical Association*, London: Allen Unwin, 1960. See also S. H. Beer in *American Political Science Review*, Vol. 50, No. 1, pp. 1–23, March 1956 and Vol. 51, No. 3, pp. 613–50, September 1957.

2 Yet the problem cries for identification as soon as businessmen are examined as a group. See Roy Lewis and Rosemary Stewart, *The Boss. The Life and Times of the British Businessman*. London: Phoenix House, 1958; a lengthy though superficial study that consistently stubs its toes on our problem without ever coming to grips with it. This is partly the penalty of examining any group in isolation, however thoroughly.

3 'The directors must act *bona fide* in what they consider – not what the court may consider – is in the interests of the company', Lord Greene M. R. in *Re Smith v. Fawcett* (1942) ch. 304, 306. See also *Hogg v. Crampthorn* as discussed in *Journal of Business Law* (1964), pp. 51–3. See also the note on commercial firms as potential patrons of the arts in *New Society* no. 83, 30 April 1964, p. 5, where Lord Greene's remarks are misquoted. The mandatory obligation on businessmen to act like businessmen is enhanced by the fact that their fiduciary duty is not to the shareholders (who might conceivably have notions of public interest) but to the company which by definition cannot have.

4 Of course there are stories about business families like *The Crowthers of Bankdam*, and businessmen – usually stereotyped – parade through many novels. But there is little interest in business as a social problem. An honourable exception is Anthony Trollope, *The Way we live now*.

5 C. P. Snow, 'Which Side of the Atlantic: The Writer's Choice' *New Statesman*, LVI (1958), p. 287–8.

6 C. P. Snow, *Strangers and Brothers*. London, 1951, p. 93.

7 See J. P. Nettl, 'A note on entrepreneurial behaviour', *Review of Economic Studies*, XXIX, 2 (1957) p. 87. See also *The Listener*, LVI, 1399 (22 December 1955).

8 Compare Marx's category of economic parasites: 'King, priest, professor, prostitute, soldier, etc.' who 'draw their revenues by grace of their social function …' *Capital*, Vol. ii, p. 429 (Transl. E. Untermann, Chicago: Chicago University Press, 1907).

9 The sociological effect of, and justification for, the award of honours in different modern societies deserves more study, particularly the question whether honours (other than for valour) relate to the quality of persons or acts.

10 I now find that the theatrical analogy of roles and the dramaturgical method of analysis has already been very ably used by Erving Goffman, *The Presentation of Self in Everyday Life*, New York, Doubleday 1959. Though not immediately relevant to this political context, I can but assert in my own defence that this interesting work only came to my notice after this article had been completed.

11 Lionel Trilling, *A Gathering of Fugitives*. Boston, 1956, p. 130.

12 It is curious that Britain, with its very real consensus, has no popular word for it – unlike nations where consensus is much less well established. Cp. the Italian expression *La gente par bene*.

13 See N. Gross and others, *Explorations in Role Analysis*. New York, 1958.

14 An examination of how the civil service came to play this role – how the consensus came to be created and how it is maintained – is outside the scope of this paper. Probably one of the key factors is the higher educational system – and the absence of social immersion in a continental or American type of compulsory military service. The army is part of the general consensus in Britain, not a separate establishment.

15 The most up-to-date and suggestive study of this problem in the United States is Raymond A. Bauer, I. de Sola Pool, Lewis A. Dexter, *American Business and Public Policy: The Politics of Foreign Trade*.

New York: Atherton Press, 1963. See also T. J. Lowi's review article in *World Politics*, XVI, 4 (July 1964), 677–715. I think this book bears out my general thesis very well (see pp. 150 ff. 209–consensus, and p. 125 ff.–location of elite).

16 Merle Miller, *The Sure Thing*. New York: Penguin, 1952. Compare the title of a businessman's reminiscences of Washington – Martin Merson, 'My education in Government', *The Reporter*, 7 October 1954 – where he compares 'Expediency vs. Efficiency: a businessman's misadventures in the Eisenhower Administration'. I owe this, and two other American references, to my colleague Professor Michael Millgate, of Toronto.

17 Eric Larrabee and David Riesman, 'Company – Town Pastoral: The role of Business in [Cameron Hawley's] *Executive Suite*' in Rosenberg and White (eds), *Mass Culture: The Popular Arts in America*. Glencoe, Illinois, 1957, pp. 326–7.

Angels in Plastic:
The Liberal Surge in 1974

James Alt, Ivor Crewe and Bo Särlvik

By the 1970s voting studies was firmly established as the most 'scientific' of all the sub-fields in the discipline, reflecting the treatment in Butler and Stokes' seminal book, *Political Change in Britain*. But some of the key features in this founding work, especially the stress on long-lasting party identifications by voters to the Conservative and Labour parties, were almost immediately called into question by the two 1974 general elections, when both major parties saw their vote shares slip simultaneously, to the benefit of third and fourth parties. Somewhere in the 1972–73 period a sea-change took place in British politics, which resulted most clearly in a big rise in the Liberal share of the vote to 18 or 19 per cent. Writing in 1977 Crewe and his colleagues were not to know that this growth was to prove more or less permanent, and their treatment of the phenomenon as a 'surge' akin to previous evanescent upward blips in Liberal support is testimony to the enduring power of a 'major party' view at this time. Yet this paper is not only the first serious effort to understand who third party voters are in Britain and what motivates them, but it has remained over many subsequent years perhaps the most impressive effort to tackle a baffling problem. For the truth is that third party voters are very hard to characterize in clear sociological or ideological terms – and like the raised level of third party voting this feature has proved an enduring one.

In the election of February 1974, the Liberal Party received nearly three times as many votes as it had in the General Election three-and-a-half years before. Survey-based research on the much smaller Liberal vote of the 1960s reached three main conclusions:

(1) The Liberal vote was electorally *volatile*: Liberal voters, unlike supporters of the major parties, could not be counted on to turn out repeatedly for their party.

(2) The Liberal vote was *socially representative*: with some local exceptions, social and economic variables did not discriminate Liberal voters from the rest of the electorate.

(3) The Liberal vote was essentially *negative*: attitudinal content linked to Liberal voting consisted of rejection of the major parties rather than appreciation of the Liberal Party or its policies.

Our central interest is in seeing how well these conclusions continue to hold up in the light of the much larger Liberal vote of 1974.

The most frequently commented-on feature of the Liberal vote is its volatility. Butler and Stokes report less than 1 per cent of those in the electorate in both 1959 and 1970 as voting Liberal on both occasions.[1] Among a sample of middle-class men interviewed on five occasions between 1959 and 1970, Himmelweit and Bond report only 2 per cent voting or intending to vote Liberal on four or more occasions.[2] The aggregate Liberal vote holds up only because at each election the

© *Political Studies Association, 2000.*
Published by Blackwell Publishers, 108 Cowley Road, Oxford OX4 1JF, UK and 350 Main Street, Malden, MA 02148, USA

Liberal Party draws off a small proportion of the major parties' former supporters to compensate for massive defections from among its own ranks. In the next section, we show that the volatility of Liberal support can be exaggerated, though it is indeed the case that the Liberal Party has only a small core of regular supporters. We then propose a typology of Liberal support which takes into account attitudes and behaviour at more than one election, and show that this typology compels us to revise considerably the conventional view of the Liberal Party as socially representative.

(a) *Volatility of Liberal Support.* It is certainly the case that the Liberals are less able to retain their support from one election to the next than are either the Conservatives or Labour. In each successive pair of elections since 1959, both major parties have retained on average close to 80 per cent of their support from one election to the next, and never much less than 70 per cent. The weakest retention by a major party in this period is by the Labour Party, which retained only 69 per cent of its 1966 voters in 1970. The *average* Liberal retention of its vote from one election to the next in this period was only 60 per cent: it was never higher than 71 per cent (1970 to February 1974) and has been as low as 52 per cent (1964 to 1966). The extent to which a party retains its support from one election to the next depends on whether it is winning or losing, and on the interval between elections:[3] since Labour's electoral position relative to the Conservatives has improved between 1959 and 1974, it appears that Labour is slightly better able to retain its votes. Nevertheless, and even though the Liberals do retain three votes in five from one election to the next, they are far less able than either major party, on average, to retain a large bloc of constant support.[4]

One reason for this lower rate of vote retention might have to do with the smaller number of candidates fielded by the Liberal Party. There are some Liberal voters at one election who find themselves without a Liberal candidate at the next election, a situation which does not arise among voters for the major parties. However, the number of Liberal candidates increased steadily from 1959 to 1974 so that the absence of candidates does not have a large effect. Moreover, the great majority of those who vote Liberal live in seats where the Liberals stand every time, for the seats where the Liberal Party drops out are those in which they do worst, and thus where the fewest of the voters live. It is probable that not more than 10 per cent of 1966 Liberal voters found themselves without a Liberal candidate in their constituency in 1970, and the proportion must have been smaller in 1974. Liberal vote retention since 1959 in those constituencies with Liberal candidates each time probably increased from 60 per cent to 65 per cent, but this is still far lower than the corresponding figure for the major parties. Similar adjustments for other structural factors in the Liberal vote – like geographical mobility – would not make much more difference.[5]

Even though the Liberal vote is apparently more volatile than the major-party vote, Liberal voting is clearly not the result of a transient whim. Nor is the Liberal Party markedly less able than the major parties to retain the votes of recent converts. Table 1 gives some evidence on this point, averaged over all triples of consecutive elections since 1959. As Table 1(a) shows, of people voting Liberal in each of the first two elections of the triple, 70 per cent voted Liberal at the third

Table 1: Three-election vote retention and conversion

(a)

Vote at first election was: Vote at second election was:	Conservative Liberal	Liberal Liberal	Labour Liberal
At third election, proportions			
Voting Conservative	25	11	4
Voting Liberal	55	70	53
Voting Labour	9	9	28
Other	11	10	15
	100%	100%	100%
(base)	(173)	(225)	(143)

(b)

Vote at first election was: Vote at second election was:	Liberal Major Party X	Major Party X Major Party X	Major Party Y Major Party X
At third election, proportions			
Voting Liberal	25	5	9
Voting Major Party X	55	82	55
Voting Major Party Y	9	3	22
Other	11	10	14
	100%	100%	100%
(base)	(74)	(4,510)	(270)

The cell frequencies reflect the average of four triples of elections: 1959–64–66 (Source is Butler–Stokes 1966 cross-section sample, weighted n = 1,836); 1964–66–70 (Source is Butler–Stokes 1966–70 panel sample, weighted n = 1,258); 1966–70–February 1974 (Source is British Election Study February cross-section, n = 2,462); and 1970–February–October 1974 (Source is British Election Study October cross-section, n = 2,365). In (b), major parties X and Y reflect the average of Conservative and Labour, as appropriate: the middle column reflects staying with the same major party at the first two elections, and the final column those who switched between them.

election. On the other hand, those who vote for the same major party twice in a row are more likely to do so again the third time: according to Table 1(b), 82 per cent do so. This is consistent with the figures relating to two-election vote retention given above. Where between the first two elections people have switched votes from one of the major parties to the Liberals, then 55 per cent of Conservative–Liberal converts and 53 per cent of Labour–Liberal converts remain Liberal at the third election. This proportion is lower than the 70 per cent of two-time Liberals remaining Liberal, but far higher than the 25 per cent of Conservative –Liberal converts and 28 per cent of Labour–Liberal converts returning at the third election to their original party. (Of the remaining 20 per cent or so of converts, abstention in the third election was far more common than switching *again* to the other major party.)[6] When we turn to the major parties, a similar pattern appears: in each case about 55 per cent of converts are retained, while fewer (25 per cent to the Liberals, 22 per cent to the other major party) return to their party of origin. Thus the appeal of the Liberals appears to be only relatively, rather than absolutely, ephemeral: their ability to retain converts the next time round is comparable to that of the major parties. On the other hand, their ability to call out a 'core' vote time and again is weaker. Because the core vote is smaller converts are a numerically larger part of the Liberal vote at any election. Even though a clear majority of converts may stay with the party, its overall vote is nevertheless more volatile than that of the major parties.

(b) *A Typology of Liberal Support.* In fact nearly half of those who voted Liberal in February 1974 failed to do so again in October. Thus despite the apparent stability in the aggregate Liberal vote, and the fact that Liberal losses appear to have been distributed relatively evenly over constituencies, there was a massive turnover of Liberal support. Something on the order of two-and-three-quarter million February Liberals did not repeat their vote. That the Liberal vote held up as well as it did was due to the conversion of a further two million new Liberals in October. Of course, to be abandoned is not to be forgotten: half of those who voted Liberal in February but not in October reported thinking about voting Liberal in October, or said that they 'really preferred' the Liberals but felt they had no chance of winning, or claimed that, had they voted at all, they would have voted Liberal. Of those October Liberals who had not voted Liberal in February, again nearly half had reported thinking seriously about voting Liberal in February or claimed they would have done had they voted at all. Indeed, there were some who thought about it both times, and voted Liberal neither time. Because short-term, local and personal factors may have influenced Liberal voting considerably, and because there is a large turnover in the actual Liberal vote, it will simplify the study if we re-define Liberal support accordingly.

To do this, we construct the scale of Liberal support shown in Table 2. The scale rests on responses to several questions. In addition to reported or recalled vote and the 'probable' vote of reported non-voters, the scale includes reports of serious consideration of voting Liberal, likelihood of voting Liberal if a Liberal candidate had stood in the constituency or had had a better chance of winning, or a 'real preference' for the Liberals not carried out in voting because the Liberals had no chance of winning the constituency. Each respondent is assigned only to the highest category he or she fits: for instance, many Liberal voters would also qualify for inclusion in the various categories reflecting consideration of a Liberal vote.[7] The two elections are treated as one continuous event, and each respondent is assigned to the category describing his/her 'closest' approach to the Liberals in 1974. As the Table shows, the Liberal 'core' – those who voted Liberal three or more times in 1966–70–74 – amounts to just 4 per cent of the electorate. A further 8 per cent have voted Liberal twice in that period, and 13 per cent have voted Liberal once (almost all of them in 1974). Thus a quarter of the electorate have some recent experience of Liberal voting. For each of these individuals there is another who did not vote Liberal but who came close to it on one of the four grounds which in Table 2 define 'potential' Liberal supporters.[8] In 1974 this figure was an extra 22 per cent. In order to study the Liberal support in 1974, Table 2 suggests that our sample of the electorate can be split in half, depending on whether or not the respondent ever at least considered the Liberals, and that the Liberal half can be further split, again roughly in half, according to whether or not the respondent has ever gone so far as to vote Liberal. A very small proportion of

Table 2: Index of Liberal support

Type of supporter	Definition of group	Per cent
Stalwart	Voted Liberal at least three times 1966–70–February–October 1974	4
Occasional	Voted Liberal twice in the period	8
	Voted Liberal once in the period	13 = 21%
Potential	Never voted Liberal, but:	
	Generally speaking, thinks of self as Liberal, feels closest to Liberals	4
	Really preferred the Liberals, but votes for some other party as the Liberals had no chance in the constituency	4
	Very likely vote Liberal if they had a candidate (February), if Liberals had better chance of winning (October)	7
	Liberals were second choice of SNP voter; were the party a non-voter would have voted for; voter for some other party 'seriously thought' he/she might vote Liberal	7 = 22%
Pure Major Party	Some connection with a major party; no evidence even of consideration of Liberals	51
Residual	Only connection with minor parties; no vote or party identification	2
		100%
(base)		(1,830)

Source is British Election Study, February–October panel sample, with recall of vote in earlier years.

the Liberal vote can be further split off as the stable core of the Liberal Party's support. We shall refer to this last group as the 'stalwart' portion of Liberal support. Those who have voted Liberal, but less often, we shall call 'occasional' Liberals. The 22 per cent who never voted Liberal, who gave some indication of having liked them, or considered voting Liberal, we shall call 'potential' Liberals, for it is in this group that the Liberals had their best chance of further conversions. Paradoxically, this group represents both the Liberal success and failure of 1974: success in the sense of having attracted so much potential support, and failure in terms of having actually converted so little of it into votes.[9] The half of the electorate which neither voted Liberal, nor showed any sign of having considered it, we shall call 'pure' major party supporters, or major party supporters 'untouched' by the Liberal advance of 1974.

We shall return to this classification repeatedly in the following sections. Of course, we shall be interested in anything which explains the fundamental division of the electorate we propose – the distinction between that half touched by, and the half apparently oblivious to the Liberals in 1974. We shall also attempt to find factors which discriminate between people who only leaned towards the Liberals, and people who voted for them (if only occasionally), as well as between both these groups and the small core of Liberal stalwarts. Of particular interest are cases where the group of stalwart Liberals appear to have more in common with their major party counterparts than with either group of less committed Liberals. It is unlikely that we shall find one single characteristic shared by all those who either considered or voted for the Liberals, but we shall present such evidence as we have found.

(c) *Social Composition of Liberal Support.* Liberal voters have for some time represented more of a cross-section of society than have voters for either of the major parties. Both major parties tended to be disproportionately deserted by their 'class-deviant' 1970 voters in February 1974, and therefore appeared to increase in homogeneity of class composition in February.[10] Thus, while February Liberals were slightly more middle-class, slightly better-educated, and somewhat younger than the electorate as a whole, they nevertheless continued to appear far less socially distinctive than either Labour or Conservative supporters. Over the years, there have been numerous attempts to find some social antecedent for Liberal voting; most frequently these attempts have centred upon hypothesising Liberals to be subject to some form of social cross-pressure and thus 'underdetermined' socially in terms of voting (e.g. upwardly mobile), or in marginal class positions.[11] We have shown elsewhere that defection to the Liberals in February 1974 was particularly heavy among that portion of the 1970 Labour vote which was middle-class and better-educated. On the other hand, it should be borne in mind that the majority of 1970 Labour voters who defected to the Liberals were nevertheless working-class. Similarly there were *numerically* but *not proportionately* more converts to the Liberals among middle-class as opposed to working-class 1970 Conservatives. While it is probably the 'class-deviant' supporters of each major party who are more likely to defect, because of the large class bias in support for the major parties, the bulk of the converts the Liberal Party attracts from each major party will come from the class predominantly supporting that major party.

Are there any background characteristics which unite those who thought about or even occasionally voted Liberal from those who never considered it, as well as from those who repeatedly voted Liberal in recent elections. One difference is of course that potential or occasional Liberals are far less likely to have a very strong identification for one of the major parties: potential Liberals are half, and occasional Liberals less than one-third, as likely to have a very strong identification as are their major-party counterparts untouched by the Liberals. Because of this, there are similarities between the account we give of the Liberal upsurge and the explanation of the decline of two-party partisanship in Britain.[12]

In general, potential and occasional Liberals were drawn from among younger electors. In 1974, 23 per cent of potential Liberals and 28 per cent of occasional Liberals were under 29, while only 18 per cent of untouched major party supporters were. Stalwart Liberals are by definition older, since they would have had to be in the 1970 electorate to have a chance of voting Liberal three times but they are also slightly older than their stalwart major party counterparts. The real difference between the more stalwart and occasional Liberals, however, lies in social origin. As table 3 shows, the potential Liberals of 1974 – those who consider the Liberals but never went so far as to vote for them – are in terms of social grade, a perfect cross-section of society. They are, in fact, socially representative in each case of the party for which they voted: there is no evidence that those Labour or Conservative voters who only thought about the Liberals were atypically drawn from among some social component of their party's support. Occasional Liberals – those voting Liberal once or twice in the period from 1966 to 1974 – are somewhat atypically middle-class, with 18 per cent coming from managerial grades A and B, and 31 per cent from non-manual grades C1a and C1b, as against 16 and 27 per cent respectively in the whole electorate.[13]

Table 3: Social Origins of Liberal Supporters

Proportions in social grade:		Potential Liberals	Occasional Liberals	Stalwart Liberals	Electorate
A	Higher managerial or professional	9	8	14	7
B	Lower managerial or administrative	8	10	20	9
C1a	Skilled or supervisory non-manual	16	19	18	16
C1b	Lower non-manual	11	12	13	11
C2	Skilled manual	36	33	19	34
D	Semi-skilled/unskilled manual	18	14	13	19
		100%	100%	100%	100%
	(base)	(392)	(354)	(62)	(1,741)

Source is British Election Study, February–October panel sample, n = 1,830. Individuals whose social grade could not be ascertained, or who fall within Residual category E, have been eliminated from the percentage base of each column. Percentages reflect the averages of percentages calculated separately for data relating to February and October.

What is most remarkable, however, is the social difference between stalwart Liberals and the party's more occasional recruits. The small but steady core of the Liberal vote is very largely middle-class. The proportion of this steady vote coming from managerial grades A and B – 34 per cent – is higher than the proportion (usually about a quarter) of the Conservative vote in any election coming from these social grades. (Of course, the Conservatives still get numerically the largest vote in these social grades.) The steady Liberal vote also over-represents those in lower non-manual occupations, and only a third of the stable core of the Liberal vote comes from those with manual occupations. Partly as a reflection of this, it appears that half of the stalwart Liberal core live in safe Conservative seats, but the middle-class nature of the Liberal core is not due to bias in Liberal candidates. It appears then that the usual portrait of the Liberals as a cross-section of society is misleading. Liberal support really contains two quite different parties: a small stable core of supporters who are heavily middle-class and middle-aged, and a larger group of more occasional supporters who are the social cross-section.

Notes

1 D. Butler and D. Stokes, *Political Change in Britain*, 2nd edition. London, Macmillan, 1975, p. 267.

2 H. T. Himmelweit and R. Bond, 'Social and Political Attitudes: Voting Stability and Change', Report to the Social Science Research Council, 1974.

3 There is a relationship between defection rate from a party and interval between elections, given by the equation $D = 22 + 0.17M$, $(r^2 = 0.18)$, where D is the percentage of those eligible to vote at two consecutive elections who voted for one major party at the first occasion and did not vote for the same party at the second occasion, and M is the interval between elections, in months. Estimation is by ordinary least squares regression, and the observations are ten party-election pairs between 1959 and October 1974. This equation really appears to contain two separate relationships, one for the party winning the first election (e.g. defection rate from Labour 1966–70 or from the Conservatives 1970–February 1974): $D = 17 + 0.28M$ $(r^2 = 0.55)$

and one for the losers: $D = 25 + 0.04M$ $(r^2 = 0.04)$.

The equation for the party losing an election suggests that it will be abandoned by about 25 per cent of its present support at the next election, regardless of the interval between elections. For winners, it suggests loss of 17 per cent of its support, plus an extra 0.28 per cent each month, or about 3.5 per cent each year, until the next election. The idea that a Government loses more of its support with the passage of time, while the Opposition is unaffected by time, is consistent with ideas outlined by J. Mueller, 'Presidential popularity from Truman to Johnson', *American Political Science Review*, LXIV (1970), 18–34; and W. Miller and M. Mackie, 'The electoral cycle and the asymmetry of government and opposition popularity', *Political Studies*, XXI (1973), 263–79. Be warned, however, that these separate regressions are each based on only five pairs of elections, and are put forward as a suggestive hypothesis which future research may well deny.

4 Unless otherwise specified, conclusions relating to years before 1974 are based on surveys of the British electorate conducted by David Butler and Donald Stokes between 1963 and 1970. Data from these studies was supplied by the Inter-University Consortium for Political Research at the University of Michigan. Conclusions relating to 1974 are mainly based on the panel of 1830 electors interviewed after both elections of 1974 in surveys conducted by the authors and financed by the Social Science Research Council. All conclusions presented in this paper, however, are the responsibility of the authors.

5 Structural analyses of Liberal voting can be found in H. Berrington and T. Bedeman, 'The February Election', *Parliamentary Affairs*, XXVII (1974), 317–32; and in Michael Steed's Appendices to the most recent Nuffield studies, especially in D. Butler and D. Kavanagh, *The British General Election of February 1974*. London, Macmillan, 1974. However, characteristics like constituency marginality, while they may affect the actual level of Liberal voting, can hardly be argued to affect vote retention. (By and large, the same constituencies are marginal from one election to the next.) There are circumstances in which a party's small size will automatically give it the appearance of lower vote retention rates. In the simplest system, an exchange of an equal *number* of electors between two parties of unequal size will leave the relative sizes of the parties unchanged, but give the *smaller* party the appearance of lower vote retention. However, real vote flows are more complicated, and as soon as one allows third parties and particularly non-voters there is no reason *a priori* that a small party should not be as able as the larger parties to retain its votes from one election to the next.

6 Notice that while 'homing' – i.e. returning to one's party of origin after defecting to another party – is more common than abstaining or defecting to yet another party at the third election, all these alternatives *together* are less likely than staying with one's newly-joined party the third time.

7 For instance, an October Liberal voter who said in February that he was 'very likely' to vote Liberal had they had a candidate in his constituency is counted only among the voters, and not also among the 'potential' support.

8 It would be difficult to give any meaningful evidence of order among the four categories of potential Liberal supporters who did not vote Liberal. There is also a great deal of overlap between questions: two-thirds of those who 'seriously thought' they might vote Liberal also felt it 'very likely' they would have voted Liberal if they felt the party would have done better. The four categories seem to us to be

alternative ways of saying that there was something about the Liberals which attracted the respondent, who was nevertheless not prepared to vote for them. We shall usually analyse these categories together.

9 Question wordings and omissions bedevil comparisons, but two things are very likely. One is that the analogous 'potential' support of the major parties is far smaller relative to their actual vote. Probably each of the three parties was considered or voted for by about half the electorate, but each of the major parties got the votes of a much greater share of the sub-population whose interest it attracted. The other point is that, like their vote, the Liberals' potential support in 1974 was far greater than in earlier years. Again, comparisons are difficult, but it is highly unlikely that in 1966 the sum of those with some recent experience of Liberal voting plus their potential support exceeded one-third of the electorate. At that time, with fewer candidates, the Liberals got the votes of even fewer of their possible supporters.

10 I. Crewe, B. Särlvik, and J. Alt, 'The Decline of the Two Party System', paper presented to the Annual Conference of the Political Studies Association, Oxford, March 1975.

11 None of the studies have provided much satisfactory evidence, except of the difficulty of finding social antecedents of Liberal voting. Cf. Rose, 'Britain: simple abstractions and complex realities', esp. p. 530, and J. Bonham, 'The middle class revolt', *Political Quarterly*, XXXIII (1962); or B. Jessop, "Which party can provide the goods?', *Times Higher Education Supplement*, 22 March 1974.

12 I. Crewe, J. Alt, and B. Särlvik, 'The Erosion of Partisanship in Britain 1964–74', paper presented to the Annual Conference of the Political Studies Association, Nottingham, April 1976.

13 This classification is in terms of social grade of the head of household, based on respondents' current occupations, or husbands' occupations in the case of married women not employed full-time, and 'normal' occupation when working in the case of retired persons. The actual classification into seven grades follows the revised Market Research Society classification devised by Butler and Stokes, and is fully described in J. Spence, 'The British Election Study of October 1974: Methodological Report' London, Social and Community Planning Research, 1975.

Thatcherism and the Conservative Party

Paul F. Whiteley, Patrick Seyd, Jeremy Richardson and
Paul Bissell

In the 1980s the Conservative ascendency under Margaret Thatcher raised important questions about the previous pluralist assumptions of consensus and centrist politics. To address these issues required new methods of understanding the internal dynamics of the political parties, and especially of the Tories. But party members constitute only a tiny fraction of the electorate, so that even in the largest election studies too few cases could be gathered for analysis. By securing the main parties' approval for large-scale mail questionnaires being sent to their memberships, Whiteley and colleagues considerably extended the political science toolkit, and were able to gain a much more precise quantitative understanding of party members' views and how they changed over time. Their findings pointed up the relatively fragile or contingent acceptance of full blooded Thatcherite positions within the Tory ranks, and suggested that by the early 1990s John Major sat a good deal closer to the party's ideological centre than his predecessor.

A Framework for Classifying Conservatism

Our reading of contemporary accounts of Conservative party ideology suggests that ideological divisions within the party divide into three broad categories: traditionalism, individualism and progressivism. These distinctions have largely grown out of the experiences of the Conservative party both in government and opposition, since its growth into a mass party in the latter half of the nineteenth century.[1]

Traditionalism is perhaps the oldest ideological tendency in the party, being rooted in the values of the land-owning aristocracy. It stresses patriotism and authority but often takes an anti-modern attitude to social and political change such as the emancipation of women, racial integration and the availability of abortion and easy divorce. In echoing Joe Chamberlain's 'Social Imperialism'[2] it tends to be rather anti-European, and covertly, if not occasionally overtly, racist. Traditionalists are also strong supporters of the idea of social 'discipline' and law and order; they tend to favour capital punishment and emphasize the importance of punishment as a means of dealing with crime. Another feature of traditionalism is support for existing political institutions, so that traditionalists tend to oppose constitutional changes in society, preferring to retain old forms of government in the belief that the longevity of institutions gives them particular legitimacy. They are strongly attached to the monarchy and institutions like the House of Lords and opposed to constitutional changes like the introduction of a Bill of Rights.

Progressive Conservatism also has a long pedigree, being originally associated with Disraeli's 'One Nation' Toryism.[3] It was, however, revitalized by the post-war election defeat and the perception that the party needed to adapt to the changes introduced by the post-war settlement and the 1945–50 Labour Government. Progressives support the Beveridge welfare state and up to the 1980s this also went with an acceptance of Keynesian methods of macroeconomic management. These ideas, often associated with R. A. Butler,[4] stress the importance of a social safety net to deal with poverty, limited redistribution of income and wealth, and a paternalistic commitment to caring for all members of the community. Along with support for limited redistribution goes agreement with government intervention to regulate markets in the interests of both consumers and producers.

Individualism has its origins in nineteenth century Cobdenite market liberalism which emerged within the Liberal party but migrated to the Tories after the Liberal split over Irish home rule in 1885.[5] Individualism is pre-occupied with petty-bourgeois concerns about private property and the interests of the small businessman. It supports the ideal of laissez-faire and reduced government intervention in the economy. The most enthusiastic supporters of the Thatcher government's privatization programmes can be found among this group. Individualists believe that the welfare state undermines self-reliance and enterprise, and that the government should cut taxes and de-regulate business. They tend to be anti-welfare and are inclined to blame the victim when it comes to explaining the origins of poverty or unemployment.

These three broad dimensions of contemporary Conservative ideology are operationalized in terms of a variety of issue indicators, set out in Table 1. The classification in this Table is made on the basis of *a priori* judgements about the components of Conservative ideology, but these are subsequently subjected to a confirmatory factor analysis to test the validity of this classification scheme.

The indicators in Table 1 are all Likert statements or close variants of such scales and are used to measure ideological beliefs in terms of attitudes to various controversial issues within the Conservative party and British politics. In addition there are two 'left-right' scales, of the type which have been successfully used to identify ideological variations in the electorate in a variety of democratic systems.[6]

The indicators of traditionalism focus on national sovereignty, issues of constitutional reform, moral issues to do with abortion and divorce, capital punishment and attitudes to defence spending. As they appear in this Table, they are worded so that traditionalists will tend to agree with them.[7] Thus traditionalists will resist further European integration, oppose constitutional reforms like the Bill of Rights, support the repatriation of immigrants, deplore the social changes leading to easier divorce and abortion, and oppose cuts in defence spending. In addition they will be strongly in favour of the reintroduction of capital punishment.

In contrast the indicators of progressivism focus primarily on domestic welfare issues such as government spending on poverty and the National Health Service, the redistribution of income and wealth, unemployment compensation and the regulation of markets and industries. In addition there is a general indicator of support for centrist policies in the Conservative party. Again the indicators in Table 1 are worded in such a way that progressives would be expected to agree with the statements.

The indicators of individualism focus principally on privatization, fiscal orthodoxy, the regulation of trade unions and criticism of the welfare state. Individualists should favour the privatization of the coal industry, the introduction of market mechanisms into the National Health Service, reduced government spending in general and cuts in income tax and the proposition that the welfare state undermines

Table 1: Indicators of Ideological Groupings in the Conservative Party

Traditionalism
'A future Conservative government should encourage repatriation of immigrants.'
'All shops should (not) be allowed to open on Sundays.'
'A future Conservative government should make abortions more difficult to obtain.'
'The death penalty should be reintroduced for murder.'
'Conservatives should resist further moves to integrate the European Community.'
'There is no need for a Bill of Rights in this country.'
'The reduction in East-West tensions (doesn't) mean that Britain can make significant cutbacks in defence spending.'
'Divorce has become too easy these days, and the divorce laws should be tightened up.'
'The Government should (not) give more aid to poor countries.'
'Child Benefit should be abolished.'

Progressive
'The Conservative party should adjust its policies to capture the middle ground of politics.'
'The next Conservative government should establish a prices and incomes policy as a means of controlling inflation.'
'Income and Wealth should be redistributed towards ordinary working people.'
'The consumer needs much stronger protection from the effects of the free market.'
'Unemployment benefit should ensure people a reasonable standard of living.'
'Britain's present electoral system should be replaced by a system of proportional representation.'
'The Government should spend more money to get rid of poverty.'
'The Government should put more money into the National Health Service.'
'The Government should give workers more say in the places where they work.'
'The public enterprises privatized by the Conservative government should be subject to stricter regulation.'

Individualism
'A future Conservative government should privatize British Coal.'
'High income tax makes people less willing to work hard.'
'Introducing market forces into the National Health Service means that the quality of our health will improve.'
'The welfare state undermines individual self-reliance and enterprise.'
'Schools should (not) be encouraged to opt out of local education authority control.'
'Government should encourage private education.'
'Government should encourage the growth of private medicine.'
'The Government should reduce government spending generally.'
'The Government should introduce stricter laws to regulate the trade unions.'
'The Government should cut income tax.'

General
'In Conservative party politics people often talk about the "left" and the "right". Compared with other Conservative party members, where would you place your views on this scale below?'
'And where would you place your views in relation to British politics as a whole (not just the Conservative party)?'

individual self-reliance and enterprise. Finally, they should be anti-trade union, seeing unions as monopolistic, rent-seeking organizations.

Attitude Structuring among Conservatives

A confirmatory factor analysis using the thirty-two indicators produced a total of four significant orthogonal or independent factors, using the criteria that a factor should have an eigenvalue greater than 1.5.[8] The rotated factor matrix from this exercise appears in Table 2, which includes all loadings greater than plus or minus 0.40.

Table 2: A Confirmatory Factor Analysis of Attitude Indicators

Indicator	Factor One	Factor Two	Factor Three	Factor Four
Spend more on poverty	0.62			
Protect consumers from free markets	0.61			
Introduce a prices and incomes policy	0.61			
Spend more on the NHS	0.58			
Make unemployment benefit reasonable	0.56			
Redistribute income and wealth	0.55			
Capture middle ground of politics	0.52			
Give workers more say in workplace	0.50			
Regulate privatized industries	0.49			
Introduce proportional representation	0.42			
Encourage private education		0.63		
Encourage private medicine		0.62		
Markets in the NHS improve the service		0.59		
Privatize British Coal		0.54		
Cut income tax		0.52		
Introduce stricter trade union laws		0.51		
Left-right scale for Conservatives		−0.47	−0.47	
Left-right scale for British politics		0.43		
Reintroduce the death penalty			0.65	
Encourage repatriation of Immigrants			0.61	
Resist further European Integration			0.55	
Give more foreign aid			−0.54	
Abolish Child Benefit			0.44	
Make abortion more difficult				0.73
Divorce is too easy				0.70
All shops should open on Sundays				−0.56
Eigenvalues	4.41	3.32	1.80	1.64
Variance explained	13.8	10.4	5.6	5.1

Notes: Factor one: Progressivism   Factor two: Individualism   Factor three: Traditionalism (general)
Factor four: Traditionalism (moral)
(N = 2.467)

The four factors explain about 34 per cent of the variance in the issue indicators, which suggest that while attitudes are structured among Conservative party members, the degree of structuring is not high. This point is reinforced by the fact that some of the thirty-two indicators do not load significantly on the factors, and thus are unrelated to the dimensions identified by the factor structure.

The first factor in Table 2, which explains 13.8 per cent of the variance is clearly a progressive factor, since it includes all ten of the indicators of progressivism. Thus Conservatives who support public spending on poverty are also likely to be in favour of the regulation of markets, the redistribution of income and wealth, incomes policy and the provision of adequate unemployment benefits. Similarly, they are likely to favour giving workers more say in the workplace.

The second factor is unambiguously an individualism factor, since six of the indicators of individualism load highly on it. However, it is rather narrower than was envisaged in Table 1, focusing exclusively on the issues of privatization and tax cuts. All the measures of privatization, relating to the coal industry, private education and medicine and market mechanisms in the National Health Service, load significantly on this factor. Indicators of anti-welfare attitudes do not load highly on this factor, nor does the measure of attitudes to cuts in government spending. However the two left-right scales do load highly on it, both with negative signs. This indicates that left-wing Conservatives, as measured by these scales, are likely to disagree with privatization and tax cuts.

The third factor is clearly a traditionalism factor, since it loads significantly on attitudes to immigration, the death penalty and opposition to further European integration. Interestingly enough, the left-right scale for the Conservative party also loads highly on it, as well as on factor two. Again the negative sign of this loading suggests that liberal Conservatives oppose the death penalty and further restrictions on immigration, and they tend to favour European integration.

An important feature of the traditionalism indicators, however, is that the measures of moral traditionalism load on a separate factor from those of traditionalism in general. This suggests that traditionalism, as it is operationalized by these indicators, is more heterogeneous than progressivism or individualism. Factors three and four are independent of each other, which implies that respondents who favour the death penalty or the repatriation of immigrants do not necessarily favour restrictions on abortion or divorce.

Overall the factor analysis, which uses a wide variety of issue indicators, confirms the existence of the dimensions of progressivism, individualism and traditionalism in contemporary Conservative party ideology. But the results also show that traditionalist attitudes are rather more fragmented than can be captured in a single dimension. In addition, individualism is rather narrower in scope than the measures set out in Table 1 would indicate. Finally, the left-right scale applied to the Conservative party appears to provide an excellent summary measure of important components of individualism and traditionalism. In the light of this analysis, the next section examines Thatcherism as a distinctive set of ideas within Conservative ideology.

Thatcherism and Conservatism

There is a fair degree of consensus about the ideological characteristics of Thatcherism, though much less consensus about its achievements. Peter Riddell provides a summary description of Mrs Thatcher's approach to politics, which fairly represents the range of views about the meaning of Thatcherism. He writes:

> Her approach has revolved around a number of themes – a belief in Britain's greatness and the assertion of national interests, a prejudice against the public sector (at any rate in economic and industrial affairs), a backing for the police and the authorities in fighting terrorism and upholding law and order, a strong dislike of trade unions, a general commitment to the virtues of sound money, a preference for wealth creators over civil servants and commentators, and a support for the rights of the individuals to make their own provision for education and health.[9]

In a similar vein Peter Jenkins regarded part of Mrs Thatcher's appeal as a championing of the taxpayers, particularly the skilled working class, against what she saw as overbearing organizations such as the Treasury, the trade unions, and local government landlords.[10] In this respect he believes that Thatcherism is an echo of the radical Toryism of Joseph Chamberlain.

In terms of the four factors discussed above, Thatcherism represents a clear shift away from progressive ideas towards individualism and traditionalism. With regard to individualism it favoured privatization, de-regulation, tax cuts and free-market solutions to economic problems. But it also represents a shift towards traditionalism exemplified by Mrs Thatcher's support for capital punishment, her vocal opposition to European integration and her attitudes to restrictions on immigration and abortion.

One difficulty in trying to classify Thatcherism is the possible mismatch between the image and the actual behaviour of the Thatcher government in office. The popular conception of Thatcherism is, in fact, quite different from the historical post-1979 record of public policy. In practice there was no such phenomenon as pure 'Thatcherism' against which one can measure party attitudes. Even the apparently straightforward notion of privatization, which is enthusiastically supported by individualists in the party, proved to be a much more complex phenomenon in practice.[11]

Thus if Thatcherism is taken to mean less public expenditure, lower taxes and above all, less government intervention in society, it bears little relation to the massive output of public policy in the period 1979–90. If anything, this period was one of massive intervention in most aspects of society. In a very real sense therefore, two rather different tests might be applied to the attitudes of Conservative party members. The first, and the one we focus on in this paper, examines the relationship between popular conceptions of Thatcherism as articulated by the media and for the most part by Mrs Thatcher herself. The second, and more difficult comparison, is between the attitudes of Conservatives and the actions of the Conservative government during the Thatcher period. Clearly, party members can support aspects of Thatcherism in theory while also supporting a rather different reality of Thatcherism in practice.

Setting that distinction aside, if Mrs Thatcher succeeded in radicalizing the Conservative party we should expect to see significant majorities of grassroots members opposing most of the progressive indicators and favouring the individualism and traditionalism indicators. Thus they should oppose spending more money on poverty or the unemployed; they should favour privatization and cuts in income tax, and be opposed to further European integration. Finally, they should favour restrictions on abortion and a tightening up of the divorce laws. In the next section we examine the evidence to see if this gives an accurate picture of opinions within the contemporary Conservative party.

Grassroots Conservatives and 'Thatcherism'

Table 3 contains a breakdown of the distribution of opinions among the grassroots Conservative party members on the indicators of progressivism.

Table 3: The Distribution of Opinions on Indicators of Progressivism

Indicator	Strongly agree	Agree	Neither	Disagree	Strongly disagree
Protect consumers from free markets	13	44	18	22	3
Introduce prices and incomes policy	12	31	12	32	14
Make unemployment benefit reasonable	14	60	13	11	2
Redistribute income and wealth	5	22	21	41	11
Capture the middle ground of politics	16	54	14	14	2
Regulate privatized industries	25	48	13	13	1
Introduce proportional representation	5	18	12	42	22

	Definitely should	Probably should	Doesn't matter	Probably should not	Definitely should not
Spend more on poverty	29	52	8	9	2
Spend more on the NHS	31	49	7	11	2
Give workers more say in the workplace	16	48	13	18	4

It is readily apparent from this Table that a majority of grassroots Conservative members tend to gravitate towards the progressive end of the scale. Thus clear majorities of members favour pursuing policies designed to 'capture the middle ground of politics'; they strongly favour making unemployment benefit adequate to support a reasonable standard of living. In addition they strongly favour protecting consumers from the free market and regulating industries which have been privatized. Equally, majorities favour spending more money on the Health Service, on reducing poverty and giving workers greater say in the workplace. Only two of the progressive indicators have majorities opposed; these are the indicators of redistribution of income and wealth, and electoral reform. Thus some 52 per cent of respondents oppose the redistribution of income and wealth, and 64 per cent oppose the introduction of electoral reform in the shape of proportional representation. It is particularly interesting to note that incomes policy, the keystone of the Heath administration's macroeconomic policy after 1972, is favoured by some 43 per cent of respondents, only marginally less than the number who oppose it. This is true despite the fact that the Thatcher administration strongly opposed such 'corporatist' approaches to macroeconomic management.

If there is evidence in Table 3 that grassroots Conservatives opposed many of the policy positions taken up by Mrs Thatcher and her supporters, there is clear evidence in Table 4 that there was widespread support for other aspects of Thatcherism, notably privatization and tax cuts. It can be seen from Table 4 that clear majorities favour privatization of coal and the introduction of market mechanisms into the National Health Service. Majorities also support a policy of encouraging private education and private medicine. However, there are also significant minorities of respondents who oppose the privatization of the coal industry and have doubts about encouraging private medicine. So support for the privatization programme has its critics within the grassroots party. A similar point could be made about cuts in income tax; clear majorities of Conservative party members favour cuts in income tax but slightly more than a third of respondents

Table 4: The Distribution of Opinions on Indicators of Individualism

Indicator	Strongly agree	Agree	Neither	Disagree	Strongly disagree
Markets in the NHS will improve the service	15	53	15	14	3
Privatize British Coal	11	43	17	22	6

	Definitely should	Probably should	Doesn't matter	Probably should not	Definitely should not
Encourage private education	28	36	20	12	3
Introduce stricter TU laws	27	38	12	20	3
Cut income tax	20	40	13	22	4
Encourage private medicine	17	35	16	26	7

**Table 5: The Distribution of Opinions on Indicators of Traditionalism –
General and Social**

Indicator	Strongly agree	Agree	Neither	Disagree	Strongly disagree
General					
Reintroduce the death penalty	36	33	7	17	7
Encourage repatriation of immigrants	32	38	12	15	4
Resist further European integration	19	34	16	28	3
Give more foreign aid to poor countries	2	21	25	41	11
Abolish child benefit	7	13	12	53	15
Moral					
Divorce is too easy	18	42	13	23	4
All shops should open on Sundays	16	31	10	23	20
Make abortion more difficult	12	21	19	35	13

are opposed or indifferent to these. So it would not be true to say that opinions on these issues are uniform within the party. However, there is fairly strong support for this aspect of Thatcherite politics.

Table 5 contains information about the distribution of opinions on the two traditionalism factors and in this case it is apparent that grassroots Conservatives are more divided on these issues; they strongly support some aspects of Thatcherite beliefs, while at the same time opposing others. For example, they strongly favour the death penalty, they are very anti-immigrant and they are opposed to further European integration. At the same time, however, they are clearly not in favour of restricting abortions or abolishing Child Benefit. Similarly, a plurality opposes any restrictions on Sunday trading.

Table 6 presents the distribution of opinions along the two left-right scales, which load significantly on the individualism and traditionalism factors. It is clear from the distribution of opinions that most Conservatives think of themselves as being on the centre-right, both within the Conservative party and within British politics. The mean score on the two nine-point scales is 6.0 and 6.7 respectively, suggesting that Conservatives think of themselves as being more centrist in relation to the party than in relation to British politics as a whole.

Overall, these results suggest that while there is support for distinctive Thatcherite policies such as privatization, capital punishment and opposition to further European integration, grassroots Conservatives are much more progressive than

**Table 6: The Distribution of Opinions on the Left-Right Ideology Scales
(percentages)**

Left-right scale in the Conservative party

1.9	1.8	4.0	7.0	26.7	17.5	20.8	8.3	12.0

Left-right scale in British politics

0.3	0.3	0.8	2.6	19.2	18.4	27.9	15.0	15.5

conventional wisdom would suggest. It is hard to make the case that the Conservative party has been converted to Thatcherism on the basis of these results.

Contrary to Thatcherite rhetoric, members favour a centrist electoral strategy and they support welfare for the poor and unemployed. It is true that they are supporters of the privatization programmes but they also want the newly-privatized industries to be closely regulated in order to safeguard the interests of consumers. Similarly, while they support stricter laws to regulate trade unions, a majority supports the idea of giving workers more say in the workplace. Perhaps most significantly, while the average grassroots members think of themselves as being on the centre-right of the ideological spectrum within the party, some 41 per cent of them can be found in categories 1 to 5 of the left-right party scale, i.e. in the left-wing to centrist positions. Only just over 20 per cent can be found in categories 8 and 9, i.e. in the right-wing position. Having said that, it is clear that party members tend to be rather chauvinist, both with respect to immigrant minorities in Britain, and with regard to the European Community. Equally, the strong support they give to the reintroduction of capital punishment is very much in line with Thatcherite opinions.

But it would be a distortion to suggest that these attitudes are the result of a Thatcherite programme of 'educating' the Conservative party. This is because majorities of voters in Britain, both Conservative and non-Conservative, have been anti-immigrant and pro-capital punishment for many years, long before Mrs Thatcher became party leader.[12] Moreover, scepticism about the benefits of European integration has been a perennial feature of public opinion in Britain for many years.[13] In so far as voter attitudes are a guide to the opinions of party members, these results suggest that Thatcherism may be merely aligned with pre-existing attitudes within the Conservative party, rather than a force which has shifted opinions in a new direction.

Next, we examine the influence of these ideological tendencies among the Conservative grassroots on attitudes to Mrs Thatcher and her successor, John Major. The aim is to see if ideological differences translate into differences in support for the two leaders within the grassroots party.

Ideology and Attitudes to the Leadership

The survey of Conservative party members contained thermometer scale indicators of attitudes to both Margaret Thatcher and John Major.[14] Table 7 contains the

Table 7: The Effects of Ideology on Support for Margaret Thatcher and John Major

Indicator	Thatcher thermometer		Major thermometer	
Conservative Party thermometer	0.30**	0.35**	0.59**	0.62**
	(13.2)	(17.8)	(29.3)	(35.5)
Progressive scale	0.11**	—	–0.02	—
	(5.3)		(1.2)	
Individualism scale	–0.21**	—	–0.10**	—
	(9.7)		(4.9)	
Traditionalism scale (general)	–0.18**	—	0.07**	—
	(8.7)	(3.8)		
Traditionalism scale (moral)	–0.06**	—	–0.03	—
Left-right ideology scale for Conservative party	—	0.20	—	0.00
		(10.3)		(0.1)
R	0.25	0.21	0.40	0.39
F statistic	123.5	306.6	238.7	712.3

Standardized coefficients, t statistics in parentheses
** significant $p < 0.01$; * significant $p < 0.05$.

regression models of the four indicators of ideological tendencies within the party, together with a control for attitudes to the Conservative party, as predictors of the Thatcher and Major thermometer scales.[15] The control for affective feelings towards the Conservative party is included in these models in order to isolate attitudes to the party leader from feelings about the party as a whole.

Not surprisingly the strongest predictor of attitudes to Mrs Thatcher is the Conservative party scale, implying that strongly attached Conservatives thought very highly of the ex-Prime Minister. This variable, however, represents a generalized loyalty to the party, which a party leader of any political tendency is likely to benefit from and is included in the model purely as a control. As far as the four ideology scale variables are concerned, the results show that the progressives were significantly less likely to think warmly of Mrs Thatcher than traditionalists or individualists.[16] The strongest predictor of attitudes to the ex-Prime Minister, apart from the Conservative party thermometer, was the individualism scale, closely followed by the general traditionalism scale. Thus strong individualists and strong traditionalists thought much more highly of Mrs Thatcher than other party members. The weakest effect was associated with moral traditionalists, although once again this group were marginally more likely to favour Mrs Thatcher than members in general.

Since the left-right ideological scale applied to the Conservative party was significantly associated with two of the scales, the second model in Table 7 examines the influence of this measure on the thermometer score for Mrs Thatcher, once again controlling for feelings towards the Conservative party. It can be seen that the ideology scale is almost as good a predictor of attitudes as the four factors were since the variance explained by the second model is only marginally smaller than the variance explained by the first. Again, the positive effect indicates that right-wingers liked Thatcher much more than left-wingers.

Overall, these findings support the idea that Mrs Thatcher did indeed win the support of traditionalists and individualists within the grassroots party, while progressives were much less supportive. The grassroots party may be more pro-gressive on some issues than conventional wisdom suggests but Mrs Thatcher nonetheless won support from two of the broad ideological groupings within the party, providing her with a secure base of support overall.

Turning next to the John Major model, not surprisingly the Conservative party thermometer is an even stronger predictor of his thermometer score than was true for Mrs Thatcher. Again, this reflects a generalized loyalty to the Conservative party which naturally is acquired by the leader. With regard to the ideology variables two things stand out in comparison with the Thatcher models; a change of signs on the progressive and general traditionalism factors and the non-significance of the progressive and moral traditionalism factors as predictors of the Major thermometer score.

The lack of any significant relationship between progressivism and the Major thermometer score implies that progressives are neither more nor less likely to feel warm towards the new party leader, in comparison with other party members. Whereas progressives were cool towards Mrs Thatcher, they are essentially neutral towards John Major. This suggests that they are more supportive of the new leader than they were of his predecessor. A similar point could be made about moral traditionalists, who were more supportive of Mrs Thatcher than of John Major, but who are not actively opposed to the new leader. The change of sign on the general traditionalism variable indicates that anti-traditionalists feel warmer towards John Major than other party members. In this respect his support is different from that of Mrs Thatcher. However, he continues to receive warm support from indi-vidualists, although it is not as strong as the support they gave to his predecessor. The fourth model indicates that when the Conservative party thermometer score is taken into account the left-right ideology scale for the party does not significantly influence the thermometer score for the new party leader. This reinforces the point that his support was more broadly based in the party at the time of the survey than that of Mrs Thatcher.

Overall it would be fair to conclude that at the time of the survey John Major had shifted the ideological base of his support towards the progressive end of the spectrum, without alienating the individualist or moral traditionalists within the party. He was, however, significantly less popular among the general traditionalists in comparison with Margaret Thatcher. On the whole, though, he appeared to have a broad ideological base of support within the Conservative party.

Conclusions

These results confirm the hypothesis developed by Norton and Aughey and by Crewe and Searing that the basis of support for Thatcherism within the

Conservative party was a combination of traditionalism and individualism. However, the results also suggest that Thatcherism as a doctrine has done little to 're-educate' the Conservative party, by transforming it into a more strongly traditionalist and individualistic organization. In the absence of longitudinal data, we cannot know if the attitudes of grassroots members have shifted over the years that Mrs Thatcher held the leadership. But if they have, the shift does not appear to be very large, since there is a lot of support in the party for 'One Nation' Tory policies like incomes policy, regulation of markets and social welfare spending, which are anathema to died-in-the-wool Thatcherites. Chauvinism aside, many grassroots Conservatives are quite progressive in their attitudes to many of the contemporary issues in British politics.

The change of party leadership appeared to have shifted the ideological centre of gravity in the party to a significant extent, with John Major winning support among progressives which his predecessor did not have, without appearing to alienate individualists and to a lesser extent traditionalists. Over-all, the evidence suggests that with the possible exception of the issue of privatization Thatcherism was as evanescent a phenomenon within the Conservative party as it was in the wider electorate.

This conclusion, however, brings only partial comfort to the spatial theorists of party competition. While the strategy of 're-educating' party and public opinion clearly did not pay off, the leadership of Mrs Thatcher was nonetheless successful for many years in the face of significant ideological opposition both within the Conservative party, and from the wider electorate. If voters and parties choose their leaders exclusively on the basis of issue preferences Thatcherism would not have existed. Thus the theoretical problems for both spatial models of party competition and the Westminster model of British politics remain.

The success of Thatcherism can be explained in terms of factors which lie outside the theoretical concerns of spatial models of party competition, such as the weakened Labour party, which made voters doubt the credibility of the main alternative to the Conservatives; the importance of leadership styles, particularly the appearance of decisiveness and conviction;[17] and to a certain amount of good fortune, exemplified by the 'Falklands factor'.[18] In addition, her final election victory as Prime Minister in 1987 was considerably aided by a pre-election manipulation of the macroeconomy.[19] But none of these factors were permanent; eventually events caught up with her and precipitated the leadership crisis.

In conclusion these results suggest that spatial models and the Westminster model both fail because they are too narrow in scope as theoretical accounts of party strategy and the determinants of electoral success. Spatial models fail because they focus exclusively on issues. Voters do not (nor should they) rely exclusively on issues in an uncertain world, where leadership reputations may be a better guide to policy outcomes than pre-election issue positions. The Westminster model fails because it assumes that effective policy instruments exist for achieving widely agreed economic and social policy goals. We now know, with the benefit of hindsight and the failure of neo-Keynesian and more recently monetarist policies, that this is not the case. So, it is not surprising that consensus politics was a relatively temporary phenomenon in British politics.

Notes

1 R. Blake, *The Conservative Party from Peel to Thatcher*. London: Methuen, 1985.

2 R. Jay, *Joseph Chamberlain: a Political Study*. Oxford, Clarendon, 1981.

3 Blake, *The Conservative Party from Peel to Thatcher*, p. 124.

4 R. A. Butler, *The Art of the Possible*. London: Hamish Hamilton, 1971.

5 D. Marquand, *The Unprincipled Society*. London: Fontana, 1988. pp. 125–7.

6 See S. Barnes and M. Kaase, *Political Action*. Beverly Hills and London: Sage, 1979.

7 Several indicators are worded in the questionnaire in such a way that traditionalists are likely to disagree with the statements. These appear with (not) or (doesn't) in the Table, to indicate this fact. The same approach is taken for indicators of 'Individualism' and 'Progressivism'.

8 Table 2 contains rotated factor loadings from a principal components analysis of the indicators, with pairwise deletion of missing values. The requirement that a factor should have an eigenvalue of 1.5 is more stringent than the standard Kaiser's criterion, which requires an eigenvalue of only 1.0. Kaiser's criterion, though widely used, is rather undemanding since an eigenvalue of 1.0 only represents the variance which is likely to be explained by an 'average' variable (see H. Harman, *Modern Factor Analysis*. Chicago: Chicago University Press, 1967). Accordingly, we apply a stronger criterion.

9 P. Riddell, *The Thatcher Decade*. Oxford: Basil Blackwell, 1989, p. 4.

10 P. Jenkins, *Mrs Thatcher's Revolution*. London: Pan, 1989, p. 53.

11 It is quite misleading to see an issue like privatization simply in terms of a laissez-faire approach to the economy, and as part of an ideology which encourages a reduced role for government in economic management. Privatization under Mrs Thatcher has seen a very marked increase in regulation compared with the public ownership of industries which it replaced.

12 Butler and Stokes report that 71 per cent of the electorate wanted to retain the death penalty and 83 per cent thought that too many immigrants had been let into Britain, in their first survey of the British electorate conducted in 1963: see D. Butler and D. Stokes, *Political Change in Britain*. London: Macmillan, 1974, pp. 461 and 465.

13 See Butler and Stokes, *Political Change in Britain*, p. 464.

14 Respondents were asked to 'Please think for a moment of a thermometer scale that runs from zero to 100 degrees, where 50 is the neutral point. If your feelings are warm and sympathetic towards something or someone, give them a score higher than 50; the warmer the feelings the higher the score. If your feelings are cold and unsympathetic, give them a score less than 50; the colder your feelings, the lower the score. A score of 50 means that your feelings are neither warm nor cold'.

15 The ideological variables are factor scores from the varimax rotation of the four factors and the variable measuring attitudes to the Conservative party is a thermometer scale similar to the Thatcher and Major scales.

16 The signs of the coefficients are purely an artifact of the coding of the various scales. A low score on the progressive scale, for example, denotes a very progressive outlook, and a high score the opposite. Thus the positive relationship between the progressive scale and the Thatcher thermometer scale indicates that progressives gave Thatcher a low score and anti-progressives gave her a high score. In the case of the individualism scale strong individualists who got a low score on the scale, rated Thatcher more highly than anti-individualists who got a high score on the scale.

17 I. Crewe and D. Searing 'Ideological change in the British Conservative party', *American Political Science Review*, 82 (1988), 361–84, p. 364.

18 H. D. Clarke, W. Mishler and P. F. Whiteley, 'Recapturing the Falklands: models of Conservative popularity, 1979–83', *British Journal of Political Science*, 20 (1990), 63–81.

19 H. D. Clarke and P. F. Whiteley, 'Perceptions of macroeconomic performance, government support, and Conservative party strategy, 1983–87', *European Journal of Political Research*, 18 (1990), 97–120.

COMPARATIVE POLITICS and EMPIRICAL THEORY

Introduction by Patrick Dunleavy

The perceived uniqueness of the British constitution and polity amongst liberal democracies lead to rather country-specific theoretical and empirical approaches to studying both British politics and much of normative political theory also. So together with the study of radically different political theory traditions, the comparative analysis of other countries and the development of 'positive' or empirical political theory played a large part in opening up the UK profession to wider influences. In the early post-war period the sources of influence were fairly limited. Comparative work in *Political Studies* tended to be single-country papers focusing on parts of the British Commonwealth (where political practices were often of course strongly influenced by the Westminster model), the USA and France (both long-lived liberal democracies and wartime allies of the UK). During the 1960s a strong movement began in the UK profession, which reached fruition in the 1970s and 1980s, moving away from single-country comparisons and towards a much more systematically organized comparative politics. It included a wider range of countries and regimes (especially the Soviet Union and a range of less developed countries) and looked more analytically at discrete themes such as party politics, bureaucracies, or revolutions. In the 1980s and 1990s the erstwhile clear boundaries between 'comparative' and UK politics were re-blurred by the development of studies treating the UK as a fully European state. The growth of specialist journals with a specific area or comparative or European focus meant that purely empirical studies in these genres tended to feature less in *Political Studies* than papers with wider appeal.

Empirical political theory focusing on 'positive' analyses modelling how states or political processes actually operate (as opposed to the normative focus on how they *should* operate) also developed across this period as an increasingly central element of political science debates. The behavioural revolution played a large part up to the late 1960s in extending the range of comparative analyses and in systematizing the methods used. A shift towards broader political sociology research into structures of power and patterns of state formation was influential in encouraging the closer integration of comparative work with debates about the theory of the state, especially within liberal democracies. Methodologically more sophisticated work on public policy-making also encouraged more systematic and quantitative analyses from the 1970s on. A further strong stimulus in this direction came from public choice theory founded on a more deductive style and using assumptions of rational actors who maximize their benefits net of costs, and from broader political economy approaches influenced by 'soft' public choice theory. Public choice work has been an especially important motor of change but new forms of more inductive pluralist theory were constantly originating as authors involved in empirical studies stood back and tried to make sense of their findings. And towards the end of the 1990s post-modern critiques also began to have resonance in empirical work.

Our selection of papers is particularly restricted in this section, partly because much of the published comparative work in the journal relates to contemporary report-age and up-dating, or to developments and issues subsequently resolved. Many other studies form important scholarly building blocks in long-running collective efforts to build up a coherent empirical picture, especially in more recent times; but they deal with fairly specialized subjects which do not lend themselves easily to extraction for a collection such as this. We have thus focused on some examples with continuing relevance from single-country studies, from the era of broadening into the state debates, and from path-breaking empirical theory work.

Towards an Explanation of McCarthyism

Nelson W. Polsby

University of Wisconsin

Nowadays political science methods and toolkits have penetrated extensively into the media's discussion of electoral politics and public opinion, but in 1960 this influence was still in its infancy. Polsby's article sets out to critically test the conventional media interpretations of the origins of public opinion backing for Senator Joe McCarthy's populist anti-Communist campaigns, widely recognized then and since as a critical test for post-war American democratic processes. He demonstrates in detail that the available poll evidence shows little or no confirmation of many widely accepted elite explanations. Instead of being a maverick with diverse sources of political support, McCarthy's appeal was in fact chiefly confined to Republicans and fitted closely into the pre-existing left-right dimension in American politics. As a corollary of this revisionist view, Polsby also argues that McCarthy's political impact in terms of being able to destabilize or pressurize established party politicians was also much more restricted than contemporary observers estimated.

Three Hypotheses

Numerous ingenious explanations of the McCarthy phenomenon have been proffered.[1] Furthermore, sophisticated students have seldom relied upon any single explanation. In reducing previous explanations to three hypotheses, then, I have no doubt greatly simplified the viewpoints of the writers who first suggested them.

One hypothesis which attempts to account for McCarthy's rise to prominence lays heavy stress on 'atmospheric' conditions surrounding the position of the United States after the Second World War. Instead of being allowed to relax into their customary inter-war posture of 'normalcy' Americans were faced with the necessity of continuing their foreign entanglements, owing to the hostility of the Russians and the debilitation of our overseas allies. This hypothesis suggests that many Americans were unhappy at this turn of events, and that many of them interpreted these events as the inexorable result of involvement in 'foreign' wars. These citizens opposed large-scale spending for foreign economic aid, were progressively angered by the fall of China and the discovery of atomic spies both here and abroad, had always been sceptical of alliances with Great Britain, and became bitterly frustrated at the seemingly endless manoeuvres of the Cold War and the Korean conflict. Senator McCarthy's approach to politics, so runs the argument, gave support to the nostalgia of isolationists, many of whom had ancestral ties with Germany, and was congenial to those who harboured populistic and anglophobic sentiments.[2]

From this hypothesis we should deduce that McCarthy would find support among people of German extraction, among isolationists, and among those who preferred dramatic activity to patience in the conduct of foreign affairs. Evidence on these points is not conclusive, but certainly suggests the plausibility of this hypothetical description of McCarthy supporters. For example, Samuel Lubell has reported two chief sources of strength for Senator McCarthy:

> One was the frustrations that arose out of the Korean War, which often took the form of voters demanding 'Why don't we clean up these Commies at home with our boys dying in Korea?' ... The second main source of McCarthy strength came in areas which opposed our entry into the last war.[3]

Lubell also indicates that McCarthy ran better in those Wisconsin townships with high German populations than he did in the rest of the state.[4]

Hodges, Graham, and Anderson, in a study of Pierce County, Wisconsin, discovered that McCarthy supporters could be found disproportionately among those of German extraction, and among those who are 'sceptical about foreign involvements on the part of the United States...[favouring] discontinuing both economic and military aid to Asiatic and European nations, and [feeling] that the Korean conflict was a mistake'.[5]

Information from various Gallup surveys is also relevant. A study of New London County, Connecticut, indicated that one of the major reasons people gave for supporting McCarthy was that 'They admire greatly his "courage" and "sincerity", feeling that he is not afraid to "get tough".'[6] Gallup also reported a similar response among citizens of East Stroudsburg, Pennsylvania, where many citizens favoured McCarthy because of his 'fearlessness', and because he 'gets a lot done the way he goes about things'.[7]

It seems likely that the political atmosphere contributed in some general sense to McCarthy's rise, and supplied his followers with rationalizations for supporting him. But presumably this atmosphere existed for everyone, and, save in the case of the relatively small German-American group, the hypothesis does not explain, for the purpose of assessing his political possibilities at any time, where in the population most of McCarthy's supporters could have been located.

Many people have been persuaded that McCarthy's potential was considerable, since for a great length of time Gallup surveys recorded that a substantial proportion of the population 'approved of' McCarthy in some sense.[8] A trend line on Senator McCarthy's popularity was released on 12 November 1954 by the American Institute of Public Opinion. The results are shown in Table 1. McCarthy also ran fourth in the Gallup nationwide survey of 'most admired men in the world', in 1954. The atmospheric hypothesis differentiates only crudely between those favourable to McCarthy and those unfavourable, on the basis of generalized attitudes towards historical events, and identifies more exactly only a small portion of McCarthy's alleged followers.

A second hypothesis derives from the researches of Adorno and his associates[9] and identifies McCarthy as an authoritarian leader. Authoritarianism implies a host of rather misanthropic social attitudes including 'toughness', superconformity, intolerance, generalized hostility, and an unusual concern with sexual 'goings on'. Many observers, pointing out that Senator McCarthy exhibited more than his share

Table 1: Trend line on Senator McCarthy's popularity

Date	Favourable (%)	Unfavourable (%)	No opinion (%)
June 1953	35	30	35
August	34	42	24
January 1954	50	29	21
March	46	36	18
April	38	46	16
May	35	49	16
June	34	45	21
August	36	51	13
November	35	46	19

of these hostile attitudes, deduced that throughout the population those individuals who were most authoritarian would be most likely to be McCarthyites.[10] This hypothesis has gained some confirmation, but contrary evidence suggests the need for more precise specification of the personality characteristics which are supposed to have caused pro-McCarthy sentiments.

Hodges, Graham, and Anderson report that McCarthyites were 'more conformistic, agreeing that there are too many "odd-balls" around, that the "good" American doesn't stand out among his fellow Americans, and that children should not develop hobbies which are ... unusual'; and more misanthropic, 'concurring with statements that "people are out to cheat you", and that "there is wickedness, cheating and corruption all about us"'.[11]

However, some students have noticed that there were relatively intolerant groups in the population whose members nevertheless seemed markedly impervious to McCarthy's charismatic charm.[12] And, conversely, it has been established that members of other groups which were not notably intolerant have supported him to a disproportionate degree.[13] A third hypothesis attempts to account for these findings by making reference to the needs and aspirations of certain groups within the population which were satisfied, it is suggested, through McCarthyite activity.

The authors of *The New American Right* have advanced this hypothesis in its most full-blown and persuasive form. This volume is a collection of essays by a distinguished group of social scientists, all attempting to explain the social sources and consequences of McCarthyism. The nature of American politics has changed, they say, so as to render the McCarthy movement unintelligible to conventional forms of political analysis. They call for a 'new' type of analysis, one that recognizes the significance of the emergence of status groups as entities making important demands upon the rest of American society, through the political system.[14] In times of economic distress demands are made along class lines; economic 'interests' divide the nation's wealth and income by putting pressures of various kinds upon one another and on the government, which acts as a mediating and legitimizing agent for society and as a forum for the expression of dissatisfactions and the

Table 2: Groups Comprising the New American Right (i.e. McCarthyites)

I. *Named in six out of seven essays*: New rich.
II. *Named in five essays*: Texans, Irish, Germans.
III. *Named in four essays*: Middle class, Catholics, Midwesterners.
IV. *Named in three essays*: Lower middle class, up-mobile, less educated.
V. *Named in two essays*: 'Cankered intellectuals', old family Protestant 'shabby genteel', recent immigrants, down-mobile, minority ethnics, Old Guard G.O.P., ex-Communists, Midwest isolationists.
VI. *Named in one essay*: Lower class, small town lawyers, auto dealers, oil wildcatters, real estate manipulators, small business men, manual workers, elderly and retired, rentier class, youth, Southern Californians, South Bostonians, fringe urbanites in middle-sized cities, transplants to city, Polish Catholics, hick Protestants, patriotic and historical group members (e.g. DAR), Scandinavians, Southern Protestant fundamentalists, soured patricians, small town residents, neo-fascists.

Source: The New American Right.

promulgation of panaceas. In periods of prosperity the continuing adjustments of interests to each other and to the resources of the economy yield the centre of political attention to the demands of status groups, which use the arena to insist on the improvement or maintenance of their status position in society. In times of economic well-being the 'dynamic of dissent' resides in those status groups who wish to change the *status quo* – and of course consider themselves at a disadvantage in the status hierarchy. The McCarthy movement, the authors agree, expresses a non-economic form of protest which can only mean that those in society who supported McCarthy did so because of status dissatisfactions.[15]

The authors could have predicted from this hypothesis those groups which should be pro-McCarthy and those which should be anti-McCarthy. Secondly, they could have checked these predictions against the available evidence. In fact, they took only one of these steps, deducing who McCarthy's followers might be. It can easily be seen from an inspection of Table 2 that the 'status politics' hypothesis is much too inclusive to have very much explanatory power. Although it may accurately estimate why specific members of each of the groups named may have found McCarthy an attractive political figure (i.e. because of their status anxieties) it neither differentiates successfully among groups, nor provides criteria by which some groups can be excluded from its purview.

A second step would have been to check deductions against facts. Only Lipset, among *The New American Right* essayists, attempted to do so, and he presents only his conclusions from findings, rather than the findings themselves. At the time of publication of *The New American Right* there were several sources available which might have confirmed at least partially some of the predictions made in these essays. I present the relevant conclusions of these sources in Table 3.

Table 3: Groups Comprising the New American Right, According to Empirical Evidence

Group	Gallup	Bean	Harris
5			
(1) Germans	—	No	—
(2) Irish	—	—	No
4			
(3) Catholics	Yes	Yes	—
3			
(4) Less educated	Yes	Yes	
2			
(5) Minority ethnics	Yes & No	Yes & No	Yes & No
(6) Republicans	Yes	—	—
(7) Recent immigrants	Yes & No	Yes & No	—
1			
(8) Lower class	Yes	Yes	—
(9) Manual workers	Yes	—	—
(10) Polish Catholics	—	Yes	—
(11) Elderly	Yes	—	—
(12) Youth	No	—	No
(13) Scandinavians	—	No	—
Groups not named in *The New American Right*			
(1) Farmers	Yes	Yes	—
(2) New Englanders	Yes	—	—

Notes: The vertical axis ranks groups according to the number of essays out of seven in which they are explicitly mentioned in The New American Right. *The horizontal axis lists sources of empirical data in support of (Yes) or against (No) the listing of groups as nuclei of New American Right sentiment.*
Sources: American Institute of Public Opinion (Gallup Poll), Influences in the Mid-Term Election, 1954 *(Bean),* Is There A Republican Majority? *(Harris).*

As Table 3 indicates, the 'status anxieties' hypothesis yields rather indifferent results, since it apparently fails to account for two groups in the populace found to have been disproportionately pro-McCarthy, yet on the other hand evidence indicates that some groups named as McCarthyite in fact were not.

Other criticisms can be made of *The New American Right*. The assertion that 'status groups' are at the heart of the McCarthy movement is essentially trivial. The task was to determine *which* status groups were peculiarly situated so as to be especially favourable to McCarthy. And the identification of some of the groups named as McCarthyite is simply implausible. This should weigh heavily in the case of the book under discussion, where the basic argument depends on plausibility rather than more 'scientific' demonstrations of truth. For example, it is unclear why members of the DAR should release status anxieties by joining in an attack on the very social groups whose history their organization celebrates. That status anxieties can drive people to attack others – especially the weak – is a reasonable enough argument, but if it is in principle possible to negate *The New American Right* thesis in any way, surely the cases of white Protestant 'shabby genteel' McCarthyites succeed in doing so. Finally, it should be noted that the introduction of ethnic and status considerations into political analysis can hardly be said to have originated with the authors of *The New American Right*, as they themselves, aware of the practices of 'ticket balancing', the folklore of political 'availability', and long-standing academic interest in the group conflict theory of politics, no doubt realize.

Since the publication of *The New American Right*, Martin Trow has come forward with new data bearing on the 'status anxieties' hypothesis.[16] He concludes from his study of Bennington, Vermont, that: (1) Supporters of McCarthy were not more politically intolerant than non-supporters of McCarthy when formal education was held constant. McCarthy received a disproportionate share of his support from the less educated members of the community, who are always less tolerant.[17] (2) McCarthy received much greater support from those members of the middle class who were *economically* at a disadvantage (e.g. small business men) and who expressed hostility towards modern forms of political and economic organization.

These findings support all three hypotheses in so far as they identify McCarthyites as members of a movement of generalized protest. But they also indicate that economic and political factors may have been as important as status anxieties in explaining the social sources of McCarthyism.

A Political Interpretation

I want to turn now to a fourth hypothesis, one which attempts to explain McCarthyism as a political phenomenon. It is a surprising fact that analysts have discounted so heavily the purely political aspect of his success. Therefore I want to review now the rather heavy evidence supporting the hypothesis that McCarthy succeeded at the grass roots primarily among Republicans.

For example, I present in Table 4 the results of a re-analysis of a Gallup survey. In this re-analysis I have attempted to differentiate between those who were for and those against McCarthy. Pro- and anti-McCarthy populations were selected by tabulating responses to the following question: 'In general, would you say you have a favourable or unfavourable opinion of Senator Joseph McCarthy?'

The data at hand were limited; none the less they provided an opportunity to test in some approximate way the predictions of each of the hypotheses thus far offered to account for McCarthy's grass roots support.

Authoritarians, it is said, tend to be politically confused and badly informed.[18] The nationwide survey asked a series of questions designed to elicit political information of various kinds. McCarthyites and non-McCarthyites were able to identify Far Eastern political leaders correctly to about the same degree, but, once again, the slight differences recorded were all in the expected direction. This is also

Table 4: Popularity of Senator Joseph McCarthy

In general, would you say you have a favourable or unfavourable opinion of
Senator Joseph R. McCarthy?

	N	%
Favourable	456	31
Unfavourable	693	46
No opinion	287	19
Don't know him	41	3
Total	1,477	99

Source: Gallup Survey 529 K, 6 April 1954.

true of the questions asking about participation in the last election, and in elections generally (see Tables 5 and 6).

The same thing happens when crude tests of the 'status' hypothesis are applied, the assumption being that a higher proportion of McCarthyites come from the Catholic, lower class, and less educated parts of the population. The Tables (7, 8, and 9) show, once again, tendencies in the direction of confirmation.

Table 5: Political Information of those Favourable and Unfavourable to Senator J. McCarthy

Will you please tell me which of these men you have heard of?
And will you tell me what country he is from?

	Favourable			Unfavourable		
	Chiang (%)	Mao (%)	Nehru (%)	Chiang (%)	Mao (%)	Nehru (%)
Yes, correct country	89	34	60	88	42	67
Yes, incorrect or don't know country	6	19	12	8	20	9
Not heard of, no answer	5	47	28	4	38	24
Total	100	100	100	100	100	100
	(N = 458)	(N = 455)	(N = 454)	(N = 700*)	(N = 689)	(N = 690)

Source: Gallup Survey 529 K, April 1954.
* The fact that the Ns here exceed the total unfavourable population of 693 is perhaps on account of double responses in a small number of cases.

Table 6: Political Participation of those Favourable and Unfavourable to Senator J. McCarthy

Question I.   Have you ever voted in any election, or don't you pay any attention to politics?

Question II. In the election in November 1952, did things come up which kept you from voting, or did you happen to vote?

	Favourable		Unfavourable	
	I (%)	II (%)	I (%)	II (%)
Yes, voted	86	77	89	81
No	3	20	2	14
Never	11	—	9	—
No, too young	—	3	—	5
Total	100	100	100	100
	(N = 456)	(N = 455)	(N = 692)	(N = 687)

Source: Gallup Survey 529 K, April 1954.

Table 7: Religious Preference of those Favourable and Unfavourable to Senator J. McCarthy

Question: What is your religious preference: Protestant, Catholic, or Jewish?

	Favourable (%)	Unfavourable (%)
Protestant	68	71
Catholic	28	20
Jewish	1	5
Other	2	3
Total	99	99
	(N = 452)	(N = 685)

Source: Gallup Survey 529 K, April 1954.

But this relatively meagre empirical confirmation is unimpressive when set against comparable figures describing the two populations by their political affiliations (see Table 10).

Table 8: Social-economic Rating of those Favourable and Unfavourable to Senator J. McCarthy (Rating by interviewer)

	Favourable (%)	Unfavourable (%)
Upper	3	3
Above average	32	34
Average	2	1
Below average	47	45
Lower	11	14
Total	95*	97*
	(N = 433)	(N = 675)

Source: Gallup Survey 529 K, April 1954.
*Totals are less than 100 per cent apparently because interviewers failed to rate some respondents.

Table 9: Educational Levels Attained by those Favourable and Unfavourable to Senator J. McCarthy

	Favourable (%)	Unfavourable (%)
Up to 8 years school	27	22
9–12 years	53	51
Over 12 years	17	24
Total	97	97
	(N = 441)	(N = 682)

Source: Gallup Survey 529 K, April 1954.

These findings speak for themselves, but do not stand alone. The distributions of McCarthy's vote in Wisconsin, where, it should be admitted, 'The impact [of McCarthyism] on the political and cultural life of the state was not particularly great',[19] indicate strongly that McCarthy ran best in the most heavily Republican areas, and conversely. James G. March has demonstrated this point conclusively with respect to the 1952 primary election.[20] Samuel Lubell has observed that Senator McCarthy in 1952 ran well ahead of his state average in townships populated heavily by people of German extraction, but this also was true of other Republicans, including Senator Taft in the 1952 primary, and Republican Presidential candidates in 1944, 1948, and 1952.[21] Inspection of election returns bears out the thesis that McCarthy ran best where the Republican Party was strongest. McCarthy's strongest showing in 1952, for example, generally took place in those counties giving Walter Kohler, Republican candidate for Governor, their heaviest support. Out of the 71 counties in Wisconsin, 30 gave McCarthy a margin

Table 10: Party Sympathies and Voting Records of those Favourable and Unfavourable to Senator J. McCarthy

Questions
I   Did you vote for Eisenhower (Republican) or Stevenson (Democratic)?
II   If the elections for Congress were being held today, which party would you like to see win in this state—the Republican Party or the Democratic Party?
III (If undecided) As of today, do you lean more to the Republican Party or to the Democratic Party?
IV   In politics, as of today, do you consider yourself a Democrat, Republican or Independent?

| | Favourable (%) | | | |
Question	I	II	III	IV
Republican	76	53	37	46
Democratic	21	29	23	30
Undecided	—	17	27	—
Other	3	1	13	24
	100	100	100	100
	(N = 350)	(N = 456)	(N = 77)	(N = 456)

| | Unfavourable (%) | | | |
Question	I	II	III	IV
Republican	49	29	28	24
Democratic	49	57	38	58
Undecided	—	13	26	—
Other	2	1	8	24
	100	100	100	100
	(N = 560)	(N = 693)	(N = 88)	(N = 693)

Source: Gallup Survey 529 K, April 1954.

of 2–1 or better, and of those 30, 24 were counties in which Governor Kohler beat his opponent by 3–1 or more. In the 29 counties where he made his strongest race, capturing 75 per cent or more of the two-party vote, Kohler received only 28 per cent of his state-wide vote. But in the 30 counties where McCarthy received 65 per cent of the vote or more, fully 35 per cent of McCarthy's state-wide vote was concentrated.[22]

These figures demonstrate that the McCarthy vote was concentrated in areas of Republican strength, and was neither scattered, nor distributed in some pattern unique to McCarthy, nor particularly strong.

Did McCarthy Affect Election Outcomes?

Deciding where McCarthyites at the grass roots were located is of course not sufficient to explain his success in official Washington. Many cogent reasons for

McCarthy's success have been given, and since they are mutually complementary it is unnecessary to choose between them. McCarthy was, at first, the weapon of a desperate Republican Party. Senator Taft's famous advice, 'If one case doesn't work, then bring up another',[23] is a measure of the lengths to which Republicans were willing to go in those days to embarrass a long-entrenched Democratic administration. Secondly, there was McCarthy's protected position as a member of the Senate.[24] While he was never even remotely a significant member of the Club, attacks on him might have been construed by powerful Senators as attacks on Senatorial prerogatives and practices. McCarthy's place in the Senate also gave him the protection of immunity from libel suits, the services of the staff of a committee, and the powers to hold hearings and issue subpoenas.

Third, one can scarcely discount his personal effectiveness as an imaginative political entrepreneur who exploited the mass media by accommodating his 'exposés' to the exigencies of deadlines, and who employed the bulging briefcase, the non-existent 'document', garbled figures, and so on, with stunning effect.[25] A fourth reason for McCarthy's success was no doubt the vulnerability (real or imagined) of the Truman administration on the issue of Communists in government, and a fifth reason would certainly be the emasculation of administrative resistance to McCarthy's activities, by order of President Eisenhower.[26]

All of these are 'factors' which contribute to an explanation of McCarthy's phenomenal success in demoralizing federal employees, in blackening the name of the United States abroad, and in dominating the headlines for more than four years. But they do not explain the remarkable fear of McCarthy that seems to have afflicted those somewhat outside his line of fire – newspaper people, professional folk, most academicians, and his colleagues in Congress. This fear can be accounted for, I think, by adding one more factor, a critical assumption made by almost all those for whom McCarthyism was of daily concern. This assumption was that McCarthy was in fact uniquely powerful at the grass roots; that he had a vast following which cross-cut party lines and loyalties, which he could call upon to defeat his enemies. Richard Rovere reports: 'After the 1952 elections, it was believed in the Senate that McCarthy was responsible for the presence there of eight men – which meant that he was responsible for the absence of eight others.'[27]

Surely a useful task for policy science would have been to test such beliefs of policy-makers against the available evidence. It is disquieting to wonder how history might have been changed if the evidence had shown a more modest number of scalps on McCarthy's belt – or none at all. After all, the only thoroughly documented victory of this kind for McCarthy was the replacement of Republican Senator Raymond Baldwin by Democratic Senator William Benton of Connecticut – hardly a net gain for the right wing of the Senate. Baldwin has made no secret of the fact that abuse at the hand of McCarthy during the investigation of the Malmedy massacre was the determining factor in his decision to leave Washington.[28]

It does not seem entirely pointless to undertake an analysis of at least one of the other seven cases. There are those who still believe that McCarthy was a powerful influence with voters all over the nation and that these voters rose up and smote some of his most distinguished adversaries. It seems important to make at least a token effort to verify this belief. If it is correct, the usual supposition by political scientists that political support is in general not transferable from one figure to another must go by the board. We would have to conclude that American politics is a more dangerous and unstable game than we had suspected, if a demagogue can criss-cross the country and impose his will upon the electorates of states far from his own.

Political observers seem most willing to grant that McCarthy was important in the defeat of Senator Tydings in 1950, and of Senator Benton in 1952. Rovere says: 'McCarthy, a nobody in 1949, threw his weight against Tydings in 1950, and, lo, Tydings lost',[29] and, '... he had, in fact, attended to Senator Benton's expulsion by the voters of Connecticut'.[30] McCarthy's reputation for grass roots political effectiveness outside his home state rests most heavily on these two cases. The easy availability of appropriate statistical materials prompts me to select the Benton case for further examination here.[31]

William Benton was appointed Senator from Connecticut in 1949 by Governor Chester Bowles, his erstwhile partner in the advertising business, to succeed Raymond Baldwin, who retired to the Connecticut Supreme Court of Errors. There was some question at the time of Benton's appointment as to whether he was a *bona fide* resident of the state of Connecticut, but he was duly qualified, and took his seat. Benton's occupational record was unusually distinguished. He had been an advertising executive, Vice President of the University of Chicago, President of the *Encyclopedia Britannica*, and an Assistant Secretary of State. In 1950 he stood for election to the seat he had held by appointment, and won with 50.06 per cent of the state-wide two-party vote.

Returning to the Senate, Benton went out of his way to tangle repeatedly with Senator McCarthy, urging an investigation of McCarthy's finances, among other harassments. McCarthy struck back with characteristic resourcefulness, and managed to have Benton investigated too. When Benton stood again for election for his full term, in the fall of 1952, McCarthy campaigned briefly in Connecticut against him. Benton lost, polling 45.80 per cent of the vote.

Rovere, and presumably others, concluded that McCarthy 'got' Benton. But no reasonable construction of the evidence at hand seems likely to sustain this conclusion. A few elementary facts about Connecticut politics should be noted. First, Connecticut had no primary system, a situation which has since been changed; hence at the time there was little incentive for most voters to reveal their party affiliations to registrars of voters, and only a minority did so. However, Connecticut voters generally vote straight tickets, for all the reasons for which straight tickets are popular in other parts of the country, and also because the voting machines in use in Connecticut make a split ballot difficult. In order to split a ticket, it is necessary first to pull a party lever and then cut individual candidates off the ballot, replacing them with other candidates.[32]

It should surprise no one to learn, then, that just as Benton's vote went down in 1952 as compared with 1950, so Democratic fortunes generally declined in the same period. For each of these years, the Democratic percentage of the two-party vote for the 'top' of the ticket (excluding the race in which Benton figured) was calculated, giving Democratic 'norms' for each year.[33] For both years Benton's

Table 11: Democratic Percentage of Two-party Vote in 1950 and 1952, Connecticut

	1950 (%)	1952 (%)
Benton	50.06	45.80
Democratic norm	50.19	45.87

percentage corresponds exactly with the Democratic norm, as Table 11 demonstrates.

Now, how are we to account for this general depression in the Democratic vote? It would be too much, I think, to attribute these results to McCarthy's efforts, since a more parsimonious explanation is readily at hand. Clearly Connecticut Democrats in 1952 were caught in the landslide that elected Dwight D. Eisenhower President.[34]

It still might be argued that Senator McCarthy affected the outcome of the Benton race by robbing Benton of support he had in 1950 and which he could not replace elsewhere. This argument would be based on the premises that Benton would have improved his position as compared with the rest of the Democratic ticket if McCarthy had not campaigned against him.

How to test this assertion? Each of Connecticut's 169 towns reports election returns separately, and so it is possible to detect changes in the location of a candidate's political strength within the state. Figure 1 shows that Benton deviated by more than 3 per cent in 1952 from his 1950 relationship to the norm in only two towns in the entire state. Benton gained on the norm in 71 towns, stayed the same in 51, and fell behind in 47. Nine of ten towns where Benton fell behind by 3 per cent or more are located in the home county of the 1952 Democratic ticket leader, Abraham Ribicoff, who ran for Senator (short term) in that year, and lost by a narrow margin. Thus Benton's comparatively poor showing in these towns can be attributed to Ribicoff's unusual popularity, and not to some disability of his own.

We have in effect judged McCarthy's impact against two base-lines, by comparing Benton's performance in 1952 with his performance in 1950, when McCarthy did not campaign against him, and, secondly, by comparing Benton's performance with that of the rest of the 'top' of the state-wide Democratic ticket in 1952, against whom McCarthy did not campaign. This evidence shows that Benton's record deviates hardly at all from the record of his party in state-wide elections for both years. In general, it appears that Benton maintained or improved upon his 1950 record in 1952, a fact obscured by the effects of the Eisenhower landslide. In the light of these findings, the granting of credit to McCarthy for Benton's defeat is no doubt unjustified, if not entirely erroneous.

Policy Science and McCarthyism

It cannot be overemphasized that most of the facts on which this analysis has been based were available while McCarthy was still very much alive, and in the headlines. I think this analysis shows McCarthy to have been more dependent on

Figure 1: Net Change, 1952–50, in Senator Benton's percentage of the two-party vote compared with the Democratic norm, by towns in Connecticut

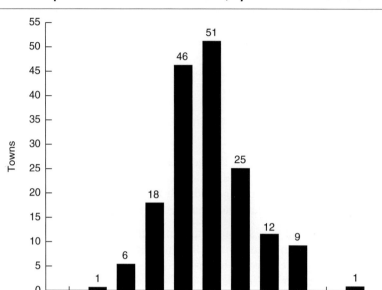

Percentage of the two-party vote by which Benton gained (+)
or lost (–) on the Democratic norm.

his party, and personally much less effective at the grass roots, than has been commonly supposed. The erroneous supposition that McCarthy was a powerful figure with some politically meaningful segment of 'the people' no doubt served to make him so in the peculiarly isolated subculture that is official Washington. The consequences of this error are well known to all those who were 'tuned in' to news media anywhere in the world over the last decade.

Let me summarize, in conclusion, what policy scientists could have established about McCarthyism during the period when it was still a live issue. First, they could have confronted myths about McCarthy with facts. It would have been especially useful if they had mobilized information about the actual consequences of crossing McCarthy and diffused it to those in a position to withhold from him the freedom he enjoyed for so long to create the political atmosphere in which he thrived. Second, they could have indicated the extent to which pro-McCarthy sentiments were ineffectively mobilized politically, revealing that McCarthy was unusually dependent upon regular Republican support both in the Senate and in his home state. McCarthy was more deeply a political phenomenon, perhaps more vulnerable to a change in the definition of his position by Washington politicians, than these politicians themselves realized. Third, policy scientists could have assembled information about current states and locations of pro-McCarthy sentiment. By tracing the ebbs and flows of McCarthy's popularity, inferences could have been made about the kinds of events triggering gains and losses in his popularity, hence about the size and locations of the margins of McCarthy's political appeal.

A latent function of making concerted demands for these kinds of data would no doubt have been a general improvement in the sources of supply for such data – notably the commercial polls. Issues that capture extra-ordinary public attention are precisely those in which polling organizations are willing to make their greatest investment; hence it is uniquely possible in these cases for policy scientists to help decision-makers to make rational choices, to help data-collection agencies to improve on the relevance of their inquiries, and, finally, to help themselves by cultivating increasingly meaningful and useful sources of information. The brief demonstration I have made in the case of McCarthy is meant to suggest that such developments as these are not only desirable but feasible.

Notes

1 See an excellent review which extracts explanatory propositions from mostly hortatory literature on McCarthyism: Dennis H. Wrong, 'Theories of McCarthyism', *Dissent*, I (Autumn 1954), pp. 385–92.

2 See, for expositions of this hypothesis, Samuel Lubell, *The Future of American Politics* 2nd ed., Garden City, NY: Doubleday, 1956, p. 164; Samuel Lubell, 'The Question is Why', review of *The New American Right* in the New York *Times Book Review*, 11 Dec. 1955; Peter Viereck, 'The Revolt Against The Elite', in Daniel Bell (ed.), *The New American Right*. New York: Criterion, 1955, pp. 91–116; Talcott Parsons, 'Social Strains in America', in ibid., pp. 117–40.

3 Samuel Lubell, *Revolt of the Moderates*. New York: Harper, 1956, p. 268.

4 Ibid., p. 269.

5 Harold M. Hodges, Jr., Charles Graham and Philip Anderson, 'A Sociological Analysis of McCarthy Supporters', a paper delivered at the Fifty-second Annual Meeting of the American Sociological Society, Washington, D.C., August 1957.

6 John M. Fenton, '"Barometer" Area Divided on McCarthy', American Institute of Public Opinion news release, 22 January 1954.

7 George Gallup, 'Two Pennsylvania "Test-Tube" Towns Split Sharply in Views on McCarthy', American Institute of Public Opinion news release, 26 June 1954.

8 George Gallup, 'Ike Tops Ten Most Admired Men', American Institute of Public Opinion news release, 26 December 1954.

9 T. W. Adorno, Else Frenkel-Brunswik, Daniel J. Levinson and R. Nevitt Sanford, *The Authoritarian Personality*. New York: Harper, 1950.

10 The 'authoritarianism' hypothesis is advanced by Richard Hofstadter, 'The Pseudo-Conservative Revolt', in Bell, op. cit., pp. 33–35, and David Riesman and Nathan Glazer, 'The Intellectuals and the Discontented Classes', in ibid., pp. 56–90. See Immanuel Wallerstein, 'McCarthyism and the Conservative', unpublished M.A. thesis, Columbia University, 1954; James A. Wechsler, 'Where proof of innocence becomes damning evidence of guilt', *Washington Post*, 3 May 1953; Richard Rovere, op. cit., *passim*; and Michael Straight, *Trial By Television*. Boston: Beacon, 1954, *passim*.

11 Hodges, Graham, and Anderson, op. cit.

12 This criticism is in effect a special application of more general strictures against the Authoritarian Personality study. See Richard Christie and Marie Jahoda (eds), *Studies in the Scope and Method of the Authoritarian Personality*. Glencoe: Free Press, 1954. For indications that non-followers of McCarthy may be at least as authoritarian as his followers see Samuel A. Stouffer, *Communism, Conformity and Civil Liberties*. Garden City, NY: Doubleday, 1955, p. 129; Seymour Martin Lipset, 'Democracy and working class authoritarianism', *American Sociological Review*, 24 (Aug. 1959), p. 484. Hodges, Graham, and Anderson, op. cit., found that McCarthyites in Pierce County tended to be more anti-Semitic than non-McCarthyites, but were not more anti-Negro. This too suggests that a general 'authoritarian' personality syndrome is not an adequate category for the analysis of McCarthyism.

13 See Stouffer, op. cit., p. 129; Martin Trow, 'Small businessmen, political tolerance, and support for McCarthy', *American Journal of Sociology*, 64 (November 1958), pp. 270–81.

14 Daniel Bell, 'Interpretations of American Politics', in Bell, ed., op. cit., pp. 4 ff.

15 Ibid. Hofstadter, pp. 33, 34, 43 f.; Lipset, 'The Sources of the "Radical Right"', pp. 167 ff. This hypothesis suggests a new application for the concept of 'relative deprivation', which urges that disprivilege be considered not as an objective social position, but rather as a state of mind which

occurs when the aspirations of a group exceed its current resources. See Alice S. Rossi and Robert K. Merton, 'Contributions to the Theory of Reference Group Behaviour', in Robert K. Merton, *Social Theory and Social Structure*. Glencoe: Free Press, 1957, revised ed., pp. 225–80.

16 Martin Trow, op. cit.

17 See Stouffer, op. cit., and Lipset, 'Democracy and Working-Class Authoritarianism', loc. cit. Herbert McClosky has some findings which indicate that greater degrees of intolerance, hostility, and misanthropy also characterize those persons subscribing to 'conservative' ideology. Herbert McClosky, 'Conservatism and personality', *American Political Science Review*, 52 (March 1958), pp. 27–45. This presents an interesting puzzle for the student of McCarthyism. It is generally well recognized that the content of McCarthy's political 'programme' – such as it was – was destructive and profoundly anti-conservative, as well as politically intolerant, hostile, and misanthropic. It is entirely possible that McCarthy's followers were either conservatives responding favourably to the tone of his approach, or radicals responding to its manifest content – or both. Regrettably, McClosky's data do not relate personality characteristics and ideological predispositions to current political sympathies or activities, hence this puzzle must go unsolved.

18 See Adorno *et al.*, op. cit., pp. 658 ff.; Fillmore H. Stanford, *Authoritarianism and Leadership*. Philadelphia: Institute for Research in Human Relations, 1950, p. 159. Low levels of political information have been found to correlate with low personal involvement in politics, and these in turn would lead us to assume that authoritarians participate less in politics than non-authoritarians. See Morris Janowitz and Dwaine Marvick, 'Authoritarianism and Political Behavior', *Public Opinion Quarterly*, 17 (Summer 1953), pp. 185–201; Paul F. Lazarsfeld, Bernard Berelson, and Hazel Gaudet, *The Peoples' Choice*. New York: Duell, Sloane and Pearce, 1944; and Morris Rosenberg, 'Some determinants of political apathy', *Public Opinion Quarterly*, 18 (Winter 1954), pp. 349–66. The relationship is regrettably not so simple, as Robert E. Lane has demonstrated: 'Political personality and electoral choice', *American Political Science Review*, 49 (March 1955), pp. 173–90. Apparently, when class is controlled, authoritarians have been found to participate in elections about as much as non-authoritarians, but probably for different reasons. I include figures on participation here, first because they were available, and second because they reinforce both my own conclusion – that McCarthyites differentiate themselves slightly by their lower rates of participation – and Lane's conclusion – that the differences between presumably authoritarian and non-authoritarian populations with respect to their political participation is negligible.

19 Leon D. Epstein, *Politics in Wisconsin*. Madison: University of Wisconsin Press, 1958, p. 4.

20 James G. March, 'McCarthy can still be beaten'. *Reporter*, 7 (28 October 1952), pp. 17–19.

21 Lubell, *Revolt*, op. cit., p. 269.

22 It should be remembered that we are not talking about Wisconsin's more populous counties in this analysis, which no doubt explains why a majority of the state-wide Republican vote is not located in those counties giving Republicans their heaviest majorities. See also Bean, op. cit.

23 William S. White, *The Taft Story*. New York: Harper, 1954, p. 85; Jack Anderson and Ronald W. May, *McCarthy: The Man, The Senator, The 'Ism'*. Boston: Beacon, 1952, p. 353.

24 One analysis which covers these points especially well is Aaron B. Wildavsky's 'Exploring the content of McCarthyism', *Australian Outlook*, 9 (June 1955), pp. 88–104. See also John B. Oakes, 'Inquiry Into McCarthy's Status', *New York Times Magazine*, 12 April 1953.

25 See Rovere, op. cit., and Cecil Holland, 'Short course on McCarthy techniques', *Washington Star*, 11 April 1954.

26 See Martin Merson, *The Private Diary of a Public Servant*. New York: Macmillan, 1955, pp. 72–81.

27 Rovere, op. cit., p. 37. Rovere has named only five of the eight casualties in his book, and as I write has not responded to a letter asking him to name the other three. He includes Raymond Baldwin and William Benton of Connecticut, Millard Tydings of Maryland, Ernest McFarland of Arizona, and Scott Lucas of Illinois.

28 McFarland is generally supposed to have been the victim of the uncommonly vigorous campaigning of his opponent, Barry Goldwater, and Scott Lucas was thought by many observers to have fallen prey to the aftermath of the Kefauver crime investigations. Rovere may be claiming more for McCarthy here than most people ever gave him credit for.

29 Rovere, op. cit., p. 37.

30 Ibid., p. 189.

31 Those interested in the Tydings case might consult the long, but for our purposes inconclusive, Hearings and Report of the Subcommittee on Privileges and Elections of the US Senate Committee on Rules and Administration, *The Maryland Senatorial Election of 1950*. Hearings, 20 February–11 April 1951. Senate Report 647 (82 Cong., 1st session), or Stanley Keeley, Jr., *Professional Public Relations and Political Power*. Baltimore: Johns Hopkins University Press, 1956, pp. 107–43.

TOWARDS AN EXPLANATION OF McCARTHYISM

35 But even without this mechanical aid to straight ticket voting, Connecticut voters seem generally to favour the straight ticket. In 1956, in Wallingford, Connecticut (pop. 11,994), where an overwhelming majority of voters was registered as independent, I conducted a pre-election survey of between 3 and 4 per cent of the population, using paper and pencil ballots, and over 80 per cent of all ballots were straight tickets. The results and methods of this survey are reported in the Wallingford (Conn.) *Post*, 1 November 1956.

36 In 1950 I averaged the Democratic percentage of the two-party vote for the offices of Governor, Lieutenant Governor, Senator (Long Term), and At Large Representative. In 1952 I averaged the Democratic percentage of the two-party vote for President, Senator (Short Term), and At Large Representative. In 1950 Benton ran for the Short Term, and in 1952 for the Long Term Senatorial Seat. His percentage of the two-party vote is in both cases excluded from the Democratic norm. For their painstaking help in collecting and tabulating these statistics, I want to thank Daniel D. Polsby and Linda O. Polsby.

37 Two plausible alternative explanations might be mentioned. The first is that 1950 Democratic voters changed over to the Republican Party in 1952 not because they were attracted by Eisenhower but because they were repelled by Benton. This explanation is not testable, given the data available. The second is that McCarthy and McCarthy-generated issues supplied a substantial part of General Eisenhower's personal appeal in 1952. This seems highly unlikely on the basis of much evidence: (1) McCarthy was much less well known than Eisenhower: (2) Eisenhower had a tremendous personal appeal to voters, apart from *any* issues; (3) Eisenhower ran better in 1956, after McCarthy became passé, than in 1952. Consult Stouffer, op. cit.; Angus Campbell, Gerald Gurin, and Warren E. Miller, *The Voter Decides*. Evanston: Row Peterson, 1954; and, especially, Herbert H. Hyman and Paul Sheatsley, 'The political appeal of President Eisenhower', *Public Opinion Quarterly*, 17 (Winter 1953–4), pp. 443–60.

The Propensity to International Transactions

Karl W. Deutsch

Gauging what has been widely seen as the growing extent of interactions between nations and different parts of the world is an issue of peculiar resonance throughout our period. It has become especially topical since the 1980s, when an alleged push towards 'globalization' has been held up as imposing increasingly restrictive limits on the capacities of liberal democratic governments to vary their policies in response to the balance of domestic political forces. Deutsch's very early article in the field discusses the difficulties in characterizing countries' relationships with the rest of the world. Like Polsby (above) he insists on the need for clear criteria and a careful look at empirical evidence to fix any trends or changes in a precise way, rather than relying on diffuse impressions or a conventional wisdom.

In the thinking of some economic theorists, a 'propensity' is the average share of efforts or resources allocated to a specific class of activities. Thus, the 'propensity to save' is the average percentage of income which people allocate to saving. Such percentages can then be plotted against other variables which are believed to be relevant, in order to find out whether, and how, changes in each variable are correlated with changes in the proportions of resources allocated to the activities in question.

In this manner the average percentages of their incomes which the people of some country save can be plotted against the levels of their incomes, as found in different income groups. Very roughly put, it may then appear that those who are richer save a bigger share of their incomes; someone may infer from this that the 'propensity to save' rises with the level of the income; and this inference may be tested by investigating whether, and to what extent, the same people, when and as they get richer, do in fact increase the proportions of their incomes which they save. Similar studies can be carried out for the behaviour of members of other social groups, so that one might speak of the 'propensity to save' of farmers, or workers, or Protestants, or Negroes [sic], or of more narrowly defined sub-groups; and other types of behaviour can be studied in similar terms, such as the 'propensity to invest', the 'propensity to hoard', and so forth.[1]

It is impractical to go here beyond this extremely crude sketch of what is actually a considerably more complex field of economic theory and measurement. Yet the main points should be clear. A propensity is a quantitative concept; it is a proportion, derived from the measurement of some class of past activities of the members of some defined group, and applied to the tentative prediction of the future frequency of similar activities – and sometimes of related ones – within the same social group, or within similar ones. In its relation to other variables it can be depicted as a curve on a graph, and expected values can be read from it for various conditions. This concept and this technique have long been applied, successfully, in economics.

Published by Blackwell Publishers, 108 Cowley Road, Oxford OX4 1JF, UK and 350 Main Street, Malden, MA 02148, USA

They could be applied to other fields; and it is the purpose of the present paper to propose their application to the field of international relations.

In its broadest terms, a propensity to engage in international transactions would cover a considerable and ill-defined range of different activities. It might be better, therefore, to break it down into several more specifically defined propensities, referring in each case to a more narrowly definable class of activities, such as trade, postal communications, news reporting and readership, travel, migration, or the allocation of governmental expenditures. These propensities would have to refer in each case to the behaviour of the members of some defined group, such as the population of some country.

This approach would call, therefore, for measuring for at least one of these activities the volume of relevant transactions entered into by the members of this population, and for measuring further the proportions of such transactions which cross the boundaries of the country, as against those that remain entirely within it. Considerable statistical data are available in published sources – on national incomes and foreign trade, on the flow of domestic and foreign mail, on residence and migration, on governmental budgets, and on the content of newspapers and other media of mass communication – from which proportions of this kind could be computed.

From such computations propensities could be inferred. It could be supposed tentatively that such proportions should turn out to be fairly stable over longer periods of time; that they should be fairly similar for similar countries; that their variations should appear to be non-random and capable of being accounted for in an orderly manner; and that conspicuous changes or differences in these proportions should suggest interesting questions and potential insights, as to the underlying social and political structure of the countries and communities involved. These suppositions can be tested. In the course of several preliminary studies it has turned out thus far that the proportions discussed here do meet in fact, by and large, the qualifications just listed.

The collection and analysis of such data should be of interest to students of society and politics. The proportions found might be interpreted tentatively in terms of propensities, as defined above, and thus not necessarily in terms of any supposed psychological predispositions or national character traits. Such cultural or psychological assumptions would require additional and independent evidence to count as even strongly indicated. The empirical behaviour, measured by the propensities, might be caused simply by external arrangements or constraints, or by broad factors of geography, or industry, or occupation, or religion, or general type of culture, rather than by any peculiarities of inner group structure or individual decision. The study of propensities should start a process of more deep-probing analysis, not terminate it.

With these cautions, however, even tentative findings could serve as more general indicators of the levels and trends of international involvement on the part of groups or nations. In regard to the politics of each country, such findings might tell us something about the relative strength of those political and social interest groups that are directly involved in international transactions, as against those whose primary concerns are domestic. The relative strength of such internationally involved groups, and the share of economic resources involved in direct international transactions, have a direct bearing on the generation and distribution of political power in a country, and on the purposes to which it is applied. In addition to the power process, the processes of communication and decision-making are affected by the proportions of purely domestic messages which compete for the attention of social *élites*, political decision-makers, and the general population, as against the proportion of messages carrying some direct concern with matters abroad. Both the power process and the attention process are inseparably interlinked in politics; and both are significantly affected by the overall proportions of domestic to international transactions.

It is possible, of course, to deny in principle the significance of such quantitative data, by proposing something like a 'vitamin theory' of the social and political importance of international transactions. Even though these were only present in small traces, it could be argued, their presence might still be essential to the functioning of the society or community concerned; and it might be asserted that any changes in the relative amounts of international transactions above this trace level should have next to no effect. Such a 'vitamin theory' of politics, however, would require some evidence to sustain it; and it would clash with much that is known about interest-group politics, the importance of economic factors, and the quantitative aspects of mass communication.

If one grants, for the time being, the potential interest of such quantitative data and proportions, what actual ratios have been found and what do they suggest. From such data, would it be possible to construct a more general scale as a background and aid in their interpretation?

A Tentative Scale of International and Interregional Integration

From a survey of the proportions of foreign to domestic mail-flows in a large number of countries, as well as of several other kinds of international and interregional transactions, a tentative scale for the integration of a relatively small community with its larger environment was proposed some years ago.[2]

The most convenient form for giving such a scale would be in terms of per cent international transactions among the total volume of transactions of the relevant class. Such percentages are often given in the published sources, and their interpretation seems intuitively familiar to many social scientists. A somewhat more sensitive yardstick for changes, particularly in cases where international transactions form a small proportion of the total, is offered by the *I/O* ratio, that is, the proportion of internal transactions to outside ones. For the purposes of the present paper it seems best to give the scale in both kinds of units – percentages as well as *I/O* ratios. This scale might be most nearly applicable to countries or communities which are relatively small relative to their total outside environment – say, not above 10 per cent of the latter.

According to this scale, and in regard to the particular type of transactions studied, one might consider countries which show between two and six times as many internal as external transactions – corresponding to a share of 14 to 33 per cent of

Table 1: A Tentative Scale of International Integration and National Autonomy (from sources given in note 1 below)

I/O ratio: internal to outside transactions	Percentage of outside transactions among total	Tentative interpretation: degree of	
		Integration to outside world	Autonomy or self-preoccupation of smaller unit
1 or less	50+	High	Low
1–2	33–50	Fair to high	Low to fair
2–6	14–33	Fair	Fair
6–10	9–14	Low to fair	Fair to high
10–15	6–9	Low	High
15 or higher	6 or less	Extremely low	Extremely high

the total for the latter – as fairly well intermediate between international integration and national autonomy, in so far as this particular type or range of transactions is concerned. Countries with more than ten times as many domestic as foreign transactions – i.e. with less than 9 per cent of the total for the latter – might count as low in international integration and high in national autonomy or self-preoccupation; and they might be rated extremely so, in both regards, if domestic transactions were to outnumber foreign ones by more than fifteen to one, reducing the international share of the total to about 6 per cent, or less. By contrast, international integration might be considered high, if domestic transactions should be equalled or outnumbered by foreign ones. Intermediate values between these 'high', 'fair', and 'low' points on this scale might then receive appropriate 'fair to high' and 'low to fair' interpretations, as shown in Table 1.

Some Specific Findings

If one applies the tentative interpretations, suggested in this table, to the data about postal correspondence for a large number of countries, it appears that the mean share of international mail was less than 14 per cent in 1880, indicating a low to fair level of international integration at that time. This average share of international mail then rose to a fair level of world integration, or at least interdependence, with almost 30 per cent in 1913, but declined again to about 25 per cent for the average of the years 1928–34, and further to about 18 per cent for the period 1946–51, while still remaining above the lower limit of the 'fair' category.[3]

International integration in regard to mail declined sharply with the area of a country, the size of its population, and the *per capita* number of letters. The last-named of these variables is correlated to some extent with literacy and *per capita* income, and apparently also with some characteristics of the general culture. Low levels of international postal integration, with less than 9 per cent of foreign mail, were found after 1928 for such countries as the United Kingdom, France, Germany, and Italy. Extremely low values, well below 2 per cent, were found for the United States, and the bottom figures of just above 1 per cent was that for the USSR for

1936 – the last year for which a figure for that country was given by the Universal Postal Union.[4]

The same scale can be applied to the results of a more recent survey of the proportions of foreign trade to national income for a large number of countries in the mid-1950's, and for a smaller number of countries at various earlier dates.[5] The first noteworthy fact here is that levels of international integration are significantly higher in regard to trade than they are in regard to mail. For a group of seventy-one countries in the mid-1950s, the median proportion of foreign trade, as compared to national income, was about 35 per cent. This is almost twice the average percentage of foreign mail found for a similar large group of countries in 1946–51, and it suggests a fair to high level of international trade integration for this group of seventy-one countries as a whole.[6] It should be borne in mind, of course, that the two periods and groups of countries are somewhat different, and that the mean value for one group is not strictly comparable to the median value for the other. The differences between the integration levels for trade and for mail seem too large, however, to be explained away by these discrepancies.

More nearly comparable figures for individual countries confirm the lagging of the share of foreign mail communications behind the levels of the shares of foreign trade. Thus France and Italy, which rated 'low' in terms of international postal integration, rate 'fair' in terms of international trade, which corresponded in 1957 to 26 and 32 per cent of their national incomes, respectively. In the same year, the United Kingdom and the German Federal Republic rated 'fair to high' in this respect, with foreign trade proportions at about 42 per cent of national income for each country, and thus more than four times as high as their corresponding percentages of foreign mail. Even the United States and the Soviet Union were less self-preoccupied in their trade than they were in the letter-writing of their populations. The share of foreign trade in the United States was a little above 9 per cent of national income in 1957, and a little below 9 per cent in 1958, leaving that country's international integration rating in regard to trade just at the borderline between 'low' and 'low to fair', but still more than four times as high as the corresponding level of the share of foreign mails.[7] The Soviet Union, finally, with a foreign trade proportion of less than 5 per cent in 1957, remained here, too, in the 'extremely low' category of international integration – including, interestingly enough, the level of its trade integration with the countries of the Communist bloc.[8] The large share which these latter countries were getting of what Soviet foreign trade there was should not obscure the remarkably small proportion of all Soviet foreign trade when compared to the Soviet national income. It may be surmised, however, that even this low level of international trade integration in the case of the USSR may still lie well above the corresponding level of its international integration in terms of the share of foreign mail, both to the world at large and within the circle of Communist countries.

The level of international trade integration tends to drop sharply with the population size of countries. In the survey of seventy-one countries referred to earlier, the median proportion of foreign trade to national income for countries with populations of about 1 million was about 50 per cent, suggesting an integration rating of 'high'. For countries with populations near 10 million, the same foreign trade ratio was about 35 per cent, with an integration level 'fair to high'. For countries near 100 million, however, the theoretical value from the regression curve would have been about 12 per cent; and for countries above 150 million, the share of foreign trade was below 10 per cent, with an apparent international integration level of 'low', or 'low to fair' at best.[9]

The fact of some decline in international integration with increasing country size should not be surprising, but the speed and extent of the decline are impressive. On the basis of these figures, any state uniting only as much as one-tenth of mankind would have to be expected to fall to a low level of international integration and to devote more than nine-tenths of its economic activities, and perhaps twice this proportion of its postal correspondence, to domestic activities. These figures might deserve the careful thought of proponents of such plans as Western European Federation, Atlantic Union, or Federal World Government, as well as that of students of integrative and disintegrative tendencies within the Soviet bloc. The trends suggested by the data need not have the inevitability of fate, but they seem to be clearly more than mere statistical artefacts, and they may well count at the very least as serious challenges to any integrative international policies or institutions.

Another type of international and interregional transactions relates to travel and migration. These processes are usually characterized by lower levels of international integration than are trade or mail, and they bring out strikingly the contrast between the high and still rising levels of integration among different regions within the same country, and the low, and sometimes even declining, levels of such integration among different countries. Thus, at censuses during the last hundred years, about 30 per cent of the American people were found living outside their state of birth, showing a long-lasting 'fair' level of interstate integration in the United States. For Switzerland, the analogous proportion in terms of Swiss citizens born outside their Cantons of residence rose from about 20 per cent in 1860 to about 40 per cent in 1950. In Bavaria the proportion of German residents born elsewhere was below 6 per cent in the 1880s; it is well above 20 per cent now, as it is in the entire Federal Republic, after the dislocations of World War II.[10] These processes may well have tended in all these countries to weaken regional separatism, and to increase the importance of national politics.

At the international level, however, developments in regard to migration have been different. Among most West European countries integration in terms of international migration must rate as 'extremely low', with the proportion of foreign-born residents well below 6 per cent. Even in the overseas countries, migration levels during the last several decades have been far below those of the pre-1913 period, and they seem unlikely to recover without deliberate changes in national policies, as well as concerted international action.

International integration is somewhat higher, on the other hand, in terms of news coverage and news attention, devoted to subject-matters beyond one's national boundaries. Here, too, however, the proportion of news space devoted on the average to foreign developments may tend to decline with the size and power of countries. According to some preliminary surveys the proportion of foreign news in the average newspaper – as distinct from the *élite* papers – of such countries as the United States and the Soviet Union may be at or below 14 per cent of total editorial content, suggesting a 'low to fair' level of international integration, or at least involvement, while such countries as the United Kingdom, France, or the German Federal Republic are apt to have comparable proportions of foreign news in the 'fair' or even 'fair to high' ranges of international integration.

The picture of national self-preoccupation is somewhat strengthened if average-reader attention is taken into account; it tends to drop for foreign news. Thus the average share of foreign and international subjects in the news space of American newspapers was a little below 9 per cent, at a time when their share of reader attention was only about 7 per cent – both figures suggesting a 'low' level of international integration.[11]

A corrective is introduced, if one notes the much higher levels of attention to foreign news in the *élite* press of most countries. To cite just one example, about 40 per cent of the editorials in both the London *Times* and the *New York Times* are devoted to international topics, and this proportion has persisted unchanged for about fifty years.[12] It is possible, therefore, that low or declining levels of international integration in the realm of material activities may be offset, to some limited extent, by a higher and conceivably even an increasing, proportion of attention to international matters in terms of news and symbols, particularly at the *élite* level.

The process of 'fundamental democratization' in the twentieth century – to recall a term of Karl Mannheim's here[13] – might then have quite different results at different stages, so far as international integration is concerned. During the first stage, mass politics might develop faster than mass acculturation to *élite* levels of international attention and interest. During the same period domestic economic development, communication, and migration might all develop faster than their international counterparts, and all these tendencies might be strengthened further through the ending of past colonial relationships. As a result of all these processes the propensities to international transactions might decline, and prolonged periods of increased parochialism and nationalism might occur in many countries just during the critical early decades of the nuclear age.

If these 'dangerous decades'[14] could be surmounted without mass destruction, however, a second stage of development eventually might permit mass acculturation to catch up, just as it might permit substantial cumulative social learning and habit-changing on the part of old and new *élites*. In this event, international attention and concern in the major countries might attain and retain sufficiently high levels of quantitative strength and qualitative competence to permit mankind to live somewhat more safely with the vast new powers of physical destruction which it has acquired. At a still later stage, structural changes in technology, economics, and social institutions may then reach a point where the material processes of international integration will enable international and supranational communities, or even a world community, to attain and exceed the present-day integrative levels of the national state.

These last points are, of course, conjectural and cannot be pursued here. The present paper will have served its purpose if it has managed to illustrate the intrinsic interest, as well as the practical possibility, of using the aid of some measurable indicators in order to trace the rise and decline of some underlying processes of international or interregional integration, and if it should find some response in the research, analysis, and criticism of other students of society and politics.

Notes

1 For an interesting attempt to extend the concept of propensities even further to aspects of economic and social behaviour that cannot be readily measured, see Walter W. Rostow, *The Theory of Economic Growth*. New York, Norton, 1950.

2 Part of the data from this survey are published in K. W. Deutsch, 'Shifts in the balance of communication flows: a problem of measurement in international relations', *Public Opinion Quarterly*, XX. 1, spring 1956, pp. 143–60; for the proposed scale, see ibid., p. 160.

3 From data, loc. cit., p. 156. Figures are for first-class mail. Between different periods, there is some variation among the countries with available data, but the overall trend seems large enough to be worth noting.

4 For details see ibid., pp. 151–6.

5 These percentage ratios of foreign trade to national income should differ conceptually somewhat from the I/O ratios, particularly in the case of countries with large import or export surpluses. If we call the domestic national product D – taking it as corresponding to the volume of domestic economic transactions – then the national income $Y = D + M - E$, where M and E stand for import and exports, respectively. The T/Y ratio then corresponds to $(M + E)$ divided by $/D + (M - E)/$, while the I/O ratio stands for D divided by $(M + E)$. For most countries, with the notable exception of the United States, this difference should be minor.

6 From data in K. W. Deutsch and Alexander Eckstein, *National Industrialization and the Declining Share of International Trade, 1890–1957*, Yale University multigraphed, 1959; publication forthcoming.

7 Deutsch and Eckstein, op. cit.

8 Ibid.

9 Ibid., 'Statistical Appendix', in collaboration with C. I. Bliss.

10 Data from standard statistical publications.

11 Cf. data in the excellent collection edited by Wilbur Schramm, *Mass Communications*. Urbana, IL, University of Illinois Press, 1954.

12 Cf. Ithiel Pool *et al., The Prestige Papers*. Stanford, Stanford University Press, 1951; and *Symbols of Internationalism*. Stanford, Stanford University Press, 1952. The results appear confirmed by more recent unpublished surveys at Yale University and The Fletcher School of Law and Diplomacy; cf. also unpublished survey data from the Center on Communications at Stanford University, collected under the direction of Professor Wilbur Schramm.

13 Cf. Karl Mannheim, *Man and Society in the Age of Reconstruction*. New York, Harcourt Brace, 1947.

14 Cf. Selig S. Harrison, *The Most Dangerous Decades*, New York, Columbia University Language Research Center, 1957 (multigraphed, with printed cover).

The New Democracy

Graeme Duncan and Steven Lukes

In the early 1960s a number of influences seemed to be coming together to routinize political science discussions of liberal democratic processes. American behavioural studies of elections had established apparently beyond question the extent to which voters operate on limited information, far removed from classical democratic theory's view of an active, informed citizenry. And beginning with Schumpeter's 'realist' view of citizens as only an audience deciding between competing party elites, many aspects of pluralist theory at this time seemed to suggest that any more extended conception of democratic processes was utopian or even potentially dangerous. Duncan and Lukes' famous paper is in retrospect one of the first signs of the dissent which was to mushroom by the end of the decade into a range of political science efforts to rehabilitate more extended conceptions of democratic control, mirrored in practical politics by major shocks to established liberal democracies, such as the urban riots in the USA and the 1968 'events' in Europe. Our selection largely omits the authors' account of classical democratic theory and focuses on their commentary on then influential contemporary writers.

It has been generally agreed that the theory of the whole electorate as politically competent and interested, expressing these qualities in democratic elections, has not proved suitable as a basis for empirical analysis. The lack of realism in many of the older descriptive accounts of elections has led a number of political scientists to work with the so-called 'competitive theory of democracy'. Joseph Schumpeter, one of the leading exponents of this theory, has defined the 'democratic method' as 'that institutional arrangement for arriving at political decisions in which individuals acquire the power to decide by means of a competitive struggle for the people's vote'.[1] Voting, which provides the electors with the opportunity to change their leaders, and competition between candidates for office, are here the key institutional devices of democracy. If 'democracy' is taken to be a political system defined institutionally in this way, empirical analysis then concentrates on the conditions for its successful operation, while the chief problem of policy becomes that of ensuring that these conditions in fact exist. The main requirement seems to be effective competition between leaders: this, in Plamenatz's view, ensures that the electorate is not 'manipulated' by the active ruling *élite*. (This view that freedom is guaranteed by free competition between *élites* derives ultimately from Mosca.) When there is no effective competition, the system ceases to be one in which the leaders are responsive to the independent wishes of non-leaders. Thus Dahl, for example, sees the main problem of democracy as that of regulating the 'great political oligopolies' – which is much as it seemed to the early utilitarians.

This 'competitive model' is adopted with variations by the writers with whom we are concerned. It is a general model useful as a point of departure in the description of existing democracies. The general picture is one of energetic and competing minorities at the top and a relatively apathetic majority, whose role is essentially that of exercising a very generalized control during the election, which is seen as a process of selecting and rejecting candidates in competition for public office. It should be seen clearly that such a model is not necessarily inconsistent with most traditional theories of democracy (except Rousseau's), for it clearly recognizes that an election in a large society can only produce clearcut and satisfactory results in this sort of way. As Schumpeter writes,

> even if the opinions and desires of individual citizens were perfectly definite and independent data for the democratic process to work with, and even if everyone acted on them with rationality and promptitude, it would not necessarily follow that the political decisions produced by that process from the raw material of those individual volitions would represent anything that could in any convincing sense be called the will of the people.[2]

The competitive model need not be incompatible with traditional notions of democracy, and it is just because classical democracy was *not* defined institutionally as a 'system of decision-making' that this is so. For, as we have seen, democracy in the traditional sense involves a great deal more than the correspondence of individual wills and collective decisions; it involves, for example, political equality, active consent about the form of government and the 'rules of the game', widespread discussion and participation, political and otherwise, through all kinds of activities and channels. To take a particular and relevant example, a study by Janowitz and Marvick,[3] which explicitly uses this competitive model, attempts to distinguish between a process of genuine consent and manipulation. The authors emphasize the importance of the quality of the voting decision, pointing out that high turnout does not necessarily reflect the process of consent. They write, in words of which John Stuart Mill would have approved:

> The underlying belief in a democracy that everyone ought to vote is indeed such a deep-seated belief that it must be regarded as a utopian goal. Reforms have been suggested above that are designed to enhance the quality of the vote by modification of the social structure. Yet in terms of practical political reform, the crucial problem is to improve the quality of competing political leaders and to increase voter competence.

The theorists of the new democracy, however, are less concerned to make the competitive 'democratic system' more democratic in the traditional sense than to justify it as an efficient and stable system, depending on compromise, 'pluralism', and a general background of apathy and political incompetence. In fact, their theory, which is intended to explain the 'democratic system', becomes in the end the new normative theory of democracy. We are driven to this conclusion by the form of their arguments. The question arises: What implications have election studies for democratic theory? The conclusion is that that theory must be made more 'realistic'. The confrontation of classical democratic ideals with actual 'democratic systems' ('what we call democracy') has no other result than the acceptance of the actual systems and their assumed conditions as entirely desirable. Electoral apathy, incompetence, and so on, which exist in most stable 'modern democracies' are now considered to be conditions of their successful functioning and are therefore taken to be the new democratic norms.

There are, of course, differences between the writers under consideration. The sociologists, e.g. Dahl and Parsons, are more concerned to produce a scientific theory of the system, whereas others, e.g. Plamenatz and Schumpeter, are much less ambitious, which is not to say that their caution is misplaced. The system is justified on a number of different grounds, and doubtless there are a number of important internal disagreements between these different writers. We can only examine a number of the most common arguments and assumptions, which may not be shared in detail by all of them.

The most notable feature of this recent democratic theory is the shift in emphasis from the needs and potentialities of the individual citizen to the requirements of the system. Despite inadequacies in individuals, the system works. In Berelson's vague words, 'The *system of democracy* does meet certain requirements of a going political organization. The individuals may not meet all the standards, but the whole nevertheless survives and grows. This suggests that where the classical theory is defective is in its concentration on the *individual citizen*.'[4] And again, in more exalted vein, 'Where the rational citizen seems to abdicate, nevertheless angels seem to tread'.[5]

It may be useful to look in some detail at Berelson's own account of the democratic system. He sees it pre-eminently as a system in equilibrium and he is followed in this by Talcott Parsons in an essay entitled '*Voting* and the Equilibrium of the American Political System'. (Parsons in fact attempts to integrate Berelson's picture into his own 'general theory of social systems'.) Berelson describes the system mainly in terms of 'balances' and the distribution of qualities in various dimensions. For political democracy to survive, the elements of the system must be distributed and related in a certain way. 'What seems to be required of the electorate as a whole is a distribution of qualities along important dimensions. We need some people who are active in a certain respect, others in the middle and still others passive.'[6] And, 'happily for the system', the voters are distributed along a smooth continuum. There must be a 'balance' between 'involvement and indifference', 'stability and flexibility', 'progress and conservatism', 'consensus and cleavage' and, finally, 'individualism and collectivism'. Low interest provides 'manoeuvring room' ('only the doctrinaire would deprecate the moderate indifference that facilitates compromise') and heterogeneity produces a balance between strongly and weakly motivated actions. Also, apart from the many factors making for social stability, 'voters carry over to each new election remnants of issues raised in previous elections – and so there is always an overlapping of old and new decisions that gives a cohesion in time to the political system'.[7] On the other hand, the least partisan are also functional to the system, making for 'flexibility' – 'for those who change political preferences most readily are those who are least interested, who are subject to conflicting social pressures, who have inconsistent beliefs and erratic voting histories. Without them … the system might prove too rigid to adapt to changing domestic and international conditions'. There is, says Berelson, 'stability on both sides and flexibility in the middle' and once again 'an individual "inadequacy" provides a positive service for the society'. Finally, there is the essential requirement of 'pluralism', which 'makes for enough consensus to hold the system together and enough cleavage to make it move'. This social heterogeneity produces a 'cross-cutting and harmonious community interest' with a 'balance between total political war between segments of the society and total political indifference to group interests of that society'.[8]

There are a number of important objections to Berelson's account. To begin with, the description of the conditions claimed to be necessary and functional to the system all embody the basic assumption of a system in equilibrium. The use, explicit or otherwise, of equilibrium concepts in the social sciences is often open to serious methodological criticisms[9] and leaves its practitioners subject to the suspicion of having based conservatism upon a pseudo-scientific foundation. More specifically, the application of an equilibrium model to actual social situations does require either careful quantification of the relevant variables (ordinally or cardin- ally) or else a situation where an equilibrium situation is directly visible (although, of course, the use of such a model may always lead to fruitful questions). Other- wise little specific sense can be made of the idea of 'balance' between elements. Yet Berelson speaks quite glibly of the balance between his various 'qualities', where neither of these conditions is fulfilled. Parsons, following Berelson, seems to accept these 'balances', translating them into his own terms as 'functional requirements'. He writes that, within a broad framework, 'if the political system is, in the relation between leadership and support, to be a relatively stable one that can integrate multifarious pluralistic interests and yet adapt to changing conditions, it must, *within broadly specifiable limits*, have certain characteristics'.[10] What we dispute is that any precise characterization has been given of these 'broadly specifiable limits' (by Berelson or by Parsons) such that we must accept their account of an equilibrium system with 'checks and balances' and the capacity for self-adjustment afforded by heterogeneity and apathy within the electorate. There is, in other words, no reason to agree that the 'democratic system' is in smoothly functioning equilibrium; and if we look hard at the assumptions behind this theory, we tend to be left with vague and questionable assertions about social harmony.

In the second place, the supposed requirements of the system are presented in an obviously value-laden and tendentious way. Berelson claims, in a rather obscure passage, that 'it turns out that this distribution itself, with its internal checks and balances, can perform the functions and incorporate the same values ascribed by some theorists to each individual in the systems, as well as to the constitutive political institutions!'[11] Berelson here seems to be trying to have the best of both worlds. Not only is his theory of democracy realistic, describing actual societies, but the old individual values are somehow incorporated in it. Apart from the verbal peculiarity (how can a distribution of qualities incorporate the values ascribed to individuals?) the claim seems hardly to have been sustained in any detail. Both he and Parsons try to show that the *system* is rational – that is, its parts are co- ordinated and it develops smoothly – but this is not rationality in any of the senses normally ascribed to individuals. Some people are active, interested and competent; others are not. Does the distribution itself, rather than any individual, incorporate these values? If this is what Berelson means, it is a roundabout and deceptive way of putting the view that, though Americans as a whole are not ideal democratic citizens, a few people do possess the required qualities and, moreover, the political system does not disintegrate.

Thirdly, the system's supposed requirements are stated very loosely – often too loosely for the validity of the account to be assessed – and sometimes tautologously, with little descriptive content. What, for example, does the requirement that there should be a 'nice balance' between consensus and cleavage, reflecting the 'health of a democratic order', really amount to? It is true but uninformative to say that if there is *too much* cleavage a democratic system – or any other system – will disintegrate: one can scarcely disagree with Berelson when he writes, 'Political parties in a democracy should disagree – but not too much, too sharply, nor too fundamentally'. Yet how can one measure these qualities to find out whether they are in balance (and what is so sacrosanct about this notional equilibrium point in any case)? This is not to say that the ideas of consensus and conflict are analytically useless; it is simply that here they are being misused, for, given that there is a measure of basic or 'higher-order' consensus, there is room for wide dispute over the nature and degree of cleavage that is tolerable or desirable (and, as Lipset shows, cleavage may itself be a factor making for consensus). And it does not help to speak of pluralism' as a 'kind of glue' which holds the system together when threatened by cleavage. Does this mean anything precise? What, for instance, is one to make of the following obscure passage from Berelson: 'The multiplicity and the heterogeneity of identifications and associations in the great society develop an overlapping, pluralistic social organization which both sharpens and softens the impact and the consequences of political activity'?[12]

Finally, there is no warrant for saying that the features isolated are requirements of the system – unless, of course, they are included definitionally as parts of it. The clearest and most important instance is that of apathy. Apathy serves, says Berelson, as a '"cushion" to absorb the intense action of highly-motivated partisans'. Apathy, it is claimed, helps the democratic system to function smoothly by facilitating change and reducing the impact of fanaticism, thus guarding against the danger of total politics'. Also, in Parsons's words, there is the 'indifference reaction', among the apathetic and incompetent floaters, which is the 'element of flexibility necessary to allow sufficient shift of votes to permit a two-party system to function effectively without introducing unduly disruptive elements into the system'.[13] Yet what is the basis for this claim that apathy must exist to hold the system together and give it flexibility, while cushioning the shock of disagreement and change? The theoretical framework seems hardly adequate to allow the role of apathy as an element of the system to be described in this way. That is to say, arguments about the necessity of apathy may always be confronted with the suggestion that any given society with democratic institutions or a democratic temper can in certain conditions tolerate an appreciably higher degree of participation than these theorists allow. The evidence, such as it is, does not in any way prove or even confirm the theory of the necessity of apathy to the survival of democracy.

Yet many of the writers under discussion support this theory, either on the basis of the equilibrium model criticized above or more generally on the basis of the evidence of scattered historical cases of differing degrees of participation. For example, Tingsten[14] makes the point, on the basis of interwar election figures in Austria and Germany, that 'an exceptionally high voting frequency may indicate an intensification of political controversy which may involve a danger to the democratic system'. His conclusion is that high political participation *may* not be a sign of the health of a democracy, but he also points out that it is misleading to speak of participation as though it were one thing whatever the community or circumstances: in other countries 'a high degree of participation cannot be judged in the same manner'.[15] Moreover, in the cases mentioned, high participation seems less a cause than a consequence of deeper-rooted social conflicts – high participation may mark some periods of crisis but it does not explain their origins. All that the evidence shows is that a high degree of electoral participation has sometimes been a symptom of crises in democracy and not even, as Lipset says, misinterpreting Tingsten's point, that 'political apathy may reflect the health of a democracy.'[16] The historical examples need careful handling – one might well argue, for instance, that the Weimer Republic fell chiefly because of apathy about the régime. In any case, neither apathy nor participation can profitably be considered in abstraction from historical contexts: apathy in the Weimer Republic can scarcely be identified with that of the affluent society of contemporary America, while increased participation, if it means a sudden 'intrusion of the masses into politics' in an artificial way is hardly equivalent to the classical prescriptions for heightened general participation in the political and other activities in the life of the community. In brief, it has nowhere been shown that apathy is either necessary or functional to democracy.

To sum up, our conclusion is that no adequate empirical theory, still less a 'scientific' theory, of institutional 'democracy' has been provided. Apart from incidental insights, the notion of a stable equilibrium system is misleading as an account of 'what we call democracy' and is deceptively presented as a development of traditional theories of democracy. Furthermore, the 'requirements' of the 'democratic system' – in particular, apathy – have certainly not been proved to be necessary to the survival of a democratic society.

It is evident that the theorists of the new democracy share a number of contemporary preoccupations which have blinded them both to the possible development and to the possible diversity of democratic societies and have led them to describe apathy as a central requirement of the functioning of such societies. Essentially, these preoccupations centre on a basic distinction between totalitarianism and liberal democracy, which underlies a great deal of recent sociological and political writing. This dichotomy, historically explicable though it is, has, in our view, distorted much recent thinking about politics among Western intellectuals. It has led to an exaggerated fear of 'ideology' and the celebration of its supposed end in the modern affluent western society, and, in addition, the familiar 'argument from the concentration camp' has often been used to condemn traditionally democratic and radical ideas which really have no necessary connexion with totalitarianism. In general, this argument takes the form of isolating a particular idea or policy from its context, either theoretical or historical, and then indicating its putative affinity with totalitarian ideas and practices. One may well question not only the specific interpretations, but also the belief that political ideas can, in any case, be more or less clearly divided into the liberal-democratic and totalitarian categories. In times of great uncertainty conservatism has a natural appeal and the advantages of stable societies are apt to be greatly exaggerated. The political system is seen as an exquisitely fragile mechanism and all possible dangers to its stability are jealously guarded against. Hence the general contemporary concern with the conditions of a stable, non-totalitarian political system and the resulting desire to avoid anything which might lead to a dangerous involvement of the masses in politics. Such a development, it is claimed, would threaten both the smooth functioning of the system and the freedom and privacy of the individual.

This background helps to explain the new directions of democratic theory. The early democratic theorists, hating the tyranny of the old régime of monarchs and aristocrats, stressed the role of vigilance and participation in protecting hard-won rights against predatory 'sinister interests'. Political participation especially was to safeguard society, protect individuals and groups and develop individual qualities as well as men's control over their social lives. The theorists of the new democracy tend to see widespread participation, interest, and conflict as substantial dangers to democracy and like to refer to the fraudulent claims of those totalitarians who see themselves as the real practitioners of democracy and the true representatives of the people. There are thus these twin dangers of 'total politics', which may disrupt the system, and totalitarian politics, which may eliminate freedom and privacy. This explains their eagerness to define the new political role of democratic man very narrowly. Meanwhile all the more radical features of the democratic tradition are abandoned in favour of a timid conservatism.

A characteristic piece of writing in this connexion is W. H. Morris-Jones's article, 'In Defence of Apathy',[17] which is often referred to in the literature and has had some measure of influence. The explicit purpose of this article is 'to suggest that many of the ideas connected with the general theme of a duty to vote belong properly to the totalitarian camp and are out of place in the vocabulary of liberal democracy'.[18] But the discussion proceeds less by detailed argument than by a process of contamination: from ideas which are part of the liberal-democratic tradition the slide is made to allegedly connected notions which are clearly totalitarian 'Political interestedness', says Morris-Jones, is the 'mark of the elect' and the obligation to vote is a dangerous idea, for 'it needs no demonstration that a totalitarian view of life easily involves an obligation not only to vote, but to do much more – and to do it, moreover, in the right direction'.[19] The trick is transparent. There is really no connexion between the obligation to vote and the obligation to act in the right direction; any idea can be simply contaminated in this way by detaching it from the theory within which it was advanced and then showing that some people have held it alongside genuinely nasty views. Apart from this, Morris-Jones advances the positive argument that parliamentary democracy should be seen less as a 'system of government resting primarily on participation and consent' but rather as 'a manner of dealing with business, a way of going about things'. In this case, the presence of the apathetic is a 'sign of understanding and tolerance of human variety' and has a 'beneficial effect on the tone of political life ... (being) ... a more or less effective counterforce to those fanatics who constitute the real danger to political democracy'.[20] The implication is obvious: to advocate widespread and general political participation is to advocate the development of intolerance and doctrinaire fanaticism.

This inference is frequently drawn in contemporary political theory and it is usually carried further, to the totalitarian conclusion that men are to be made purely political, privacy and liberty is to be invaded, and all the good things of civilized life destroyed. Examples of this kind of argument are to be found in Morris-Jones's article, in Hogan's book on *Election and Representation*,[21] in Talmon's critique of

Rousseau[22] and in Berlin's *Two Concepts of Liberty*.[23] On the one hand, the connexion is claimed to be established between the desire to participate and the totalitarian result. Berlin, for example, writes:

> The desire to be governed by myself, or at any rate to participate in the process by which my life is to be controlled, may be as deep a wish as that for a free area for action, and perhaps historically older. But it is not a desire for the same thing. So different is it, indeed, as to have led in the end to the great clash of ideologies that dominates our world.[24]

On the other hand, apathy is held to be valuable because it shows the 'limitations of politics', that men are more than political creatures and can if they wish ignore politics entirely. In Hogan's words, 'Viewed in this light, the apathy and caprice for which political democracy has been blamed is seen to be rather to its credit than otherwise. It means at any rate that people are free to interest themselves or to disinterest themselves as they please in political affairs.' This argument in terms of an ideal of freedom is deeply misleading. What is in question is not the right of men to be apathetic (and thus the enforcement of a duty to vote) but whether a society in which men concern themselves with political matters, as well as with many other matters, is likely to be more desirable than one marked by widespread apathy. If the vast majority of men were quite uninterested in politics and full general participation were demanded of everybody immediately, it is perhaps natural to infer that only constant coercion could achieve the desired result – and even more so if the desired result were unanimity. But it should hardly need saying that the ideal of general political participation is quite compatible with liberal safeguards and the rejection of coercion for partisan political goals, for instance, 'voting in the right direction'. It may be urged, with no totalitarian overtones whatsoever, that men ought to play some part in politics for their own good and for the good of society. The old democratic ideal sees apathy as dangerous because men cannot rely on others to protect their own interests and because the holders of power are likely to exercise it with too little concern for the general body of the people and for minority interests. It also considers politics to be a proper concern of the citizen and one of the fields of human excellence. In doing this, the classical theorists were very far indeed from urging constant and active participation at the behest of totalitarian masters, Stalinist Russia is as far removed from their ideals as it is from those of these modern anti-totalitarians.

As for coercion, this was the very thing that the classical theorists of democracy were concerned at all costs to avoid. The new theorists may argue that the old ideals must lead to this result, but we see no compelling reason to believe them. The now familiar dichotomies between totalitarianism and liberal democracy, between positive and negative liberty, between 'utopianism' and piecemeal pragmatism, have achieved something like a stranglehold over political theorizing. No middle way is conceded between the concentration camp and a cautious conservatism. Talmon remarks characteristically of the 'early totalitarians' that they refused 'to take the people as it was for granted; the people, that is to say the sum total of the given generation, the good and the bad, the advanced and the backward, with their wishes, enlightened or otherwise'.[25] The implicit bias of this kind of view is obvious: we must accept the existing situation in its entirety, so that the only political issue left is that of making the 'system' work more efficiently. Yet the refusal simply to accept the existing situation by no means implies the acceptance of coercion and minority domination, shaping the fabric of an existing society in the image of a utopia.

The voices of sanity and reason sound above all in times of crisis and rapid change, and their conservative tone is familiar. Edmund Burke similarly appealed to the proved virtues of stable societies against the widespread criticism of established institutions at the time of the French Revolution. The arguments of the writers we have discussed bear witness to a worthy concern with avoiding the real dangers of totalitarian politics, dangers which no one should minimize; but they have gone too far in the opposite direction. Preoccupied with stability and protecting the system against too much participation, they have in reality abandoned, without realizing it, a whole tradition of political thinking – a tradition which they claim to be developing and revising. Their arguments are, in any case, too loose to convince and too complacement to excite. This is not to say that the older democratic theories are not in need of any revision. But they have survived these particular attacks and retain their central interest and value. In particular, general political participation has not been destroyed as a desirable goal for democratic societies, nor are the new ideals that have been offered to us imposed upon us by the facts of contemporary political life.

Notes

1 Schumpeter. op. cit., p. 269. J. A. Schumpeter, *Capitalism, Socialism and Democracy*. London: Allen & Unwin, 1950, 3rd ed., part iv.

2 Schumpeter, op. cit., p. 254.

3 'Competitive Pressure and Democratic Consent' in Eulau, Eldersreld and Janowitz (eds), *Political Behaviour: a Reader in Theory and Research*. Glencoe: The Free Press, 1956, pp. 275–85, which is based on a larger study with the same title (Institute of Public Administration, Michigan, 1956).

4 Berelson, Lazarsfeld and McPhee, *Voting*. University of Chicago Press, 1954, p. 312.

5 Ibid., p. 311.

6 Ibid., p. 314.

7 Ibid., p. 316.

8 Ibid., p. 320.

9 See in this connexion an interesting paper by David Easton called 'Limits of the Equilibrium Model in Social Research', *Chicago Behavioral Sciences Publications*, no. 1 (1953), reprinted in Eulau *et al.*, *Political Behaviour*.

10 T. Parsons, *'Voting'* and the Equilibrium of the American Political System in Bwdick and Bwdick (eds), *American Voting Behaviour*. Glencoe: The Free Press, 1960, p. 114 (our emphasis). For general criticism of Parson's functional theories see Dahrendorf, 'Out of Utopia' *American Journal of Sociology* (1958), pp. 115–27.

11 Berelson *et al.*, *Voting*, p. 323.

12 B. Berelson, 'Democratic theory and public opinion', Public Opinion Quarterly, 16 (Autumn 1952) reprinted in Eulau *et al.*, *Political Behaviour*, p. 114.

13 Parsons, *Voting*, p. 114.

14 Herbert Tingsten, *Political Behaviour*. P. S. King & Son, London, 1937.

15 Ibid., p. 226.

16 Lipset, S. M. Lipset, *Political Man*. London: Heinemann, 1960, p. 32, n. 20. Lipset claims on the same page that 'the belief that a very high level of participation is always good for democracy is not valid'. This statement is true but misleading. In supporting participation the classical democrats were

thinking mainly in terms of a stable, liberal society, in which people accepted the good faith of their opponents and were prepared to work within the system.

17 *Political Studies*, vol. II., 1954, pp. 25–37.

18 Morris-Jones, 'In defence of apathy', p. 25.

19 Ibid., p. 36.

20 Ibid., p. 37.

21 D. N. Hogan, *Election and Representation*. Cork University Press and Blackwell, Oxford, 1945.

22 J. L. Talmon, *The Origins of Totalitarian Democracy*. London: Mercury Books, 1961. See especially pp. 46–7.

23 Sir I. Berlin, *Two Concepts of Liberty*. Oxford: Oxford University Press, 1958.

24 Ibid., pp. 15–16. Berlin, however, does not support the view that apathy preserves democracy and liberty. His position is that positive liberty can lead to totalitarian consequences when the meaning of the word 'self' is extended.

25 Talmon, *The Origins of Totalitarian Democracy*, p. 232.

The Myth of the 'Two Hundred Families'

Malcolm Anderson

In the mid 1960s debates between pluralists and elite theorists pushed the boundaries of the discipline towards political sociology topics. Anderson's analysis of a form of practical elite theorizing, in the shape of conspiracy models of the allocation of power in inter-war France, shows how the systematic retrieval of non-science explanations can provide new forms of material for political science. But it is also an example of how comparative and historical research can be used within wider debates about theories of the state and political processes under liberal democracy. Anderson advances a pluralist line of argument, implicitly linking elite theory with a range of unattractive political positions associated with the Third Republic's collapse from democracy under external and internal threats.

Since the Second Empire, conspiracy theories have studded the political history of France. They provided rationalizations of failure for republicans under the Second Empire, for *revanchard* radicals after Gambetta had switched the focus of radical politics from the defeat of 1870 to clericalism, for monarchists and clericals during and after the Dreyfus case, for the Left during the period of the *Cartel des gauches* and the *Front populaire*, for those deliberately excluded from power by Third Force politics during the Fourth Republic, for the supporters of *Algérie française* during the Fifth and for the extreme fringes of the political spectrum all the time. There have been recurring patterns of political eclipse and defeat accompanied by tall tales of conspiracies. The defeated have been very different sorts of men, possessing different interests and adhering to different political and intellectual traditions but they have often made use of modified versions of the same myths as a solace for and an explanation of their defeats. A striking example which unites all the typical characteristics of this process is the myth of the two hundred families.

In its developed form the myth made its appearance in the 1930s but it has a long intellectual ancestry and connexions with all the popular conspiracy theories of the nineteenth century. Indeed, the fearful notion that a small cluster of private men, hardly known to the general public, manipulated the machinery of the state exclusively for their private profit reaches far back into history. It lies at the core of the two-hundred-families mythology. But the main intellectual sources of the myth are found in the reactions to and retrospective analyses of the great political revolution of 1789 and the nineteenth-century industrial revolution. To conservatives, the overthrowing of the natural order of society and the deposition of its natural leaders was most easily intelligible in terms of small groups of men conspiring in secret societies for devilish purposes. Freemasonry provided the most popular target for those who wished to explain the collapse of the old political order in conspirational terms; the Jews later enjoyed a similar notoriety in explanations of the changing balance of economic power in society with the rise of the new capitalism.

There were analogous reactions on the left. Alarm at the consequences of changes in economic organization caused a liberal like Lamartine to characterize the holders

Published by Blackwell Publishers, 108 Cowley Road, Oxford OX4 1JF, UK and 350 Main Street, Malden, MA 02148, USA

of the new liquid wealth during the July monarchy as the *féodalité financière*, a phrase since used in many polemics against the influence of money in politics. Hostility to the new wealth of nineteenth-century capitalism linked social revolutionaries with aristocratic reactionaries in a common hatred of those groups which seemed to acquire a disproportionate share of the riches derived by exploiting new techniques of production and economic organization. Toussenel's famous work, *Les Juifs, rois de l'époque: Histoire de la féodalité financière*, ran through seven editions in the middle forty years of the nineteenth century and probably had a wider readership on the left than on the right. Jews, in the works of Toussenel and his most celebrated disciple, Edouard Drumont, were caricatures of the nineteenth-century businessmen. Antisemitism and socialism were closely associated in France until the 1890s.

Catholicism and marxism – or more precisely, counter-revolutionary clericalism and, in Popper's phrase, vulgar marxism – were sources of conspiratorial themes on which the two hundred families mythology drew heavily. The tradition established by de Maistre influenced not only ultra catholics but also social and 'liberal' catholics of the nineteenth and early twentieth centuries. Albert de Mun, the famous social catholic, gives the best summary of the conspiracy element in the 'liberal' tradition:

> If the soul of the mass of the people is separated from God, this is not the result of a spontaneous corruption: it is the reasoned work of active and resolute leaders who are united by a common plan, a conscious conspiracy of weighty interests, both public and private, against Christianity.[1]

It was usually alleged that these plotters, by successfully misleading the people in the interests of the devil, made their fortunes both politically and economically. Anticlericals turned this argument on its head; rich catholic industrialists and landowners conspired with the Jesuits and other religious orders to use religion to preserve and extend their privileges and wealth. There was agreement between clerical and anticlerical that a small powerful group was continuously conspiring to corrupt the nation; they differed only in their allegations about the membership of the group.

The vulgar marxist tradition derived from the task of translating the difficult social analysis of Marx into political propaganda directed at a wide audience. As Professor Popper writes, the essence of vulgar marxism is the belief that:

> Marxism lays bare the sinister secrets of social life by revealing the hidden motives of greed and lust for material gain which actuate the powers behind the scenes of history; powers that cunningly and consciously create war, depression, unemployment, hunger in the midst of plenty, and all the other forms of social misery in order to gratify their vile desires for profit.[2]

Vulgar marxism has encouraged and lent weight to all attempts at identifying conspirators at the centres of economic and political power.

Other political theories of both the right and the left prepared the ground for conspiracy theories in certain sectors of public opinion. Two examples are the monarchism of Maurras and the radicalism of Alain. The original Maurrasian analysis of the condition of France was not of a conspiratorial nature; it was a clear, all too simple, positivist analysis. But Maurras argued that Protestants, Jews and *métèques* modified their patriotism by considerations foreign to real French interests because they had their abiding city elsewhere; freemasons, Radicals and Socialists were also conditional in their devotion because they were committed to France as an idea and not as a concrete entity. These arguments used in a concrete political situation involved accusing 'anti-France' of deliberately and consciously conspiring to obscure the truth when it was exposed. The overtly conspiratorial element in Alain's classic exposition of Radical doctrine is small, but a suspicion of conspiracy lies at the very core of the radical political attitude. The distrust and fear of *les Gros* in parliament, administration, industry, finance, commerce, and university was based on the conviction that they shared a common outlook which was anti-democratic and prejudicial to the interests of *les petits*. If *les Gros* were aware of the implications of their own activities then they acted as conspirators.

Alain and Maurras had a wide audience during the Third Republic and they undoubtedly made many people more receptive towards conspiracy theories. But they were separated in one very important respect from the basic assumption of the two hundred families mythology. Both believed in the primacy of politics, holding that power over the machinery of state and over political decisions was acquired through direct political action. In contrast, the two hundred families mythology assumed the practical primacy of financial power, asserting that the holders of financial power could manipulate any régime, any political arrangements of their own purposes.

This places the mythology in a long tradition of political polemics. Since Lamartine described the July monarchy as being sold to the capitalists every régime has been accused of being manipulated and dominated by financiers – Jewish, protestant, foreign, or masonic.[3] The accusations rose to a crescendo during the Third Republic. In the early years of the Republic Auguste Chirac considered that Parliament had surrendered to the *'ancienne féodalité financière'*.[4] In the 1890s Adolphe Coste argued that the economy was in the hands of two hundred presidents or directors of companies who exercised formidable political power and this was a situation which would lead directly to socialism.[5] In *La Démocratie et les financiers*, a book which Daniel Halévy claimed was unobtainable because of the long arm of the financial oligarchy.[6] Francis Delaisi eloquently described the ubiquitous power of the financiers:

> Whilst the Republic, at the expense of great efforts, conquered France, the financiers have conquered the Republic. Strongly organized in power associations they control the main newspapers with which they manipulate public opinion and terrorize the deputies and ministers (whom they also console by taking an interest in their affairs). These are the people who impose a programme on the government and they supervise its execution by filling administrative offices with their creatures. In addition to being the occult masters of the machinery of State, they cover the whole country with a network of committees and newspapers with well-filled coffers ... to support 'good' candidates who are not always the least

progressive – and consequently they sometimes succeed in getting the
people to ratify their own exploitation.[7]

After the First World War Raymond Mennevée ran a periodical, *Documents politiques*,
and published a book, *Parlementaires et financiers* (three editions: 1922, 1924, 1925),
to document in detail a similar thesis.

These are only the most celebrated authors of a torrent of theorizing, accusation
and abuse, the general import of which was that French politics could not be
explained in terms of the struggle between ideologies and political principles or
the clash of interests but only by assuming the existence of a group holding key
positions in the financial system, which manipulated the public life of the country.
The myth of the two hundred families belongs to this tradition. It was enriched and
its appeal broadened by intellectual sources such as marxism, clericalism, and anti-
semitism which have already been mentioned, but its central assumptions was
a simple-minded theory of financial conspiracy which had been repeated over and
over again since Lamartine had first used the phrase, *féodalité financière*.

There were three areas in which the myth makers were building on valid
foundations. The absurdity of their final models of how the political system worked
comes near to hiding them. The first foundation is the existence of a number of
powerful and long established financial dynasties with family connexions extending over a very wide range of activities and particularly in the spheres of parliament
and public administration. This was associated with the phenomenon of *pantou-
flage*, of retiring early from the public administration to take up jobs in large private
firms. It is in this area that the conspiracy theorists provide the most valuable,
although sometimes inaccurate, documentation. The second foundation is that
powerful pressure groups in fact existed which were capable occasionally of exercising veto power over governmental policy. The third was that the world of big
finance and big business was a rather enclosed, inward-looking society. The large
capitalists, conscious of their unpopularity and apparently unconvinced that anything could be done about it, tended to avoid the public gaze. Industrialists and
financiers also acted as though they believed that secrecy was one of the sources of
their strength.

There were contingent historical circumstances which encouraged the appearance
of the myth of the two hundred families. The necessary conditions for the popularity of a conspiracy theory emerged with the breakdown of the *cartel des gauches*
in the period 1924 to 1926. For those with no sound knowledge of economics and
monetary policy (and these were in a majority in the cartelist governments) the
financial disorder and the decline of confidence were most plausibly explained by
the malevolence of the financial interests entrenched in the Bank of France.
Lacking the analytical tools necessary to regulate an awkward situation, the natural
substitute for sections of the left was a search for guilty men. Out of this grew the
legend of the *mur d'argent* which was allegedly a barrier to governments of the left.[8]
The legend was strengthened by the tendency of the men who were accused of
being part of the wall to behave in a manner which confirmed the legend.[9]

The moderate rather than the extreme left had an interest in producing an
explanation of the events of 1924–26 in terms of a conspiracy.[10] The extremists

could allege that the cartel had collapsed because there had been no attempt to pursue a correct revolutionary policy. The Radicals did not subscribe to this view for two reasons: they had held the main offices in the government and they were social and financial conservatives. Their only possible attitude, at least for public consumption, was that the correct governmental combination trying to pursue an efficacious policy had been wrecked by the deliberate machinations of its enemies. It is not, therefore, surprising that the first identifiable mention of the two hundred families came from a moderate radical source. Edouard Daladier, after denouncing 'the new feudalism' in the Chamber in 1930,[11] launched the theme of the two hundred families at the Radical party congress held at Nantes in 1934:

> Two hundred families have control of the French economy and, in effect, of French politics. They represent a force which a democratic state ought not to tolerate – Richelieu did not tolerate it in the kingdom of France.

> The influence of the two hundred families bears down on the fiscal system, on transport, on credit. The two hundred families place their delegates in power. They dominate public opinion because they control the press.[12]

He carried the idea into the electoral campaign of 1936 with attacks on the 'grandes féodalités parasitaires'. It became one of the most popular slogans of the Popular Front, used by communists, socialists, and radicals. Just before the elections of 1936 the great work of the mythology appeared, the special March issue of the muck-raking, iconoclastic periodical *le Crapouillot* edited by Jean Galtier-Boissière.

The special issue of *Crapouillot* began by repeating the story, a classic among war rumours, that the Briey foundries were saved from destruction by French artillery during the First World War through the influence of the Wendel family with the French general staff. The tone was thus set by implying that the wealthy are by definition traitors to the French nation. The main argument was that the Court of the Bank of France was the centre of the all-powerful financial oligarchy. It was remarked that the personnel of the Council of Regents remained fairly constant; some families, such as the Protestant and Jewish dynasties of Mallet, Hottinguer, and Rothschild, had been represented on it for generations. 'Let us admire the permanence of these powers, in contrast to the fluctuating situations in political life: the nation changes leaders but always has the same masters, dispensers of good and evil.' The small number of families which controlled the Bank of France were well represented in the industrial, financial, and commercial sectors of the French economy and had important foreign connexions. There were other families as powerful as those of the Regents in the major public companies but 'the regents are, in a sense, ambassadors, delegates to the central observatory with powers of attorney for the two hundred'. Representatives of the two hundred families were everywhere with only one exception. They disdained enterprises subject to competition in an open and free market. They monopolized practically all public utilities which the state had left in private hands and the companies protected by national and international ententes, trusts and cartels. A few privileged people obtained guaranteed profits at the expense of the nation. The small man had to face possible bankruptcy whilst the two hundred families were secure in enterprises subsidized or guaranteed by the state such as the railway companies, Banks, Air France, Messageries Maritimes, and so on.

Crapouillot produced much information on the overlap of personnel in government and in management of the private sector of the economy. Many ministers were company directors; diplomats, inspecteurs des finances, conseillers d'Etat, members of the cour des comptes, engineers of ponts et chaussées, prefects, and others left the service of the state to take up managerial posts in industrial and financial concerns belonging to the two hundred families. A large number of higher civil servants were prospective employees, if they were not themselves members of the two hundred families. A close identity of views and a strong supposition of an exchange of favours between the higher civil service and the two hundred families could therefore be assumed. A similar conclusion was reached about the link between parliament and the two hundred families.

As a social group the two hundred families, asserted *Crapouillot*, were extremely cohesive. Marriages were made almost exclusively within the orbit of the group. Its solidarity was preserved and strengthened by social clubs and organizations of varying exclusiveness such as the Grande Cercle and the Jockey Club. The tentacles of the two hundred families reached into the arts, the academies the university, and the press. Where the tentacles did not reach 'funds for corruption and campaigns of vindictive scandalmongering do the rest'.[13]

Crapouillot ended with a peroration on the iniquity of the two hundred families. 'A general lack of sympathy separates the people from its master and the masters conscious of their unpopularity are surrounding themselves with praetorians.' The praetorians were, of course, the fascist and ex-servicemen's leagues. The purpose of most of the contemporaneous writings on the two hundred families was to uncover 'the great fascist plot'. The best example is Francis Delaisi's book *La Banque de France aux mains des deux cents familles* published in 1936.[14] Delaisi's argument was that the two hundred families had been content to govern France through a parliamentary régime in the period of prosperity. During the lean years 1931–6, the financial oligarchy had been compelled to plunder the savings of the small man. It had consequently become necessary to destroy the democratic régime to prevent the discovery of this fraud. The Stavisky scandal was cleverly fostered in order to create conditions favourable to a coup by the leagues against parliament. A victory of the Popular Front made them ready to indulge in the worst forms of violence.

The popularity of the myth in 1936 can be regarded in various ways. It was, in the first place, the full flowering of the myth of the *mur d'argent*. It was an example of the dramatic shorthand which characterizes political debate, similar to the 'bankers' ramp' slogan of the British general election of 1931. It could also be that the propagandists of the left, realizing the weakness of the Popular Front, were creating an alibi for defeat before it happened. The myth was useful in attempting to seal the unity of the left. It was a part of the great anti-fascist theme of the Popular Front, a theme riddled with mythical elements.[15] It was an expression of widespread social frustration, a basically irrational reaction to a long economic crisis. In origin, before it was taken over by the Jew-baiting right, it was a kind of anti-semitism of the left.[16] The members of the two hundred families were regarded as being inferior to other men in moral worth but possessing a quite devilish cunning. Anything could be interpreted in terms of their machinations. Nothing except outright discriminatory measures could affect their power. An example of shifting the ground of the argument in a manner which finds many analogies in anti-semitic writings is Delaisi's treatment of the reform of the Bank of France by the Popular Front Government which destroyed the power of the Regents. In *La Banque de France et les deux cent familles* Delaisi alleged that the great economic crisis had put the most important concerns in the hands of the Bank. Whereas, before the crisis, the trusts controlled the Bank, after it, the trusts were dependent on the Bank's goodwill. Placing the real power of the Bank in the hands of nominees of a Popular Front Government, on Delaisi's argument, should have represented a crippling blow to the power of the two hundred families. But in the issue of *Crapouillot* of November 1936 Delaisi stated that the reform was only a minor setback for the two hundred families.

As well as the strong element of conscious or unconscious myth-making which fitted well into a particular political design and comprehensible feelings of social frustration, there was an element of quite genuine social and political observation.[17]

The people who have contributed to, or received with sympathy, the mythology of the two hundred families represent all strands of opinion and nearly all social groups – except those alleged to belong to the two hundred families. In three decades of political confusion it is not surprising that such a theory should have had wide appeal. The search for guilty men is a simple, easily comprehensible, human reaction of a party or faction which has had power within, or apparently almost within its grasp only to find that the reality of power eludes it, that right and efficacious policies either collapse or for inexplicable reasons are not accepted. It is not usual for political groups to admit that their general diagnosis of a situation was wrong in fundamental respects. The Radicals of 1924–26, the Socialists of 1936–38, the Vichyites, and those who insisted on charging madly down the cul-de-sac of *Algérie française* could explain their defeats only in terms of the wicked manoeuvrings of their enemies.

There is therefore no mystery as to why a comprehensive conspiracy theory of politics should be popular. But in the midst of it all, has any truth been spoken about the nature of French politics? Taken at their face value the major works in the mythology of the two hundred families are absurd. They attribute to an oligarchy a character, a cohesion, and a purpose which it did not and could not possess. Men who claimed to be opponents of the oligarchy or who contributed to the mythology have written accounts of their political defeats which give coherence to the most involuntary acts and contingent events. The inconsequential statements and tortuous policy of their enemies at the height of the struggle (de Gaulle and Algeria being the most arresting example) make it difficult not to suspect hidden and not altogether respectable designs. But there is a considerable jump both in logic and in fact from these suspicions to the allegation that a group of families are manipulating public affairs; that these conspirators, whilst affirming the public good and mouthing humanitarian sentiments, delude a gullible public and use any régime for their own private profit; that they pay an army of retainers and clients for this purpose. All this involves the conspirators in constant double-thought and double-talk. The conspiracy theorists recognize the individual and collective discipline that this requires. The conspirators are not as other men; they have been educated by a special milieu.

But the myth-makers draw attention to an indisputable fact. A financial and industrial oligarchy of a sort with considerable political influence has existed.[18] This oligarchy has not been, as the writers on the two hundred families pretend, either autonomous or all-powerful. It has not, moreover, acted as a united group. But an assessment of the position and significance of this oligarchy is essential for the understanding of the structure of French politics. Since 1880 it cannot be argued that the upper bourgeoisie has been 'in power'. It has shared power with other groups and has had great influence close to the centres of political power. A serious analysis of its role has yet to be made. The mythology of the two hundred families has pointed to a problem and at the same time obscured it.

Notes

1 *Combats d'hier et d'aujourd'hui* (1911) vol. II. p. 320.

2 Popper, K. *The Open Society and its Enemies* 2nd edn. London: Routledge (1952) vol. II. p. 93.

3 For the Second Empire see G. Duchêne, *L'Empire industrielle* (1869) and *L'Economie politique de l'Empire* (1870), M. d'Esterno, *Des Privilégiés de l'ancien régime et des privilégiés du nouveau* (1867); and O. de Vallee, *Les maniers de l'argent* (1858).

4 A. Chirac, *L'Agiotage sous la Troisième Règpublique* (1888) and *La Haute banque et les révolutions* (1888).

5 A. Coste, *Pourquoir trente ans de monopole? Observations sur le project relatif à la banque de France* (1891), and *L'Anonymat, precurseur du socialisme* (1892).

6 D. Halévy, *Pour l'étude de la Troisième* (1937), p. 80.

7 F. Delaisi, *La démocratie et les financiers* (1911), pp. 13–14.

8 For an early example of the legend see J. L. Chastanet. *La République des banquiers* (1925).

9 For example, Emile Moreau, governor of the Bank of France, boasted in his memoirs of overturning Herriot in 1926. *Revue des Deux Mondes*, 1 March 1937.

10 For the radical position see J. Kayser and J. Montigny (preface E. Daladier), *Le Drame financier: les responsables* (1928).

11 *Journal Officiel, débats de la Chambre des Députes,* 11 April 1930, p. 1711.

12 *Compte-rendu du congres Radical de Nantes* (duplicated, 1934). The actual number, two hundred, has not much significance. It was merely a convenient number neither too large nor too small to raise awkward questions. The original reference was to the two hundred largest shareholders of the Bank of France who elected the Court of the Bank.

13 There are many parallels between the two hundred families and British and American myths – Upton Sinclair's 'Wall Street', Roosevelt's economic royalists, 'The power élite', 'The Establishment', 'The Controllers' (of the *New Left Review*), are among the most obvious. The myth of the two hundred families is not the exact equivalent of any of these but shares common characteristics with them all.

14 Delaisi's work of 1911, *La Démocratie et les financiers*, was reprinted in the November 1936 issue of *Crapouillot* with a commentary on how perceptive he had been.

15 For illustration of this see J. Plumyène and R. Lasierra, *Les Fascismes français 1923–63* (1963).

16 The original works of the mythology were not overtly anti-semitic and *Crapouillot* expressly denied any connexion with anti-semitism.

17 This makes some of the works of, or related to, the mythology, such as Augustin Hamon's *Les Maîtres de la France* (three volumes 1936–8), important historical documents. E. Beau de Loménie's distinguished pamphlet in four volumes, *Les Responsabilités des dynasties bourgeoises* (1943–63) was the first comprehensive attempt to assess the rôle of finance in French politics since the first Empire. J. Lhomme, a scholarly historian has, in *La Grande bourgeoisie au Pouvoir, 1840–80* (1960), refined Beau de Loménie's hypotheses for the period for which they have most explanatory power.

18 The origins and historical evolution of this oligarchy is outlined in G. P. Plamade, *Capitalisme et capitalistes français au XIXe siècle*, A. Colin (1961). Indications of its contemporary character and role can be found in H. W. Ehrmann, *Organized Business in France*, Princeton University Press 1957; N. Deleforte-Soubeyroux, *Les Dirigeants de l'industrie française* 1961; G. F. Teneul, *Le Financement des entreprises en France depuis la fin du XXIe siècle a nos jours.* 1961; J. Sheahan, *Promotion and Control of Industry in postwar France*, Boston: Harvard University Press, 1963.

Theories of the French Party System under the Third Republic

B. D. Graham

Australian National University

For British-influenced political science up to the 1960s French politics was always an important source of insights, because of its spatial proximity and the long-time status of French as the most-learned foreign language in the UK. But in the post-war period the French Third Republic also served as a key case for analysing the forces that can weaken a major liberal democracy (see also Anderson's article above). Graham's approach is to re-interpret the academic accounts of the French party system produced from the early twentieth century into the 1930s, focusing on how contemporary authors analysed the apparently perverse impacts of the excessive 'particization' of politics for government stability and for a more coherent or simplified organization of the space of political competition. He shows how this literature rejects the post-war British conventional wisdom which linked instability primarily to a double ballot electoral system, in favour of a stress on the dynamics of party factions.

I

The idea that the main feature of French life has been the clash of two great forces, that of Progress and that of Tradition, is as old as the Republican movement itself, but it has been defined differently at different times. Perhaps the most significant interpretation of this century has been that presented by André Siegfried in his *Tableau Politique de la France de l'Ouest* published in 1913. In this book, based on a study of electoral behaviour in the western regions of Brittany and Normandy, Siegfried claimed that party politics were merely surface manifestations of more basic social forces.

> Preoccupied above all with reality, I therefore have concentrated less on parties – superficial and constantly changing categories – than on basic tendencies (*tendances*). Indeed, it seemed to me that, in the West at least, the significant dividing line between parties was not that between royalists and republicans, nor between radicals and moderates, but between the Right and the Left, or rather between the coalition of the right and the coalition of the left, that is to say, between the more or less distorted but still living tradition of the *ancien régime* – hierarchical, Roman Catholic and conservative – and the republican and democratic tradition – secular, egalitarian and *avant-garde*. This is almost the vocabulary of the July Monarchy, 'resistance' or 'movement' …[1]

Although he regarded the division between Republicans and anti-Republicans as being the essential political cleavage, Siegfried was troubled by the conflicts between various factions of the Left which he found in such towns as Nantes, Brest and Rouen.[2] He was, moreover, impressed by the fact that moderate Republicans, Radicals and Socialists were often more concerned with the differences which separated them from each other than with those which separated Left from Right. Admitting the force of the Socialists' claim that the new Left would be characterized not by Republicanism but by a concern for social justice and for the nationalization of the means of production, distribution and exchange. Siegfried conceded that 'there would be ground for thinking of another division between the coalitions of right and left based on the attitude of the parties towards the question of social reforms (au point de vue social)'. However, he qualified this remark by suggesting that 'the true "social" Left' was extremely limited, at least in the Western region.[3]

Siegfried envisaged the Left and Right tendances as traditional modes of action which expressed 'states of being and feeling' or tempéraments.[4] He identified Left and Right tempéraments with the general bodies of Republican and Monarchist ideas respectively, without treating them as distinct ideologies. However, he also distinguished a third tempérament, that of the Independent Left, the corpus of Bonapartist, Boulangist and extreme nationalist ideas,[5] which in the field of action he had treated as part of the Right tendance. In discussing the characteristics of the Independent Left tempérament, Siegfried drew attention to the persistent faith in Caesarism which was later to provide the popular support for Marshal Pétain and for General de Gaulle. Unfortunately he did not make clear the exact bearing of this third tempérament on the interplay of the two tendances.

In certain later works, Siegfried returned to his theory of tendances and refined it in several respects. In Tableau des partis en France, published in 1930, he laid much more stress on the cleavage within the Left to which he had referred in Tableau de l'Ouest. The industrial revolution, he now suggested, had affected French society just as much as had the preceding conflict between the traditions of the ancien régime and those of 1789. He felt that perhaps the most important reaction to industrial change had been the demand for collectivism both in economic organization and in social affairs, a demand which had clashed with the values of individualism and liberty held by the Republican Left. Siegfried therefore modified his earlier schema to argue that there were not two but three tendances, those of the Right, Centre and Left.[6] Later, in De la IIIe à la IVe République (1956), he used his threefold classification as a means of analysing the politics of the early Third Republic; writing of the 1870s, he emphasized the importance of the socio-economic differences separating moderates from Radicals within the Republican camp.[7]

Siegfried's view that the surface configuration of the party system was illusory and that the basic reality lay beneath in the ideas and traditions of the people was shared by François Goguel, whose La politique des partis sous la IIIe République, published in 1946, remains one of the best histories of the period. Goguel saw parties acting against 'a background of opinions, of almost instinctive – at all events irrational – assertions about the meaning of life, the nature of man, the purposes of society'.[8] There were, he maintained, two broad fronts of opinion, the Party of Order and the Party of Change (mouvement): the former had inherited the medieval view of Man as a frail creature dependent on the Church and on traditional social authorities for tutelage and guidance; the latter embodied the humanist spirit of 1789 and 1848, and credited Man with the ability to use Reason in mastering his environment and improving his government.[9] For Goguel, all the great political clashes of the Third Republic, such as those between Republicans and anti-Republicans in the period 1876–9 and between the opposing sides of the Dreyfus Affair, were examples of the continuous, underlying conflict between the Parties of Order and Change, a conflict which he maintained informed French politics at every stage, despite the tensions which had at times existed between the component groups of the Party of Change.[10]

As Siegfried had done, Goguel later modified his claim that there were only two *tendances*. In an article published in 1950, he drew attention to the defeat in 1896 of the Centre-Left Bourgeois Ministry by a combination of moderate Republicans and the Right, an incident which he described as 'the first manifestation in French politics of a division of clearly "social" origin between political *tendances*'; moving on to the period after 1905, he emphasized the differences between Radicals and Socialists much more than he had in *La politique des partis*.[11] Later still, he was more explicit and stated that the increasing importance of economic and social issues after 1905 justified a distinction being made between Left and Extreme Left within the Party of Change.[12]

While the 'tendencies theory' won wide acceptance, its exponents faced the difficulty of explaining why the basic *tendances* had not led to the formation of correspondingly large parties in parliament. Part of the reason was felt to lie in the nature of the *scrutin d'arrondissement*, the electoral method used in all but three of the sixteen contests between 1876 and 1936. Two evils were attributed to this method; namely, that it forced deputies to associate themselves with petty local interests, and that it distorted the ideological issues before the electors. In fact, the more dogmatic advocates of the theory (who included neither Siegfried nor Goguel) claimed that the provision of the second ballot had freed the electors from the responsibility of making an early firm choice between Left and Right: in the campaign for the first ballot, constituents were distracted by a medley of candidates representing every shade of opinion, and it was only during the breathless campaign for the second ballot that the election assumed its true character, that of 'a conflict of feeling between two irreconcilable conceptions of social and political life'.[13] With elections thus distorted by the ideological chaos and irrelevance of the first ballot campaigns, maintained the theorists, the *tendances* were unable to acquire the structure and identity of established parties. Coalitions of the Right and Left were formed in such crisis elections as those of 1877, 1889 and 1902, only to break up again once the tension had passed.

II

Only the unsophisticated were prepared to accept that it was the electoral system above all else which had prevented the formation of a two- or three-party system in France; however, few historians were prepared to carry out a systematic investigation of the various traditions contained within each *tendance* in an effort to determine their relative strengths and their importance as factors inducing multipartism. It is perhaps unfortunate that Siegfried, who was aware of the importance of traditions, chose to make his detailed study in the Western region, an area in which the Right had always predominated and where the factions of the Left had usually formed tight defensive alliances. Had he studied another region, he might, in developing his general theory, have attached less importance to *tendances* and more to the parties which constituted them. Even so, the *Tableau politique de l'Ouest* contains references to several districts in which Bonapartism had emerged as a distinct political force[14] and to towns in which Radical and Socialist groups had assumed separate identities.[15]

It is unlikely that at any time during the Third Republic the *tendances* possessed either the homogeneity or the continuity sometimes ascribed to them. Even in crisis situations they were seldom more than unstable and cumbersome alliances. During the 1870s and 1880s, for example, the major factions of the Right (Orleanists, Legitimists and Bonapartists) were in disagreement over a number of economic and social questions and attracted support from different social groups. Many of the landed gentry backed the Legitimists because they stood for the restoration, not only of royal absolutism, but also of the economic privileges which the *ancien régime* had provided. By supporting the Orleanists, some sections of the *haute bourgeoisie* signified their approval of both of the political order which had characterized the July Monarchy and of the liberal commercial and industrial policies carried out under Louis Philippe. The Bonapartists drew support from several important families whose members had held high administrative posts under the First and Second Empires, and from the peasantry in such regions as Picardy and the south-west, where Napoleon I had defended the peasants' newly acquired landed rights against the nobility. The importance of such differences as these indicates the danger of treating the Right of the early Third Republic as a united bloc based on a generalized conservative outlook.

In the same period, the divisions within the Left were equally pronounced. Throughout the 1880s, the Radicals and moderate Republicans differed on several important issues; whereas the latter were becoming conservative in social and economic matters, the Radicals were pressing for a more enlightened colonial policy, further revision of the Constitutional Acts of 1875 and 1884, educational reforms extending those of 1881 and 1882, the institution of progressive income taxation, and the state control of certain public utilities including the railways. In the late 1890s, the Socialists caused further divisions in the Left by raising such controversial issues as the nationalization and socialization of industry and the vesting of complete constitutional power in the Chamber of Deputies, proposals which even the Radicals refused to accept. Certain Socialist groups went so far as to suggest openly that the proletariat should lead a revolution aimed at seizing control of the bourgeois state.

Besides obscuring the significance of such cleavages within the Right and the Left, the *tendances* theory failed to explain why both Bonapartism and progressive Catholicism straddled the dividing line between the forces of Order and Change. Bonapartism had always defied attempts to class it as a movement of either the Left or the Right; both Napoleons had appealed to the people for power and both had drawn a response from social groups usually associated with the Left, such as the independent peasantry and the lower middle classes of the large towns, but Bonapartism also denied many of the values dear to the Left – Republicanism, the separation of Church and State, the tolerance of wide differences in political opinion, a strong popular chamber. An interesting modern comparison is the way in which General de Gaulle's ability to appeal to the masses enabled the RPF under the Fourth Republic, and the UNR under the Fifth, to draw away strength from the Socialist and Communist Parties. One of the paradoxes of French radicalism has always been the willingness of some underprivileged groups to countenance authoritarian methods as a means of securing social reforms, to forego political liberty in the hope of obtaining economic equality. Similarly, difficulties arise when attempts are made to label progressive Catholic movements either Right or Left. From the time of the *sillonistes* onwards some Catholics have shared with Socialists a belief in the need for economic controls and social justice without, however, accepting the anti-clerical and individualistic values of the traditional Republican Left. Under the Fourth Republic, for example, the Christian Democratic MRP held the balance between Left and Right, torn between its loyalties to the economic policies initiated by the tripartite coalitions of 1944 to 1947 and its sympathy for the corporate theories and the clerical traditionalism of the Right.

These and similar problems underlined the need to modify the *tendances* theory to take account of the political importance of ideological traditions. A book which aroused considerable interest in this respect was Albert Thibaudet's *Les Idées politiques de la France*, published in 1932. Thibaudet distinguished in French society six major intellectual traditions which he termed 'political ideologies'; these were Traditionalism, Liberalism, Industrialism (a faith in technocratic controls), Social (or progressive) Catholicism, Jacobinism (Radicalism of the 1789 variety) and Socialism. These were aligned, he suggested, with 'systems of interests' and, more remotely, 'with parliamentary groups, with a political representation'.[16] However, Thibaudet gave no systematic analysis of the relationship between ideologies and parties, and it was left to René Rémond, in *La Droite en France de 1815 à nos jours* (published in 1954), to deal with the historical evolution of the ideologies of Traditionalism, Liberalism and Bonapartism and to discuss the way in which they affected the political structure at different times, and during several crisis periods of the Third Republic.

While Thibaudet, Rémond and others did not give the concept of *tendances* a central place in their analyses, Maurice Duverger, particularly in his book, *The French Political System*, suggested an interpretation of nineteenth-century French politics which would reconcile the theory of *tendances* with the study of distinct ideological traditions. He depicted a situation in which two broadly-based groups, the Conservatives and the Liberals, were at issue over the form of the polity, the Conservatives favouring a monarchical and clerical state and the Liberals a republican and secular state. This conflict of ideas was, in his estimation, the reflection of an underlying conflict of classes in which the landowners and their loyal peasants, the Conservative forces, were pitted against the urban middle class, the mainstay of the Republican forces.[17] However, Duverger also pointed out the roles played by the separate traditions within the Conservative and Liberal movements, and showed that the rise of the Socialist Party had driven many former liberals over to the Right while giving the Left an increased identification with policies of economic planning and controls.[18]

In almost all these attempts to explain the French party system in terms of the cultural forces external to it, whether *tendances* or ideological traditions, the writers found themselves driven to speculate why such forces were deflected and distorted within the electoral and parliamentary institutions. From their inquiries arose theories of party behaviour whose primary reference was to factors operating within the political structure. These are our next concern.

III

The Constitutional Acts of 1875 were, almost from the time they came into force, the subject of close scrutiny by academic lawyers. The latter, interested to discover the institutional causes for the rapid rise and fall of cabinet ministries in France, discussed whether ministerial stability could be achieved by the use of such sanctions as the dissolution of parliament after a governmental crisis, and speculated as to why French parties appeared unable to form durable parliamentary alliances. Many of their findings were brought together in a survey, published by A. Soulier in 1939, which treated in detail the background to each governmental crisis between 1871 and 1938. In this book, entitled *L'Instabilité ministérielle sous la Troisième République*, Soulier claimed that order was achieved when all the political forces were balanced each against the other, and that the instability of Third Republican politics arose because parliament did not reflect the basic structure of electoral opinion. Having accepted the theory of *tendances*, he suggested that a temporary balance of forces was obtained whenever the alliances established during a crisis election were represented in parliament by parties arranged in two blocs, the largest of which had formed a *gouvernement de bloc*, that is, a coalition ministry reflecting its group structure in miniature.

> Thenceforth there exists between the electoral coalition and the parliamentary coalition the same relationship as between the latter and the Cabinet; the majority system [of government] can be compared to a mechanical system composed of three interdependent units which have to be brought into a state of balance; when the centres of gravity coincide, that is to say, when the Cabinet is a faithful reflection of the parliamentary majority and when the latter is itself an exact representation of the electoral majority, the stability of the system is assured.[19]

Whenever the extreme and moderate groups of the bloc in power disagreed about detailed policy objectives, however, the equilibrium was threatened. Disagreement itself would not have precipitated a crisis had there existed adequate provision for conventional bargaining or had there been a sharply defined boundary between the two blocs, neither of which condition obtained under the Third Republic. Consequently, most serious policy differences resulted in the fall of a ministry, and the dividing line between Left and Right, though it appeared to be firmly drawn during elections, was practically non-existent in parliament. The groups of the Centre-Left and the Centre-Right had much in common and found no difficulty in working together in coalition ministries. As soon as the extreme group of a governmental alliance began to press its demands against the wishes of its moderate allies, the latter would turn for support to the centre groups of the opposition. The extremists would leave the coalition, setting in train a ministerial crisis which would end in the formation of a coalition nearer to the Centre. Further crises would increase the predominance of the centre groups in the cabinet until, with the approach of another election, the shift in alliances would be reversed, the last ministry of the term being another *gouvernement de bloc*.[20] Soulier described this pattern as working itself out in the course of a single legislature or of a series of legislatures, depending on circumstances. His view of the party system was essentially mechanistic; he drew an analogy between the concept of political stability and that of equilibrium in the physical sciences, an approach which led him to treat politics at the parliamentary level as a game of skill in which the centre groups held the advantage, and to underestimate the effect of ideological differences and policy issues on party relationships.

While this may have been an acceptable attitude in the conditions of 1939, the experience of the Fourth Republic showed that even the large, coherent parties of the post-war era were unable to form stable alliances, and made it clear that the instability of multipartism could not be fully explained without reference to what Duverger called 'the non-coincidence of the main cleavages of opinion'.[21] Along with François Goguel and Jacques Fauvet, Duverger pointed out that there was seldom a straight-forward parliamentary response to all the issues in dispute at any one time. Parties which agreed on economic policy might fall out over colonial or international issues, or over problems connected with Church-State relations; group alignments formed on one question might break up on another, causing the lines of opinion-cleavage to intersect in a bewildering manner. Ministerial instability, seen in this context, was in part the result of the overlapping of various issues.[22] The application of this concept in the study of the political history of the Third Republic is as yet incomplete, but already it has clarified the way in which the cultural factors discussed earlier – the *tendances* and the ideological traditions – have affected the party system.

IV

Many of the factors operating in French party politics may be understood more clearly if they are compared with those obtaining in the politics of such countries as Holland, Belgium, Great Britain and the Scandinavian states. On the Left, the similarities emerge clearly; French Radicalism, Socialism and Communism had their counterparts in these countries, even in Great Britain where the Labour Party embodied qualities of both the French Socialist and Radical Parties. However, whereas in these countries the men of the Left were able to dominate the centre of the political stage with their emphasis on the socio-economic problems associated with rapid industrialization and urbanization, the French Left was constantly obliged to subordinate social to political concerns and to make common cause with liberals and conservatives in defending the Republic against assaults by a powerful Right which was both anti-liberal and anti-parliamentary. Had the influential social groups on which the French Right was based chosen to accept the Republican form of government and formed liberal and conservative parties like those of Belgium or Holland there would have been much more chance of establishing a stable party system in France. Instead, whenever their interests were threatened, these groups would enter politics not to bargain or to argue but to demand the overthrow of the Republic itself. *Crises de régime* became an endemic condition of Third Republican life. To some extent, Radicals and Socialists (and later the Communists) were able to establish firm identities in parliament and in urban politics, but in most elections the controversy between Republicans and anti-Republicans was conducted with such passion that socio-economic questions were largely ignored.

Although the recurrent conflicts between Left and Right gave the impression that the French party system was dualist in character, its essential multipartism became apparent during the periods of calm between crises. Even in the two short lulls which occurred in the 1880s and 1890s attention had been drawn to divisions within the Republican bloc. But the differences between Socialists, Radicals and moderate Republicans emerged clearly in the years 1906 to 1912, the interval between the controversy over Church-State relations and the onset of wartime politics. Both the Radical Socialist and Socialist Parties established strong organizations and firm electoral identities during this period. In fact, a contemporary observer might easily have formed the impression that a stable party system was at last being formed in France, and that it would consist of the Socialists on the Left, the Radicals in the Centre, a liberal party on the Centre-Right and a conservative party on the Right. The 1910 election, in particular, was fought out in terms of socio-economic rather than of crisis issues.

Soon, however, a new crisis situation took shape, during which the fierce disputes of 1913 and 1914 over the proposals for three years' military training again divided the parties into two blocs. While the long rule of the wartime *Union sacrée* and the post-war *Bloc national* tended to obscure party differences, by 1917 the Socialists and some Radicals had broken away to form a pacifist opposition, and in 1923 the bulk of the Radicals finally left the *Bloc national* to reclaim their independence. By this time, however, the Socialist movement had divided into separate Socialist and Communist Parties and the traditional distinctions between the parties of the Right had been badly blurred. During the period of relative calm which lasted from 1924 to 1933, the parties began to define their socio-economic policies with more care and to develop separate identities, but undertones of tension and the onset of the depression prevented this process from advancing very far. The election campaigns of 1928 and 1932 were largely, to use Siegfried's terms, *élections de lutte* rather than *élections d'apaisement*. The right-wing street riots in Paris on 6 February 1934 and the increasingly aggressive attitudes being taken by Fascist Italy and Nazi Germany began a final period of crisis; the rise and fall of the Popular Front, the controversies over foreign and defence policies after Munich, the military collapse and the political capitulation of 1940 marked its course.

The confusion created by the alternating periods of crisis and calm did not prevent the French party system from changing in several important ways during the last four decades of the Third Republic. By the 1930s, organizational techniques and the growth of conventions governing relations between parties had become particularly well developed. Goguel has shown[23] how out of keeping these changes were with the theory of representation which had prevailed at the founding of the Republic, when the creation of intermediate bodies (such as parties) between the Sovereign People and Parliament, the embodiment of the General Will, would have been strongly condemned. However, as he went on to observe, this theory had already become a fiction by the end of the century. Subsequently, the rise of the organized parties – the Radical Socialists, the Socialists and the Communists – had widened the areas of stability in both parliament and the electorate, and by the 1930s was forcing the groups on the Right to consider a degree of party organization which they had not previously contemplated. Writing in 1930, a Professor of Law had observed with sorrow, 'Political parties, indeed, are a fact'.[24] His conclusion that parties had perverted the parliamentary regime was shared by several of his professional colleagues, although others ventured to hope that France might at last achieve political stability through a system of large, disciplined parties. In 1945, as a new series of constitutional debates began, a great deal came to rest on that possibility.

Notes

1 André Siegfried, *Tableau Politique de la France de l'Ouest sous la Troisième République*. Paris, 1913, pp. xxiv–xxv.

2 Ibid., pp. 87–8, 198–209, and 259–63.

3 Ibid., p. xxv.

4 Ibid., p. xxvi.

5 Ibid., pp. 449–95 and 498.

6 Siegfried, *Tableau des partis en France*. Paris, 1930, pp. 55–7; cf. Siegfried, *France, A Study in Nationality*. New Haven: Yale University Press, 1930, pp. 26–7 and 38–42.

7 Siegfried, *De la IIIᵉ à la IVᵉ République*. Paris, 1956, pp. 16–18.

8 François Goguel, *La politique des partis sous la IIIᵉ République* (Paris, 1946), vol. 1, p. 26; cf. Goguel, 'Les partis politiques en France', *Encyclopédie politique de la France et du Monde*, 2nd edn., *La France et l'Union Française* (Paris, 1950–51), vol. 1, pp. 270–1, and Goguel, *Géographie des élections françaises de 1870 à 1951* (Paris, 1951), p. 9.

9 Goguel, *La politique des partis*, vol. 2, pp. 332–5.

10 Ibid., pp. 323–30.

11 Goguel, *Encyclopédie politique*, vol. 1, p. 274.

12 Goguel, *Géographie des élections*, p. 10.

13 Charles Seignobos, 'La signification historique des élections françaises de 1928', *L'Année politique française et étrangère*, July 1928, p. 259, cited by A. Soulier, *L'Instabilité ministérielle sous la Troisième République* (1871–1938). Paris, 1939, p. 401.

14 Siegfried, *Tableau politique de l'Ouest*, pp. 12–14, 126 and 312–13.

15 Ibid., pp. 87–88, 198–207 and 260–3.

16 Albert Thibaudet, *Les Idées politiques de la France*. Paris, 1932, pp. 9–10.

17 Maurice Duverger, *The French Political System*. Chicago: University of Chicago Press, 1958, pp. 84–6.

18 Ibid., pp. 88–9 and 132–4.

19 Soulier, *L'instabilité ministérielle sous la Troisième République*.

20 Ibid., pp. 399–408.

21 Duverger, *Political Parties, their Organization and Activity in the Modern State*. London 1954, p. 232.

22 For the fullest discussions of the 'overlapping of issues' phenomenon, see Duverger, op. cit. pp. 231–4; Jacques Fauvet, *Les forces politiques en France* (Paris, 1951), pp. 261–6; Goguel, *Encyclopédie politique*, vol. 1, p. 275, and *France under the Fourth Republic* (New York, 1952), pp. 137–40.

23 Goguel, 'Le problème du statut des partis', *L'Esprit*, January 1946, pp. 96–106.

24 Louis Trotabas, *Constitution et Gouvernement de la France*, 2nd edition. Paris, 1938, p. 198.

Political Economy

C. A. E. Goodhart and R. J. Bhansali

London School of Economics and Political Science

As its ambitious title suggests, this mould-breaking 63-page paper was in many ways a founding piece for a whole field of work which had not previously existed. The authors set out both to begin the systematic analysis of over-time opinion poll data using sophisticated economic modelling techniques, and to construct a theoretical apparatus which would allow the analysis of how governments respond to empirically established reactions by voters to changes in key economic variables, such as inflation rates and levels of unemployment. They also attempted to estimate quantitatively for the first time differences in the ways that voters reacted to Labour and Conservative governments and to shed light on the importance of political leadership to parties' popularity functions. We have omitted the most technical parts of their paper, and some exploratory sections subsequently superceded by later work, but retained their key model tests and broader discussions of their conclusions, along with the important iso-vote curves way of representing governments' electoral-economic choices.

The objective of this paper is to examine, with the aid of statistical techniques, the factors causing movements in the recorded observations in the polls of the popularity of the political parties and the party leaders in this country during recent years. The polls are generally considered to provide reasonably accurate indicators of the attitude of the electorate, and their findings are treated very seriously by the politically concerned. At the very least it should be of some value to find out more about the characteristics and determinants of these poll series, which themselves now play such an important role in the political process.

The basic and simple idea underlying this exercise is to take a number of variables, such as the level of unemployment, the rate of inflation, the length of time elapsed since the last election, etc., and, with the use of multiple regression analysis, to test whether variations in these selected variables have a significant effect upon political popularity as reflected in the poll figures.

The two economic variables which we took as being most likely to influence the electorate's satisfaction with the economic policy of the government of the day were the level of unemployment and the rate of inflation. Certain of the best financial journalists now writing, [Nigel] Lawson in the *Spectator* and [Sam] Brittan in the *Financial Times*, have already pointed out the links between movements in unemployment and political popularity, so that the level of unemployment seemed an obvious candidate. The second, basic economic variable chosen was the rate of inflation, as evidenced by the percentage annual change in the retail price index. Inflationary changes in prices regularly rank high among the stated complaints of the electorate. There is also some evidence that a large proportion of the electorate is prepared to accept a significant increase in unemployment in order to bring about a decrease in the rate of inflation.

A keen student of the movements of the polls will have noticed that there do appear to be recorded in the polls certain regular movements in the popularity of the government of the day between elections. Immediately after elections there appears to be a sizeable increase in the support for the newly elected government (an *ex post facto* bandwaggon effect?), which is dissipated quite rapidly. There then appears to follow a steady, but slow decline in the popularity of the government of the day as its tenure of office continues, but this unpopularity is rapidly and completely reversed during the final few months preceding the next elections.

In the exercise undertaken here we do not attempt to give a causal explanation of these seemingly regular variations. We do, however, attempt to measure the significance, strength and consistency of these posited regular variations by the use of dummy variables.

The third basic question which we attempt to answer is how strong is the influence of party leaders, the Prime Minister and the Leader of the Opposition, upon the standing of their parties. As will be seen, we did not satisfactorily succeed in answering this question.

If economic variables can influence political popularity, so also can government actions have a major impact upon the future development of the economy. If we can estimate (a) how economic variables will affect political popularity, (b) how the government will respond to changes in its popularity, and (c) how its actions will affect the economic system, then we can develop a full politico-economic model of the development of the economy, in which political as well as economic motivation will play a part in the determination of the system. We develop a prototype of such a model, drawing heavily on the hypotheses formulated by A. Downs and others.[1]

The first issue which we examined was whether it was the level of unemployment or the change in unemployment over some period that had the greatest influence on political popularity. This we tested, because Brittan in his article[2] suggested that, 'Government popularity tends to follow the trend of unemployment rather than the absolute level', while Lawson in the *Spectator* argued that it was the level that was important. So, in the first equation tested, the lead of the government of the day (G)[3] was regressed on U the current level of unemployment, dU the change of unemployment over the last six months, dP the percentage change in price over the last year, and AE the dummy variable taking positive values after elections (and zero at other times) as explained elsewhere. The results are shown in the equation below. The figures in the brackets below the coefficients are their standard deviations:

$$G = 46.6 - 0.105U + 0.091dU - 3.24dP + 1.27AE$$
$$(0.008) \quad (0.011) \quad (0.47) \quad (0.23)$$
$$R^2 = 0.676 \qquad \text{D.W.} = 0.96 \qquad \text{number of observations 96}$$

As can be seen from this equation, all the variables are highly significant and the fit is quite good, as measured by the value of R^2. But the coefficient relating to the recent change in unemployment has the wrong sign – an increase in unemployment apparently significantly *raising* the government's popularity – and there remains significant serial correlation among the residuals.

The observation of the wrong sign – in the sense of failing to accord with the standard hypothesis – for the coefficient attached to dU suggests that the strongest relation between unemployment and government popularity was between popularity and the *lagged* level of unemployment.[4] This raised the problem of trying to estimate the form of the lag.

Initially we tried several alternative lag structures of which the most successful was a simple six months lag[5] (i.e. the change in unemployment preceded the change in political popularity by six months). Subsequently cross spectral analysis between the government lead and the level of unemployment confirmed the presence of a five to six months lag.

One further question, which we sought to investigate in these first tests, was whether there was any evidence that there is an underlying preference in the country for a Conservative or a Labour government. With unemployment and inflation held constant, would the popularity of the government be higher when the governing party was Conservative or Labour? In order to throw light on this question a second dummy variable was introduced taking the value 1 when the Conservatives were in office and 0 when Labour was in power. This dummy variable in the equation below is given the symbol Q. The results of this equation[6] are shown below:

$$G = 46.11 - 0.099U - 3.47dP + 1.26AE - 1.91Q$$
$$(0.009)^{t-6} \ (0.45) \quad (0.24) \quad (1.25)$$
$$R^2 = 0.669 \quad \text{D.W.} = 1.00$$

An examination of the residuals from this and all the other equations for this period in this preliminary study showed consistent systematic pattern whereby the support for the government of the day, the Conservatives, was overestimated by the equations employed over the months, July 1961–May 1964, and then underestimated over the period, June 1964–October 1964. One possible reason for this is that there may be normally an anti-government trend during the life of a government which is reversed in the months immediately before an election. This had not clearly shown up in the case of the Labour government by September 1967 (the end date for our preliminary study), because it was too soon since their March 1966 electoral success for such longer trends to become obvious.

There was thus considerable statistical evidence of a continued and persistent decline in the popularity of the Conservatives from 1959 till mid 1964 – rapidly reversed thereafter – which was not adequately explained by the variables already included in the regression equations. As an experiment, to see how much the statistical fit was improved and to observe the effect of its introduction upon the coefficients attached to the original variables, it seemed worthwhile and potentially interesting to introduce a new dummy variable, acting as a proxy for the unknown factors causing this swing in Conservative popularity, into the equations and then to re-run. This dummy variable took the value 27.5 in period 1 (October 1959), declined by 1 per period until it reached a value of –27.5 in period 56 (June 1964) and then returned to 0 in period 61 (October 1964), continuing at 0 thereafter. This new dummy variable (D) was highly significant and its inclusion considerably raised the values of R^2 in the equations tried.

From this preliminary work the following tentative conclusions were drawn: first, the level of unemployment, with a lag of somewhere around four to six months, and the rate of inflation do influence political popularity significantly; second, there may well be a natural path of government popularity between elections, with an immediate burst of support – in addition to that actually received at the elections – rapidly dissipated, followed by a long-run, but slow, decline in popularity, which in turn is sharply reversed in the run up to elections.

In those cases when the absolute magnitude of the coefficient relating to the impact of unemployment upon political popularity increases, so also does the size of the constant term. With quite impressive regularity the value of the constant is between 400 and 450 times the value of the coefficient relating to unemployment. This implies that, if inflation is not existent ($dP = 0$) and with other things being equal, a governing party which allows the level of unemployment, seasonally adjusted, to exceed 450 thousand six months before the election is likely to lose, while if it can reduce unemployment below 400 thousand at this time it should win.

As inflation is greater, so unemployment must be the less to maintain the same level of popularity. The second point to observe is that when the value of the coefficient relating to unemployment is greater in absolute size, so the coefficient relating to the rate of inflation also tends to rise, thus suggesting that the trade off between the evils of unemployment and inflation has remained roughly constant over time in the eyes of the electorate. In a large number of cases, with these various data, an increase of 100,000 in unemployment has about the same adverse effect upon political popularity as an increase of 2.5–2.75 per cent per annum in the rate of price increase.

There is some statistical evidence for the existence of the type of regular pattern of swing in the support for the government over the life of a Parliament, which was noted earlier by casual empiricism. It seems as if the regular anti-government swing over the life of a full Parliament may amount to as much as 10 percentage points, which deficit can be expected to be whittled away in the run up to the elections, leaving very little natural pro- or anti-government bias at the election itself (so much for the pendulum theory). It also means that, as the life of a government continues, one should discount much of the apparent unpopularity of the government of the day as a purely transient phenomenon to be reversed as the election approaches.

[We also set out to model the influence of economic variables and the election cycle on party popularity for the Conservatives and Labour – to see if different variables influenced the two main parties popularity].

Owing to the number of variants of the basic hypothesis tried, over several differing periods for the two parties separately, the resulting Table is rather lengthy, containing 24 equations. The main results can, however, be summarized as follows:

(i) The influence of the two economic variables on both parties was notably stronger after 1959 than before. The sensitivity of the (support for the) Conservative Party to changes in economic conditions is greater than that of the Labour Party over all periods (i.e. the size and significance of the coefficients attached to *both* economic variables is generally greater for the Conservatives than in the equivalent equation for the Labour Party). This we had not expected. We had imagined beforehand that the support for the Labour Party would be particularly likely to ebb and flow with the tides of cyclical unemployment, but it appears that the Conservative Party popularity is even more sensitive to such variations.

(ii) The difference in the size and significance of the coefficient relating to the *unemployment level* between the two parties is, however, on average quite small. Thus changes in unemployment can be expected to affect the standing of the Conservative Party only marginally more than it will affect the popularity of the Labour Party – in, of course, the opposite direction. On the other hand (the popularity of) the Conservative Party is much more sensitive to the *rate of inflation* than is the Labour Party. The size and significance of the coefficient related to dP is generally much less in the Labour Party equations than in the equivalent Conservative equations.

This result was predictable. Professor H. G. Johnson in a paper on 'Problems of Efficiency in Monetary Management' wrote that, 'From one important point of view, indeed, the avoidance of inflation and the maintenance of full employment can be most usefully regarded as conflicting class interests of the bourgeoisie and the proletariat respectively, the conflict being resolvable only by the test of relative political power in society and its resolution involving no reference in an overriding concept of the social welfare.'[7] Thus one would have expected anyhow that the rate of inflation should have a greater effect on the support for the Conservative Party: but it is always pleasant to have one's hypothesis upheld.

(iii) These results suggest that the posited regular inter-election swings in popularity, as approximated by the three dummy variables, *EU*, *TR*, and *BA*, are rather weaker and less consistent than would appear from the earlier tests on the lead of the government. In a substantial proportion of these equations one, or more, of these dummy variables is not significant and in quite a number of them one of these variables is even of the wrong sign. While the results of the equations, taken as a whole, continue to reveal a tendency for the suggested pattern of variation of support for the parties to occur, this pattern would not appear to be markedly consistent or reliable.

(iv) It is not really possible to calculate the impact of the popularity of the leader of a party upon the popularity of that party simply by regressing the one series upon the other. In the first place the series for the leader's popularity may merely act as a proxy for significant independent variables omitted from the equation (e.g. if world-wide peace was declared between Russia and the USA the popularity of the government and Prime Minister of the day might well rise together, however slight our influence on this outcome). We have already suggested that this factor explains the high correlation between the popularity of the Prime Minister and the lead of the government of the day. Again there is the possibility of simultaneous, two-way causation, so that the popularity of a leader can hardly be said to be 'independent' of that of his own party. This problem must be taken especially seriously because of the finding that there is no clear lag structure whereby movements in the popularity of a leader lead or lag that of his party (at any frequency).

Such interrelationships may well bias the coefficient for the impact of a leader's popularity on that of his own party upwards. It is difficult to see how a downwards bias could result. The coefficients shown, relating the influence of a leader to the standing of his own party, may, therefore, be regarded as maximum possible estimates with the true relationship being lower by some unknown extent.

The coefficients shown in the equations are all of the right sign (i.e. positive for own leader, negative for leader of the other party) and have the expected relative values (i.e. absolute size and significance of coefficient greater for own leader than for leader of opposition party). The coefficient for the popularity of own leader is generally statistically significant; the coefficient for the leader of the opposition party is often not significant. The addition of these two variables to the equation generally improves the fit, as measured by the corrected R^2, but not by very much. The value for the coefficient for the popularity of own leader seems to be generally in the range of 0.15 to 0.20, while the coefficient for that of the leader of the opposition party is lower, being around −0.5 to −0.10. These values seem reasonable and sensible, though as we warned they may be biased upwards. It suggests that if the leader of a party became significantly more popular, his party would benefit marginally. For every 10 point surge in a leader's popularity his own party might pick up a 1.5 per cent increase in popularity and the opposition party might lose 0.5 per cent. The influence of a leader's popularity on his party's standing is not *nearly* as strong or as important as the influence of domestic economic conditions, but in a tight race it could still be decisive. Unfortunately, even this judgement must be regarded as tentative, because of the difficulties involved in isolating the independent influence of the leader on his party for purposes of quantitative examination. It is to be hoped that this party of the study can be much improved by further work using improved statistical methods.

The Dynamics of Politico-Economic Interaction

We have up to this point concentrated entirely upon the impact of variations in economic conditions upon political popularity. Yet, politicians have adjusted and will continue to adjust their policies in order to maintain their control of power by retaining popular esteem. Thus the swings in political popularity will cause subsequent changes in policy, and, after a further lag, in economic and social conditions. In other words we perceive a potentially cyclical closed system.

We [have] presented the results of our empirical tests, showing the effects of changes in economic variables upon political popularity. This exercise was conducted on a purely pragmatic basis. We could equally well test the effects of changes in political popularity upon subsequent changes in policy and economic conditions in a similar pragmatic and statistical manner. From this pair of tests we could estimate all the coefficients necessary to calculate the path over time of our politico–economic cycle, which would describe the time path not only of unemployment and prices but also of political popularity.

We preferred, however, at this stage to move from empirical analysis to theoretical model building. Instead of estimating how the party in power had over past years reacted in policy terms to changes in its popularity, we simply adopted the hypothesis that in a democratic society all political parties would so act as to maximise the percentage of the votes likely to be cast for them at the next election.[7] We have already estimated approximate forms of society's political preference functions in Section 3. On this hypothesis the party in power will simply act so as to maximize this function. The difficulty involved here for the politicians is that both unemployment and inflation are disliked by the electorate, but that a reduction in unemployment (resulting from an increase in demand) is almost certainly going to result in an increase in inflationary pressure. Thus the party in power would have to seek an optimal 'political' solution where the marginal rate of substitution in the eyes of the voting electorate between inflation and un-employment was equal to the marginal rate of transformation between unemploy-ment and inflation in the economy. This analysis can be followed more simply with the aid of a figure.

We take as the basis for this figure (Figure 1) the equation from the period 1959–67, using Gallup data,

$$G = 46.11 - 0.099U_{t-6} - 3.47dP + 1.26AE - 1.91Q$$

assuming the Labour Party to be in power. But any of the other equations could have been used as the basis for the diagram. It is now possible to construct a political difference map, showing those combinations of inflation and unemploy-ment levels which will result in the same lead for the government. Incidentally this indifference map can measure popularity on a cardinal scale. We further posit, purely for expository reasons – since we are not concerned at this juncture with establishing the validity of this concept – that there exists within the economy a stable functional relationship, such that $dP = f(U)$, i.e. that the rate of inflation is a function of the level of unemployment within the economy. We suppose for the sake of exposition that this relationship takes the form shown by the dashed line in Figure 1.

If the curve $dP = f(U)$ does not cross the zero indifference line, then no government can be viable, since it would be impossible structurally for the government of the day to establish that combination of high employment and stable prices which would induce the electorate to re-elect it. As we have drawn this curve $dP = f(U)$, it does cross the zero lead indifference line twice, and the area bounded within these two curves is hatched on the diagram, and entitled the area of political viability. The larger the size of this area, naturally the easier it should be for a government to organize the economy of the country so as to maintain power. As we have drawn the curve $dP = f(U)$ it would suggest that the politically expedient course would be to aim for an unemployment rate of 200,000 to 250,000 with an expected rate of inflation of some 5 per cent per annum, at least on election day.

There is, however, a difficulty lurking here, for the assumption that the Phillips curve, $dP = f(U)$, is stable over time seems to imply money illusion on the part of the trade unions, and possibly on the part of other large sectors of the economy also.[8] If we expect prices to rise by 5 per cent next year, and we were concerned with our *real* earnings, we would press harder for higher money wage increases at any level of unemployment and state of demand, than if we expected no inflation at all. Thus we would expect the function to take the form, $dP = f(U, EI)$, where

Figure 1 ISO – vote lives and the Phillips curve.

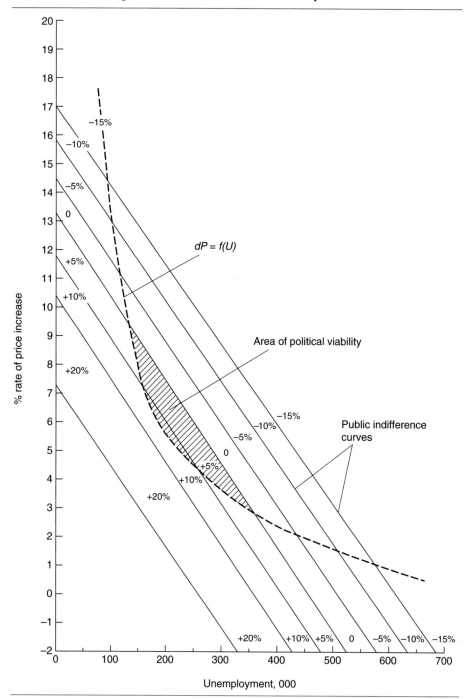

EI represents the expected rate of inflation. Generally we would assume that expectations would be generated in a way approximated by the equation,

$$EI = (1-a)\sum_{j=0}^{\alpha} a^j dP_{t-j}$$

This implies, of course, that if at time, *t*, the Phillips curve $dP = f(U)$ was at the point shown in Figure 1, and the government sought to maximize its popularity, then we would observe continuous inflation over a period. This would cause *EI* to rise, and the curve, $dP = f(U)$, in Figure 1 would shift upwards. This would result economically in a steadily increasing rate of inflation and politically in growing instability since the area of political viability would be continuously eroded. Thus from our model we reach the politico-economic conclusion that a pure democracy with all parties seeking to maximize public support is doomed to increasing inflation and political disintegration.

This is a challenging assertion and certainly points to real dangers. These dangers are met in three ways in practice. First, as a result of experience of past periods of massive inflation and forms of government other than democracy, the electorate's political preference function may eventually switch towards giving price stability a sufficiently high weight and unemployment a sufficiently low weight in order to maintain a steady, non explosive, economic and political path. This seems to have been the case in Germany in recent years: the continued readiness of the German governments not to inflate demand in search of popularity unless price stability is maintained will be an indication of the health of their democracy.

Second, the problem may be met by keeping certain key economic powers out of the control of the democratically elected government. This, in short, has usually been the rationale behind the demands to maintain a Central Bank, independent of the government, charged with the responsibility for maintaining the value of the currency, irrespective of the political popularity of such actions. This is certainly not an optimal solution, not only because it infringes upon the very principle of democracy, but also because to maintain two actually independent foci of economic control would most likely lead to major difficulties in directing the future of the economy.

Third, the problem will be diminished in so far as our basic hypothesis that all parties in a democracy are seeking only to maximize their vote is falsified. If the leaders of our parties are concerned with the welfare of the people, the future judgements of history and the development of particular kinds of society, such overriding concerns will, hopefully, cause them to follow policies which, though good for the country, may not be so good for their standing at the polls.

Conclusions

The determinants of the parties' popularity

On the basis of our preliminary study we formed the hypothesis that the popularity of the two parties (and, therefore, of the government of the day) would be largely determined by two sets of factors, domestic economic conditions, and a regular inter-election swing in party popularity. The two key economic variables were the level of unemployment, whose full impact upon political popularity does not occur until after a six months' lag, and the rate of price inflation. Other economic variables were tried in the equations but were not satisfactory. This posited regular inter-election swing, consisting of a post-election short-lived burst of additional support for the winning party followed by a steady but slow erosion of its popularity which in turn is reversed in the run-up to the next election, was observed from casual empiricism and was given no causal foundations. It was, however, shown to be generally significant and fairly consistent.

These two sets of factors were able to explain a large proportion of the variations in the recorded popularity of the two parties. The fit is clearly much less good for the early post-war years, when political popularity was apparently much less sensitive to domestic economic conditions. For the years after 1959 the basic equation succeeds in achieving a remarkably good fit, especially in view of the extent of random variation in the political series. Indeed, the apparent sensitivity of political popularity to economic conditions, as shown by the equations, seems almost too much to credit.

The residuals from the equations did, however, exhibit a considerable extent of serial correlation. But even when a lagged endogenous variable was introduced into the equation, the political series being strongly auto-regressive, the coefficients of the basic independent variables, though much reduced in size, remained generally significant – particularly for those sub-periods mainly covering the months since 1959.

The empirical tests suggested that a political party in this country, seeking to maximize electoral support for itself at any given moment, would, when in power, choose a position on the Phillips curve, showing economically feasible combinations of unemployment and inflation, that would result in a fairly low rate of unemployment, but a fairly high rate of inflation. Once, however, people came to expect this rate of inflation, the Phillips curve would shift outwards. This implies that there could well be a danger of political pressure in our system leading to a situation of steadily increasing inflation combined with a growing dislike by the public for the economic conditions which could be obtained.

The parties and the party leaders

One of the most interesting questions in this field concerns the extent to which the personal popularity of a party leader would be likely to affect the popular standing of his party. Rarely has so much been written in the press upon a subject about which so little is known with any accuracy. It is, however, a very difficult problem to estimate the strength of the relationship, since the relationship is a complex one and a simple regression between the two series (of the popularity of the party and the leader) will tend to give biased results. Despite these problems we have attempted to obtain some estimate of the strength of the relationship both via multiple regression analysis and cross-spectral analysis. The results suggest that the relationship may be a lot weaker than many might have imagined. Certainly party standing is much more closely determined by domestic economic events than by a leader's personal attraction. It seems from the results, however, to be quite likely that major changes in the popularity of a party leader (of, say, up or down 10 or

20 per cent) would have a small but significant effect on the standing of his own party (of some 2–3 per cent).

Notes

1 Anthony Downs, *An Economic Theory of Government Decision-Making in a Democracy*. Department of Economics, Stanford University: Stanford, California, 1956. Cf. Dr. A. Breton, 'A theory of the demand for public goods', *Canadian Journal of Economics and Statistics*, 32, 4 (November, 1966), 455–67.

2 *Financial Times*, 9 November 1967, p. 23.

3 This is simply calculated as the percentage intending to vote for the party then in office less the percentage intending to vote for the party in opposition.

4 The equation effectively took the form $G_t = b_1 U_t + b_2 (U_t - U_{t-6})$: if the relationship between U and G was consistently negative, but the relationship between G_t and U_{t-6} was stronger than that between G_t and U_t then we would expect b_1 to be <0 and $b_2 >0$.

5 This incidentally was also the lag suggested by Lawson in the *Spectator*.

6 This equation was recalculated using the corrected series for price inflation. The results became:

$$G = 48.30 - 0.101 U_{t-6} - 3.52 dP + 1.09 AE - 3.10 Q$$

$$(0.009) \quad (0.45) \quad (0.23) \quad (1.24)$$

$$R_2 = 0.674 \quad \text{D.W.} = 0.98$$

The value of the coefficients related to unemployment and to price inflation are barely altered. The revised equation, however, suggests a slightly greater preference for the Labour Party than calculated originally. It is important to realize that this revision means very little to the analysis, for a value of Q of -3 is only the equivalent of extra leeway to the Labour Party of 30,000 in unemployment ($30 \times -0.1 = -3$).

7 H. G. Johnson, 'Problems of efficiency in monetary management', *Journal of Political Economy*, 76, 5 (September 1968).

8 Cf. A. Downs, *An Economic Theory of Government Decision Making in a Democracy*.

9 On this point see M. Friedman, 'The role of monetary policy', *American Economic Review*, 58, 1 (March 1968), 1–17, especially pp. 7–10.

Is it Better to be Powerful or Lucky?

Brian Barry

University of Chicago

This apparently simple question provides a hook to link together Barry's original two-part article. The first part, from which this extract is taken, examines the most well-known of the established power indices devised by Shapley and Shubik and by Banzhaf, and shows that they suffer from severe limitations and difficulties. In the process Barry demonstrates that contemporary political theory can contribute a great deal to the clarification and energizing of ideas that emerge in empirical research agendas. In the second part of the paper, not covered here, Barry went on to propose an alternative power index of his own, and to challenge the then current orthodoxy that power was an essentially contested concept, arguing that it was only 'essentially messy'.

Power is desired because it gives its possessor the opportunity to change outcomes from what they would otherwise have been, in the direction that the possessor wishes. However, once we say that power is not going to be treated as an end in itself but only as a means to an end, we must define that end. Clearly, the end assumed is that of getting the outcomes you want. But what is the relation between having power and getting the outcomes you want? It should be apparent that there is no simple connection between the two. If an individual's power is defined as his ability to change outcomes from what they would otherwise have been in the direction he desires, the likelihood of outcomes corresponding to his desires does not depend solely on his power. In addition to his power, it depends on what the outcome would have been in the absence of his intervention. This is what I shall call luck. Someone with a little power (or no power) but a lot of luck may thus consistently be able to obtain more preferred outcomes than someone who has a lot of power but only a little luck.

With enough power you can get everything you want without any luck. With enough luck you can get everything you want without any power. In between these two extremes, things get more complicated.

I take political power to be the ability of an individual or of a group to change the outcomes of some decision-making process from what they would otherwise have been in the direction desired by the person or group, where the decisions made are binding on some collectivity. For many purposes of analysis, it is convenient to consider a special case, namely the case of a body that reaches decisions binding on some collectivity by fixed rules that have the effect of aggregating the preferences expressed according to some specified means by the members of that body. Call such a body a committee and call the means for expressing preferences and the rules for aggregating them a voting procedure.

There are two standard 'power indexes' which purport to measure the relative power of the members of such a committee under alternative decision-making rules (weighted voting, chairman's casting vote, and so on). The older-established of the two is the Shapley-Shubik index, which was first put forward by Lloyd Shapley and Martin Shubik in 1954.[1] The other, the Banzhaf index, was introduced in 1965 by John F. Banzhaf III, and has been used by the New York State Court of Appeals.[2]

Briefly, they work as follows. To construct the Shapley-Shubik index for the power of each member of a committee under given voting rules, we consider every possible order in which all the members of the committee might vote in favour of the measure to be decided upon. Then, for each possible order, we identify the member of the committee whose vote pushes the measure over the line so that it wins. We call that voter 'pivotal' within that particular sequence. The power of any member of the committee is then simply the proportion of all the possible voting-orders in which that member is pivotal.

Alternatively, we can consider the committee members casting negative votes in sequence, and we can then say that the pivot is the member whose vote makes the measure fail. Both ways of measuring power produce the same results, even where there are special requirements for a measure's passing, such as a qualified majority or a simple majority in two separate bodies.

Thus, take the simple case of a committee operating under a majority-rule procedure with three members who have a vote each. The possible orderings are A(B)C, A(C)B, B(A)C, B(C)A, C(A)B, C(B)A. In each ordering, the bracketed member of the committee is the pivotal one, since the second positive vote makes the measure pass or the second negative vote makes it fail. Out of the six possible permutations, each member of the committee is pivotal in two cases so each has (unsurprisingly) a score of 1/3 on the Shapley-Shubik index.

Whereas the Shapley-Shubik index is permutational, the Banzhaf index is based on coalitional considerations. To establish the scores of committee members according to the Banzhaf index, we have to consider every possible minimum winning coalition, that is to say every set of committee members sufficient to carry a measure that would become insufficient if any member of the set were to withdraw. Thus, in the example given above, there are three minimum winning coalitions, that of A and B, A and C, and B and C. To get the score on the Banzhaf index we count the number of ways in which each actor could make a winning coalition into a non-winning one by withdrawing from it. (Each here could bring down two). Then, in order to make the scores sum to unity, we simply add the individual scores and divide each of them by the total. So, in the present case, the total is six, each committee member has a raw score of two, and the Banzhaf index, again not surprisingly, ascribes each a final score of 1/3 to each.

Although the Shapley-Shubik and Banzhaf indexes are computed differently, and in any complex voting scheme usually produce different numerical results, it is generally the case that a change in voting rules that increases an actor's power on the Shapley-Shubik index also increases it on the Banzhaf index, and vice versa. In the example that was worked through above, the two indexes produced the same answer, but in such a simple case they could scarcely have failed to. If we constrain the answer so that an amount of 'power' within the committee must sum to unity and must somehow be totally allocated among the individuals who make up the committee, we must expect that any completely symmetrical voting scheme will attribute equal power to each. This must be true simply because there is no basis on which to distinguish the members.

Note that the equality thus ascribed to the committee members in no way depends on the details of the actual scheme, so long as it treats all alike. Consider, for example, a rule requiring unanimous agreement. This would make the last voter pivotal in each of the six Shapley-Shubik permutations. We can see that each committee member is going to be last twice, giving each a score of 1/3. On the Banzhaf measure, there is only one minimum winning coalition (made up of A, B and C). Each committee member is thus in the single winning minimum coalition. The total score is therefore three, so we divide each individual's score by three, giving each 1/3.

The point is, however, that we do not really need to carry out the calculations, because we can deduce directly from the symmetry of the voting rule that the power of the committee members is going to be equal. We may, of course, observe when we realize this that any measure of the distribution of power that is unable to distinguish between majority voting and a *liberum veto* is hardly telling us anything we would like to know. But that result is unavoidable right from the start once the commitment is made to treat power as something that can always be allocated to individuals in such a way that the individual scores sum to unity.

Both indexes are designed to try to capture the idea of an individual voter's chance of making a difference to the outcome. But both fail because they substitute something else – the proportion of times an individual voter is pivotal out of all pivots, or the proportion of defections from a minimal winning coalition an individual can engage in out of all such defections – and there is no reason to suppose that what we are told to count is related in any direct way to what we want to know about.

The irrelevance of the measure advocated by Shapley and Shubik is patent. In their article, they make the following claim: 'Our definition of the power of an individual member depends on [i.e., makes it depend on – B.B.] the chance he has of being critical to the success of a winning coalition.'[3] But their definition of a 'pivot' does not in the least capture the notion of being critical to the success (or failure) of something.

Suppose that a million pounds has to be raised in a given time for some purpose (for example, to prevent the export of a picture) and that as the deadline approaches contributions to the appeal are coming in at the rate of a thousand pounds a day but there is still a shortfall of a hundred thousand pounds. If some donor gives that amount, his contribution might well be said to have been critical to the success of the fund-raising effort. But if funds are flowing at a thousand pounds per day and the target is reached several weeks before the deadline, it would be an abuse of language to call the particular donation (assume it to be of average size) that carried the appeal over the line critical, because if it had not been sent the target would still easily have been reached. Similarly, if a bridge has been weakened over the years by traffic, it would be unreasonable to say that its being crossed by the particular car that caused it to collapse was critical if there is every reason to suppose that the next car in line would have done the same thing. If, however, it was being crossed by a tank that made the bridge collapse, we might reasonably say that that was critical because with normal traffic the bridge would probably otherwise have lasted for many more years.

Thus, when we say that some event is critical for something's coming about, we are necessarily involved in a counterfactual assertion that, with everything else remaining the same, in the absence of the event in question the thing would not have happened. (There is an implicit qualification here: we mean that it would not have happened roughly at the same place or at the same time or in the same form. What constitutes sufficient closeness to count depends on the context.) In particular, an event is not critical if it could be foreseen with confidence that in its absence another event with the same effects would have occurred in its place.

Now recall how the Shapley-Shubik concept of a pivot is derived.

> Let us consider the following scheme: There is a group of individuals all willing to vote for some bill. They vote in order. As soon as a majority has voted for it, it is declared passed, and the member who voted last is given credit for having passed it. Let us choose the voting order of the members randomly. Then we may compute the frequency with which an individual belongs to the group whose votes are used and, of more importance, we may compute how often he is pivotal. This latter number serves to give us our index. It measures the number of times that the action of the individual actually changes the state of affairs.[4]

I hope that it is not necessary, after the previous discussion, to belabour the point that the pivot, so understood, does *not* in the relevant sense change the state of affairs. Since we have a group of individuals 'all willing to vote for some bill', it makes no difference who happens to provide the vote that gives the measure the winning margin, since, *ex hypothesi*, if any of the remaining members of the body had replaced that person in the sequence, he would have voted for the measure instead.

In other expositions, the pivot is said to be 'decisive', and this is the term that I propose to use later in developing a more satisfactory conception of power in a committee. But again it should be clear that the pivot in the Shapley-Shubik scheme is not decisive. Thus, Steven Brams writes:

> For all the different ways in which the buildup of the grand coalition can occur through a sequence of additions of one player, there will be one player in each sequence who will be decisive to a coalition's becoming winning. We call this player, who makes the difference between a coalition's being winning or losing, the *pivot*...[5]

But obviously if what we have is 'the buildup of the grand coalition', the place of any member of the committee in the voting sequence is neither here nor there. If a simple majority is all that is required and everybody is going to vote 'aye' anyway, then nobody is decisive because nobody individually makes a difference to the outcome.

To say, however, that no individual member of the committee has any power violates ones of the postulates upon which the Shapley-Shubik index is constructed, namely that the power of the members of a committee must always sum to unity. The deeper point here is that the whole approach embodied in the Shapley-Shubik index is inappropriate. The index arises out of, and is indeed simply a special case of, Lloyd Shapley's work on the problem of the value of a game, and we need briefly to backtrack to look at that.

The question that Shapley set himself is a good one, and one of central importance to much political analysis. I shall try below to provide a framework within which it can be answered. The question is: how can we estimate *a priori* the value to someone of playing a certain game? It is evident that this is central to questions of accession and secession. The voters in the various American states had to estimate, for example, the value of the game constituted by the proposed federal constitution. More recently, the British electorate had to estimate the value of the game constituted by the enlarged EEC. When the value of the game played within a state falls below some level, we may expect that secession will begin to appeal. And so on.[6]

As Shapley wrote: 'In attempting to apply the theory [of games] to any field, one would normally expect to be permitted to include, in the class of "prospects", the prospect of having to play a game. The possibility of evaluating games is, therefore, of critical importance'.[7] Thus, we know that for zero-sum games there is a plausible case for assigning to each player his mini-max value and calling that the value of the game to him: it is what, on the basis of sound theoretical arguments, he can expect to get. The problem is how to extend the assignment of the value of a game to other kinds of game. The Shapley value of a game to each player is derived by considering all subsets of one or more players that can be formed out of the set of players and treating each subset as equally probable. Some of these coalitions will have no value, others will (in the general case) have different values depending on their composition. The value of the game for each player is based on the increment that that player brings to each coalition. In other words, for each possible coalition (subset of players) we take its value and then subtract from that its value without the player for whom we are carrying out the calculation. (Obviously, if the player is not in a coalition, the difference must be zero.) That player is then credited with the whole of the increase in the value of the coalition that his presence brings to it.

The procedure can be stated in a way that brings out clearly the parentage of the Shapley-Shubik index: we can imagine

> the random formation of a coalition of all the players, starting with a single member and adding one player at a time. Each player is then assigned the advantage accruing to the coalition at the time of his admission. In this process of computing the expected value for an individual player all coalition formations are considered as equally likely.[8]

The Shapley-Shubik index may be seen as the Shapley value for the special case where coalitions do not have a variety of values but are either winning (value 1) or losing (value 0). Adding members to a coalition thus does not increase its value until the threshold of winning is reached; then, once the 'winning' point has been reached, adding more again does not increase the value further. The pivot – the member of the committee whose addition to a coalition changes it from losing to winning – thus gets credit for the whole value of a winning coalition.

The trouble is that the basic model is inappropriate to the typical phenomena of politics. It belongs to the branch of game theory that presupposes perfectly divisible and transferable utility – something like money only even better. When we spoke above about the 'value' of any given coalition we were talking about a substance – utility – that could be divided in any way among the members of the coalition in such a way that it remained the same size. This assumption violates the first principle of political analysis, which is that a public policy is a public good (or bad). If the death penalty is reintroduced, that pleases those who favour it and displeases those who do not. Similarly, a tax break is good or bad for people according to their situation. The gains are not confined to those who voted on the winning side nor are the losses confined to those who were on the losing side. The measure creates its own gainers and losers by its content: if you are advantaged or disadvantaged by it that will be so whether you voted in favour or against or did not vote at all.

There are, of course, some cases in which people get paid off according to the way in which they vote. American presidential nominating conventions are the text-book example. Delegations are usually concerned with the symbolic/ideological characteristics of the candidates, and they also have a natural preference (at least *ceteris paribus*) for a candidate who has a good chance of winning the election. But in addition, there is some advantage, personally and perhaps for the state, in having backed the candidate who actually gets the nomination – and to have backed him before it was clear that he was going to get it. The analysis of such a case in terms of transferable utility is at any rate partially appropriate in that we can think of a fixed amount of 'patronage' to be divided up among supporters. But it is, I suggest, a basic error to take a presidential nominating convention as a paradigm of political decision-making.

In saying this, I am not committed to a particularly high-minded view of politics. We can, if we wish, follow Lasswell's formulation and say that politics is 'who gets what, when, how'. The crucial question is precisely in virtue of what they get it. What I am saying is that the standard way in which people get what they get is through the contents of public policies. Private payoffs related to the way in which they vote are a pathological by-product.

What about cases where a majority of legislators get together and cook up some scheme for providing geographically-specific benefits for their own constituents? This presents no problem for the present analysis. That it is often thought of as a counterexample illustrates just how difficult it is to keep things clear. It is still true in such a case that the outcome is a public policy that distributes benefits and costs in a certain way. The benefits derive from the adoption of the policy, not from having voted for it. Naturally, we would expect the prospective beneficiaries (or their representatives) to be the ones to vote in favour and the prospective losers (or their representatives) to vote against. But the point is that there is no advantage in 'being a member of the winning coalition' if all we mean by this is voting for the measure. If one legislator whose constituents stand to benefit votes against, and one whose constituents stand to lose votes in favour, the measure still passes and has exactly the same distributive effects. It is remarkable how much of the application of game theory to politics falls foul of this simple and elementary observation: the whole of William Riker's *The Theory of Political Coalitions*[9] is invalidated by it and so is almost every analysis of power in decision-making bodies. They operate as if the payoffs arising from a vote could be allocated according to the way people vote. They do not take account of the fact that a public policy is a public good.

On its own premises, the Shapley-Shubik index is quite correct in identifying the value to an actor of taking part in a certain decision-making process with his power. If the utility arising from any play of the game (any vote of the committee) is divisible and transferable and it all goes to whoever makes the coalition win (the pivot), then indeed power and value are directly related to one another. But the whole point about a public good is that there is no way in which the person who provides it can appropriate all the value arising from it. There can thus be 'free riders', who gain the benefits without having done anything to bring the public good into existence. Hence the distinction on which I am insisting between power and luck as alternative ways of getting outcomes that you want. You may get them by exercising power and thus making them come about when they otherwise would not have done. But if you are lucky you will be able to take a 'free ride' on the efforts of others. Provided your policy preferences are like those of people who have power you will finish up with no less than they get, even though you have done nothing to bring about the outcomes that are mutually desired. This shows plainly that if we are to talk sensibly about the anticipated value to an actor of a political process – a state, a federation, a common market or whatever, operating by known decision-making rules – we must break away from the approach embodied in the Shapley-Shubik index.

I have so far said nothing specifically in criticism of the Banzhaf index, but much less needs to be said. The Shapley-Shubik index is perfectly consistent given its premises (which happen to be inapplicable) and has a certain theoretical elegance.[10] The Banzhaf index, by contrast, is a mere gimmick, with no coherent theoretical underpinnings. It has all the drawbacks of the Shapley-Shubik index in that it too assumes that the 'power' in a committee sums to unity and can be exhaustively allocated among the members. But in addition it violates equiprobability in a very queer way by in effect assuming that each coalition should be weighted in the computation by the number of different ways in which it can be brought down by the withdrawal of a member. Thus, in a committee with weighted voting it may be that a certain coalition is vulnerable to the defection of only one particular member, while another is vulnerable to defection by any of three members. (An example will be given a little later.) Then the Banzhaf index counts the first coalition towards one member's score whereas the second coalition counts separately in the scores of three members. Yet, if one were going to depart from equiprobability, it would seem more plausible to go in exactly the opposite direction and assume that, the more different ways a coalition is open to being brought down by defection, the less likely it is to form.

Up to this point, I have treated the Shapley-Shubik and Banzhaf indexes as *a priori* indexes, which in practice means that I have followed their authors in assuming that all orderings or defections from a minimum winning coalition are equally probable. But in real life we know very well that in any actual committee it would be very extraordinary for the votes of different members not to be related in some systematic way. Any adequate treatment of power in a committee must be able to deal with departures from equiprobability, and I shall show in the next section how that can be done within the framework of analysis I propose. The attempts that have been made to modify the application of Shapley-Shubik and Banzhaf indexes, however, produce such absurdities that they underline the fundamental inadequacy of these indexes.

The method of analysis used is pretty crude. What is done is to postulate that some committee members always vote on the same side or always vote on different sides, and then see what this does to the power index for all the members of the committee. It is hardly surprising that the Shapley-Shubik index goes haywire when the attempt is made to move away from the equal probability of every ordering. The index is constructed, as we saw, by assuming that all the members of the committee vote in favour of a measure (or all against it) and by counting pivots. The introduction of the idea that some committee members vote one way and others vote the other way on the same measure therefore violates the assumption upon which the index is founded. What it does to fudge it is to assume that those who vote *before* the pivot must still all vote the same way, but that those who vote *after* the pivot can be allowed to vote either way. The Banzhaf index might appear less vulnerable, since we can always simply strike out some minimum winning coalitions on the basis of a stipulation that they will never form. But in practice both indexes give rise to exactly the same kinds of absurd conclusion.

The most dramatic illustration of this point is the so-called paradox of quarrelling members.

> We may suppose, for example, that two players are involved in a quarrel and refuse to join together to help form a winning coalition. Although one might suspect that they could only succeed in hurting each other, it is a curious fact that the quarrel between two players may actually redound to their benefit by increasing both their individual and combined voting power. We call this phenomenon the *paradox of quarreling members*.[11]

Consider an example in which there are three committee members, with weights of 3, 2 and 2 votes, and where 5 votes out of a total of 7 are needed for a committee decision. Call the player with 3 votes A and the other two B and C. Under normal circumstances the Shapley-Shubik values are 2/3 for A and 1/6 apiece for B and C and the Banzhaf values are 3/5 for A and 1/5 apiece for B and C; but if for some reason B and C never agree the figures become 1/2, 1/4, 1/4 on both indices, so that B and C gain power by quarrelling.

On the Banzhaf criterion, this is a result of the fact that when B and C quarrel only two minimum winning coalitions, that of A and B and that of A and C, are possible. Thus, A can bring down two coalitions (i.e., make them less than winning) while B and C can bring down one each. Thus, there are four possible ways of bringing down a coalition, two involving A and one each B and C. Hence the scores are: A = 1/2, B = 1/4, C = 1/4. If the coalition of A, B and C can form, however, we have an extra way in which a coalition can be brought down: by A's withdrawal from this 'grand coalition'. (Neither B nor C can bring it down by withdrawing from it since it would still have 5 votes. Thus the coalition of A, B and C is minimal with respect to A but not B or C – an awkward notion but one integral to Banzhaf's way of doing the calculations.) Therefore, if all combinations are possible, there are 5 ways in which a coalition can be brought down, in 3 of which A figures, leaving one apiece for B and C. This produces the scores of 3/5 for A and 1/5 each for B and C.

On the Shapley-Shubik index, it is a matter of the number of orderings in which each member is pivotal (i.e., makes up the required majority of 5 votes). A(B)C, A(C)B, B(A)C and C(A)B are all the available permutations where B and C disagree, making A pivotal in 2 out of 4 and B and C pivotal in one each, producing scores of 1/2, 1/4, 1/4. But if B and C do not necessarily disagree, there are also available BC(A) and CB(A) which add two more permutations where A is pivotal. (A is pivotal because B and C together do not make up the required 5 votes.) Thus, A would be pivotal in 4 cases out of 6 (2/3) and B and C one each out of six (1/6). Yet the conclusion, that the power of B and C has increased, and that 'there is an incentive for them to quarrel and increase their share of the voting power'[12] is manifestly absurd. When B and C are always on opposite sides, this has the consequence that A, by casting his 3 votes, is always able to ensure 5 votes for the side he favours, since there will be 2 votes in favour of each side automatically.

Another so-called paradox, which either reduces to the paradox of quarrelling members or makes no sense, is one that says it is better (in the sense of producing more power) to split up than vote as a bloc. Thus, consider the same committee as before, with simple majority voting. The members might as well have one vote each, since no one and any two constitute a majority. The Shapley-Shubik and Banzhaf indexes therefore assign each member a score of 1/3. 'Now assume that the 3-vote player breaks up into constituent 1-vote members.'[13] But *what* exactly are we to assume here? If the three members with one vote all vote the same way, nothing has changed. But if they vote differently (in accordance with the equi-probability assumptions of the two indexes), we have a change from (in effect) agreement between three voters to random association. The idea that a block whose members agree would split up and start voting against one another simply in order to increase their 'power' is bizarre, though not, it must be said, too bizarre to have inspired empirical research presented with a straight face.[14] In any case, if they do, the three members with a vote each increase their aggregate power from 1/3 to 3/7 on the Banzhaf index and 2/5 on the Shapley-Shubik index.[15] But obviously it is better to have two allies on a committee than not, so this is an absurd conclusion. (For those who distrust their intuitions on this point, a demonstration is offered in the next section).

Brams says of 'paradoxes' like these that 'this term is not meant to imply that they in any way invalidate the power indices. Quite the contrary: They illustrate their usefulness in showing up aspects of voting power whose existence would have been difficult to demonstrate convincingly in the absence of precise quantitative concepts.'[16] I hope it is clear that these are not paradoxes in even the loosest sense of that much-abused term. Their only use is to drive home to anyone who is not persuaded by more abstract considerations the utter inadequacy of the indexes. Brams is like someone who owns a broken thermometer and says that the fact that it does not register a higher temperature when it is put in a flame shows us something new and interesting (albeit counterintuitive) about the nature of heat.

Notes

1 L. S. Shapley and M. Shubik, 'A method of evaluating the distribution of power in a committee system', *American Political Science Review*, 48 (1954), 787–92. Reprinted in R. Bell, D. V. Edwards and R. Harrison Wagner (eds), *Political Power*. New York: Free Press, 1969, pp. 209–13. Page references are given to this reprint.

2 J. F. Banzhaf III, 'Weighted voting doesn't work: a mathematical analysis', *Rutgers Law Review*, 19 (1965), 317–43; and 'Multimember electoral districts: do they violate the "one man, one vote" principle?', *Yale Law Journal*, 75 (1966), 1309–88.

3 Bell *et al.*, *Political Power*, p. 209.

4 Bell *et al.*, *Political Power*, p. 210.

5 S. J. Brams, *Game Theory and Politics*. New York, Free Press, 1975, p. 162, italics in original.

6 See R. Rogowski, *Rational Legitimacy: A Theory of Political Support*. Princeton: Princeton University Press, 1974, for an original analysis of legitimacy in terms of expectations about the course of decision-making. Rogowski relates the acceptability of a regime to an actor to that actor's probability of 'uniquely determining' outcomes. This measure is a cousin of the Shapley-Shubik index: the total power of all actors sums to unity and each actor's score is supposed to reflect his individual responsibility for producing outcomes. Therefore the criticisms made here of the Shapley-Shubik index apply to Rogowski's treatment as well.

7 L. S. Shapley, 'A Value for *n*-person Games', in H. W. Kuhn and A. W. Tucker (eds), *Contributions to the Theory of Games II*, Annals of Mathematical Studies, 28. Princeton: Princeton University Press, 1953, 307–17, p. 307.

8 Kuhn and Tucker, *Contributions to the Theory of Games II*, p. 303. Cited in R. D. Luce and H. Raiffa, *Games and Decisions*. New York: Wiley, 1957, p. 250. See, generally, pp. 245–50 for a discussion of the Shapley value.

9 New Haven, Yale University Press, 1962. Riker's notion that 'winning' is a universal value in politics depends on precisely the equivocation identified in the text, and his 'proof' of the minimum size principle depends upon the assumption of divisible, transferable utility. Riker's theory would work if politics were nothing but a matter of allocating spoils, in other words if it had no connection with policies that are public goods or bads. For a discussion of these two aspects of politics and of the problem of integrating them in a single analysis, see my 'Review Article: "Crisis, choice, and change", part II, games theorists play', *British Journal of Political Science*, 7 (1977), 217–53.

10 Luce and Raiffa, in *Games and Decisions*, pp. 245–50 and 253–5, provide a clear exposition of this point.

11 Brams, *Game Theory and Politics*, pp. 180–81.

12 Brams, *Game Theory and Politics*, p. 181.

13 Brams, *Game Theory and Politics*, p. 177.

14 G. A. Schubert, 'The study of judicial decision-making as an aspect of political behavior', *American Political Science Review*, 52 (1958), 1022–24; W. Riker, 'A test of the adequacy of the power index', *Behavioral Science*, 4 (1959), 276–90. I am not, of course, denying that those who are pivotal in a body whose members can be arrayed on one dimension get the outcomes they want. What I deny is that it makes sense for somebody to vote against what he is in favour of simply in order to be pivotal.

15 Brams, *Game Theory and Politics*, pp. 177–8.

16 Brams, *Game Theory and Politics*, pp. 181–2.

Model or Metaphor? A Critical Review of the Policy Network Approach

Keith Dowding

London School of Economics and Political Science

In the 1980s empirical research on policy-making processes in Britain and the USA repeatedly claimed to find that public policy shifts responded to a wide range of stimuli, both external interest groups and civil society influences, and complex intra-state allocations of responsibilities between government bureaucracies, quasi-governmental and sub-national agencies, professional groups, public/private linkages, and implementation-level influences (such as 'street-level' bureaucracies). The policy network literature emerged as an inductive attempt to theorize about and systematize these patterns, and like the mushrooming of work on interest groups in the 1950s, the newly recognized phenomena attracted a lot of attention. Dowding's paper had an immediate influence in suggesting that the value-added from the new terminology was limited and that the policy networks literature lacked any theoretical core. He suggests criteria for the field to survive and mature into more than just a temporarily useful descriptive metaphor. Our selection omits some passages discussing empirical studies in more detail.

Policy network analysis has become the dominant paradigm for the study of the policy-making process in British political science and has assumed great importance in Europe and America. It is time to take stock: to see how much we have learned about policy-making from this approach, to judge whether it can develop into a genuine and fruitful theory of the policy process or whether a more fundamental theory is required. In this review I argue that whilst we have learned much about the policy process by cataloguing the policy world into different types of network, the approach will not, alone, take us much further. Policy network analysis began as a metaphor, and may only become a theory by developing along the lines of sociological network analysis. Attempts to provide a 'meso-level' theory,[1] to connect networks with state autonomy approaches,[2] or to drive network analysis by introducing 'ideas' in the form of 'epistemic communities' or 'advocacy coalitions'[3] will all fail to produce fundamental *theories* of the policy process. They will fail because the driving force of explanation, the independent variables, are not network characteristics *per se* but rather characteristics of components within the networks. These components explain both the nature of the network *and* the nature of the policy process. General theory may be developed by concentrating upon those characteristics. Theory building in this case will be reductionist. In order to produce a *network* theory; where the properties of the network rather than the properties of its members drives explanation, political science must utilize the sociological network tradition, borrowing and modifying its algebraic methods. This I argue is of limited potential.[4]

The Descriptive Approach

The origin of the terms 'policy community' and 'policy network' is essentially metaphorical. Early metaphors characterizing group-government relations include 'whirlpool'[5] 'sub-governments',[6] 'triangle',[7] 'sloppy hexagon',[8] 'webs',[9] and 'iron triangles'.[10] The 'iron triangle' concept took off in the United States to depict relations between the relevant executive agency, the relevant congressional sub-committee and interest group organizations. By 1978 Heclo complained that the metaphor was misleading and introduced the notion of 'issue networks' to suggest a less close-knit community.[11] Earlier Heclo and Wildavsky had used the idea of policy communities, suggesting that these develop around a shared framework of understanding.[12] All of these different terms were used to elucidate the same essential feature of policy-making; that the distinction between public and private organizations was flexible, the pattern of linkages within a sector affected policy outcomes, and the sub-governmental level was most important for understanding the detail of policy formation and the success of policy implementation.

Developing the US literature for Britain, Richardson and Jordan initially used the concepts of 'policy network' and 'policy community' interchangeably to indicate the close links between civil servants and favoured interest group organizations.[13] But by 1982 they had introduced a more institutionally based conception. Policy community is understood in all the literature in some sense as a common culture and understandings about the nature of the problems and decision-making processes within a given policy domain. Jordan and Richardson saw policy-making as a series of vertical components sealed off from other aspects of the policy process – other groups and departments, the public and parliament.[14] Their argument fractured the standard evaluation of pressure group/government relations as a bilateral bargain, extending analysis into domains where the state/society distinction is not so hard-edged. Recently Richardson has proposed that a theory of the transformation of policy communities is required in order to understand the dynamics of radical policy change in Britain. In a case study of water privatization Richardson *et al.* describe the process with which the water policy community failed to agree over the details of privatization particularly with regard to regulation.[15] All we learn from the study in network terms is that if a policy community breaks down an issue network evolves and other groups are able to enter the policy process more forcefully. It does not explain community breakdown, nor issue network transcendence, nor the dynamics of the change. And it cannot do so, for part of what is to be explained is the creation and destruction of communities. The imagery is simply metaphorical heuristics, though no less serviceable for that.

Attempts have been made within the descriptive approach to go beyond metaphor and provide theories of the policy process in network terms. One was developed by Wilks and Wright in order to explain the complex nature of industrial policy-formation seen in many European nations.[16] They believed that policy networks were best seen as personal relations of small groups of political actors, rather than visualizing networks as part of wider explanations of the nature of the modern state. They perceived fewer differences in the policy process across nations than had Jordan and Richardson and believed that the key aspects of the process occurred at a micro- or individual level. The Wilks-Wright team attacked the notion of grand theories of the state arguing that in the sectors they analysed across Europe there was little correlation between the degree of government intervention in different nations and the categorization of the state in those nations as interventionist or non-interventionist.[17] Rhodes and Marsh on the other hand want to integrate policy network analysis with grand theories of the state, seeing it as a 'meso-level' theory lying between micro-level theories such as rational choice and macro-level state theory.[18]

The problem here is with the very idea of a 'theory of the state'. There is a mis-apprehension about the nature state theorizing. A true theory must be general-izable to all objects to which it is supposed to be applicable. It should be able to explain variance between those objects as well as explaining similarities. Too often different state theories are about different types of state – thus some states are seen as more pluralist than others, some as more elitist than others, some as more autonomous than others. But if this is so then none of the 'theories' is about 'the state'. You cannot have a theory about dogs which only applies to alsations and not poodles, then study two dogs and conclude that one is more poodle-like and another more alsatian-like. That is not a theory; it is a system of classification.[19] Any theory of the state must specify how we expect different actors (institutions, people, groups or whatever) to behave *under different institutional arrangements*. Few extant so-called theories of the state do this.[20]

The Rhodes-Marsh typology (Table 1) offers formal definitions for demarcating the world into different types of network.[21] The heuristic value of such definitional categorization depends upon the ability to construct a proper model which causally relates the characteristics to each other and to different types of policy outcome. The problem with Table 1 is that it does not distinguish dependent and independ-ent variables. For example, in the dimension 'Type of Interest' policy community is contrasted with issue network on the grounds that the former have economic or professional interests dominating, whereas the latter encompasses a broad range of interests. In the dimension 'Consensus' there is said to be a general acceptance of the legitmacy of the outcome and a sharing of basic values within policy communities but conflict ever present in issue networks. Surely the reason why integration can be contrasted through the two types of network is because of the distinction between the types of interest. In order truly to go beyond typology the causal relationships between the entries in Table 1 need to be modelled. As used by adherents to the Rhodes model 'policy community' and 'issue network' are merely labels attached to an explanation of differences between policy formation in different policy sec-tors. The labels do not themselves explain the difference. The explanation lies in the characteristics of the actors.

The nature of power exchange in fact held together the 'Rhodes model', at least in its initial specification, in the form of the 'power dependency model'[22] which Rhodes pithily explains:

> Central-local relations take on aspects of a 'game' in which both central and local participants manoeuvre for advantage, deploying the resources they control to maximize their influence over outcomes and trying to avoid becoming dependent on the other 'players'.[23]

Table 1: Types of Policy Networks: Characteristics of Policy Communities and Issue Networks

Dimension	Policy community	Issue network
	Membership	
Number of participants	Very limited number, some groups consciously excluded	Large
Type of interest	Economic and/or professional interests dominante	Encompasses range of affected interests
	Integration	
Frequency of interaction	Frequent, high-quality, interaction of all groups on all matters related to policy issues	Contacts fluctuate in frequency and intensity
Continuity	Membership, values, and outcomes persistent over time	Access fluctuates significantly
Consensus	All participants share basic values all accept the legitimacy of the outcome	Some agreement exists, but conflict is ever present
	Resources	
Distribution of resources (in network)	All participants have resources basic relationship is an exchange relationship	Some participants may have resources, but they are limited basic relationship consultative
Internal distribution	Hierarchical; leaders can deliver members	Varied, variable distribution and capacity to regulate members
Power	There is a balance of power among members. Although one group may dominate, it must be a positive-sum game if community is to persist	Unequal powers, reflecting unequal resources and unequal access – zero-sum game

Source: D. Marsh and R. A. W. Rhodes (eds), Policy Networks in British Government. Oxford, Oxford University Press, 1992, p. 251.

This is a perfect characterization of the nature of politics within a bargaining framework. But such an approach should lead the researcher to concentrate upon the resources that actors need to enter this game. These resources include, (1) knowledge or information, (2) legitimate authority, (3) unconditional incentives to affect the interests of others, (4) conditional incentives to affect the interests of others, and (5) reputation.[24] It is unclear why the 'Rhodes model' developed away from considering the resources of actors in a game over policy outcome. Rhodes seemingly believes that concentration upon actors' resources shifts attention to the 'micro-level' and away from macro-processes such as socialization and the general form of power and interest in society:

> They [critics of power-dependency with whom Rhodes sympathizes] call for a theory of bargaining tactics *and* a theory able to capture the interactions, tactics, and sub-processes of negotiation that surround the act of bargaining itself ... Thus a focus on the distribution of resources between actors and on the socialization of actors into certain ideologies should link the analysis of negotiative behaviour to the macro-level power-interest structure of society.[25]

This then leads to his call for a 'meso-level' level of analysis. Perhaps Rhodes should not have been so sympathetic to his critics. Bargaining theory both is a theory of rational tactics and a way of describing the interactions which then take place. Whilst economists have tended simply to assume that actors have preferences and *then* model their behaviour, this is not incompatible with a theory of preference formation. New institutional economics does consider the role of preference formation given the underlying structure of resources and property rights in any given society. The Harsanyi bargaining model allows for understanding how bargaining can unconditionally change the incentive structures of other groups. For example, a headmistress and governing body which control a limited budget for their school may well take a different attitude towards a demand for a national pay-rise than if the budget is controlled by a local authority. Shifting responsibilities shapes preferences. Conditional incentives also shape preferences. Conditional incentives come in the form of threats, offers and throffers; whilst a less subtle form of preference-shaping, they are often just as effective. Analysis of policy networks and the structures of bargaining tactics can capture the various ways in which preferences are formed.[26]

This form of bargaining analysis can be applied to persons, to organizations or even with some modification, to more amorphous groupings such as social class and producer-consumer relations. It is not, as Rhodes seems to think, a 'micro-level' analysis, though it is true that most people who work with these types of models believe that applications at the macro-level require micro-level roots to explain the causal processes at work therein. There is no need for meso-level theory between the two, but merely for an analytic theory which produces testable empirical implications under different conditions.

Preference Formation and Advocacy Coalitions

Envisioning the policy process and a bargaining game between different types of actors is the traditional approach of much of political science. In most of mainstream political science and certainly within economics, little consideration is devoted to the generation of interests. Yet the first collective action problem that any group needs to overcome is the identification of its interests.[27] Rhodes perhaps shied away from the power dependency elements of his model because of doubts about its ability to capture the way in which preferences are formed. A similar concentration upon the generation of preferences motivates the approaches which have developed from the policy sciences literature. This literature has always been concerned with normative questions around policy formation – notably rational decision-making and technical issues over policy formulation and implementation. Critiques of the very possibility of rational policy-formation because of the socially constructed nature of knowledge have dominated this area in recent years. They stimulated the study of the generation of policy ideas from technical experts and professionals. From this grew the idea of epistemic communities and advocacy coalitions.

The advocacy coalition framework has four defining features.[28] First, that understanding policy change requires a time perspective of at least a decade. Secondly, that we need to concentrate upon the policy network. Thirdly, that we need to understand change through an intergovernmental framework, that is we should not concentrate attention institutionally between central, regional and local levels of government.[29] Finally, that public policies can be conceptualized as belief systems. It is the final element which most distinguishes this approach and on which I will concentrate attention.

The essential element of seeing public policy as a belief system is that beliefs change over time given the external environment around people. Issues emerge through changes in the environment, often as a shock or crisis, such as the oil crisis of the mid-1970s. The causes of re-evaluation of the belief system about public policy and new interest groups emerge. These groups form coalitions which over time may agree on a policy solution, not simply, though sometimes through the give-and-take of bargaining, but also because their beliefs about the correct solution converge. Professionals working in a given area may come to dominate the thinking of virtually all interested parties, though rival advocacy coalitions may use different expert advice. The importance of expert advice in foreign policy is the essential element of the 'epistemic communities' literature. This tries to explain how international policy has converged in a number of areas such as GATT, environmental issues, food aid, the world economy, and regulation in banking communities[30] are to see the emergence of belief systems leading to policy convergence rather than seeing international agreements as the result of power bargaining games between self-interest nation-states.[31]

The advocacy coalition literature has a more developed account of belief systems, which are thought to be composed of a set of core beliefs which will remain unchallenged; for example the primacy of the environment over economic growth for environmentalists, and the primacy of growth over the environment for capitalists; and a set of policy beliefs about how best to protect one's core beliefs. There is room for compromise over the policy beliefs, for example environmentalists and builders may agree to limited development in a given area. But such agreements may break down once room for compromise is over, say, the potential for limited development is ended and developers want to continue into new areas. Munro discusses California water politics and shows how in the 1960s room for compromise between two sets of advocacy coalitions made brokerage by successive governors impossible.[32] Similarly this contest between environmentalists and capitalists broke from uneasy compromise to open battle in Sabatier's story of Lake Tahoe.[33]

An excellent account of two policy coalitions – environmental groups such as the Audobon Society and the Sierra Club, and the major oil companies battling for the

support of four government agencies, Department of the Interior (DOI), Department of Energy (DOE), the Environmental Protection Agency (EPA) and National
Oceanic and Atmospheric Administration – is contained in Jenkins-Smith and
St Clair's analysis of the politics of offshore energy.[34] Jenkins-Smith and St Clair
built up an ideological map of the groups over time. They chart them in four time-
periods and demonstrate changes in three broad coalitions of the environmental
groups, the oil companies and trade associations, and the governmental agencies
occupying ground between the two. In the first time period there exists a tight
conservation group, a slightly more diverse pro-development group (including the
DOE) with the EPA closer to the environmentalists and the DOI closer to the
developmentalists. Under Carter the DOI and DOE switched positions and both
moved closer to the environmentalists. With the onset of the energy crisis the
government agencies moved back to the pro-development fold and the environmental coalition also became less tightly knit. In the final period, once again, the
system had become increasingly polarized, with the coalition groups tighter-knit
but remaining just as far away from each other. Jenkins-Smith and St Clair
conclude that this analysis shows the importance of exogenous shocks to the
system, and the importance of core sets of beliefs. We might also note the
significant role of change in the White House, and that opposed coalitions form
tighter bonds when it becomes more difficult to broker compromise. This study tells
us little about the power of different groups, including government agencies, to
shape policy, apart from suggesting that changes in the external environment affect
power, though it does demonstrate the usefulness of quantitative techniques to map
the relationship of different coalitions. This approach therefore does not seem to be
a *rival* to those examining the bargaining power of different groups in different
institutional settings. The focus of the research problem seems rather different.[35]

In some policy-areas there may be virtual unanimity over the correct solution.
Brown and Stewart demonstrate that over a period of twenty years, the issue of
airline deregulation in the US altered from should we deregulate, to how are we
going to deregulate, to in the 1980 presidential election how good at deregulation
was Carter versus how much better would Reagan be.[36] Similarly in Britain we can
see how views on management of the macro-economy have changed from the
time of the famous letter to *The Times* signed by 364 economists against the
Conservative government's economic policies.[37] Wickham-Jones is correct in his
argument that monetarism triumphed not because of the quality of its ideas but
because of political power within the Conservative Party; the coalition welded
together transformed the dominant assumptions. Only recently have ideas in the
Labour Party about full employment re-emerged as a credible alternative economic
package to some form of monetarist policy. Another example is Barke's account of
changes in Federal communications policy.[38] He suggests that the views of the
Federal Communications Commission, largely insulated from dominant political
forces in the White House and Congress, changed over time largely because of
technological innovation and a sea-change in general attitudes towards the
market's ability to ensure quality.

The importance of this approach can be seen when we consider how some policy
arenas seem to generate policies which are against the grain of the ideology of the
government of the day. Think of the 1989 'Children's Act' which seemingly ties the

hands of social workers and the police when dealing with criminalized children. How was this passed by a 'hang 'em and flog 'em' Thatcherite Conservative government? It was helped by the publicity given to child molestation at this time, but was inspired by a policy community of experts who argued that if children were respected they might become more responsible and invested them with the rights of adults. Government policy was led by a professional advocacy coalition put together over at least a twenty-year period.[39] Similarly the 'Health Service and Community Care Act' was driven by a convergence of professionals believing in a new type of care and the Treasury seeing the opportunity to slash social health budgets. Often, the technical solution offered by professionals can in retrospect be seen as disastrous, particularly as it is interpreted by other interested parties.[40]

The advocacy coalition framework has generated enormous interest because it reintroduces the concept of ideas and their origins in the study of policy change. By concentrating on beliefs as a generator of policy change they force attention away from seeing public policy simply as a battle between groups, though knowledge is a forceful source of power, and one way of using knowledge is in open rational debate. The policy advocacy coalition proponents do not demonstrate, however, that public policy is a result of open rational debate, and would not want to try. The approach is perfectly compatible with bargaining models of the policy process. By concentrating upon two primary causes of policy change, the values of coalition members and exogenous shocks to the system, the advocacy coalition framework perhaps misses out on the way in which such ideas are used and misused by other agencies, notably government agencies such as the Treasury to save money. Nevertheless, as the leading exponent of the advocacy framework coalition has maintained, together with institutional rational choice the framework may prove one of the most useful theories of the policy process.[41] Institutional rational choice links together properties of individuals within a decision-making process and properties of the structure under which decision-making takes place.[42] I have argued that the policy network approach is driven by properties of the actors, but the sociological network approach concentrates attention upon network characteristics.

The Sociological Network Approach

The descriptive approach uses 'network' as a metaphor. There is nothing methodologically wrong with this, until the metaphors are overblown into classifications posing as explanatory models. The sociological tradition does employ explanatory network models and has been used by numerous European and North American political scientists. In this section I will explain what they are, how they may be used in conjunction with a bargaining model of power; and suggest why this approach is limited. Formalism in political science is to be encouraged, but we should not have inflated expectations of how much it will teach us. In the end the descriptive approach, bounded by a formalized theory, will prove most fruitful.

Consider Figure 1. In 1(i) we have four dots on a page, each joined to the others by six lines forming the complete set of possible single-joinings. In 1(ii) and (iii) we have the dots joined in subsets of ways in 1(i). All these figures can be called networks. The first can be seen as the logically complete set of single-line interactions

Figure 1

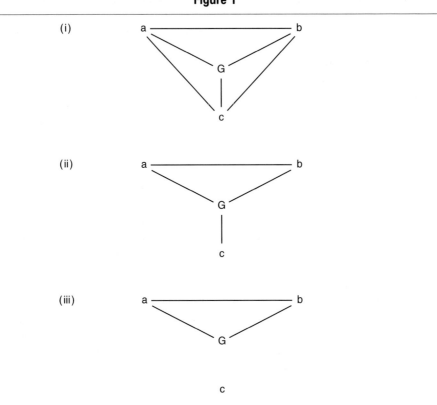

between the four dots. The second two are subsets of the first. If the lines represent contacts at the political level then we can see exclusion in (ii) as one dot has no line to others. In (iii) we can see one dot is only linked to G and not the other dots. This might represent a group outside the cosy 'policy community' represented by {*a*, *b*, G}. How influential *c* is cannot be determined by the diagram; that requires empirical research. Now, note the difference between l(i), (ii) and (iii) are contained in the fact that they have different lines. The dots and their labelling are exactly the same. If the dots stand for actors (whether people, organizations, classes, or groups in the Bentley/Truman sense) they are invariate across the networks. What makes the networks different are the lines which represent the relationships between the dots. Networks are distinguished one from another by the relations between the actors. In other words, the networks denote different structures. Network analysis is, necessarily, structural.[43] These linkages or different structural features of different networks can be examined by a number of mathematical techniques. Relational data on organizations drawn as a network can be represented in data matrices which can be transformed in various ways to reveal underlying structures.[43] In the sorts of networks we are considering there is likely to be a focal point – a government agency – or rather a set of focal points. The social network literature has developed different measures of centrality to map important individuals within certain social networks.[45] Modifications of such measures, taking into account the greater exchange power of government agencies, could be developed to try to measure the closeness of community in certain networks. Graph theory has developed to try to measure the density (inclusiveness and number of connections between actors) of different networks.[46] These measures may all stand as independent variables, for they are measures of characteristics of the *lines* between the dots and are not characteristics of the dots themselves. They are thus features of the network and not of its members. Figure 2 for example specifies two types of network with the members with the same individual characteristics, and the same two types of network with members with different characteristics. If the dots are, say, professional actors linked to a government agency G, the policy community may vary in the type of policy outputs given the different type of network relations in network 2(i) and 2(ii). In 2(iii) and 2(iv) we have the same two types of network as defined by the lines, but here the crosses stand for, say, producer groups with different sets of resources to the professional actors. Hence, these two networks, whilst sharing network characteristics with the professional networks, may have a different type of policy process. We can see here that we may generalize across network type, 2(i) and 2(iii) sharing network features, and 2(ii) and 2(iv) sharing network features, and across network member type, 2(i) and 2(ii) sharing membership features, and 2(iii) and 2(iv) sharing membership features. Table 2 specifies the characteristics that may be of most interest to the network members and the characteristics of the network. The characterization of the relationship into properties of members and properties of the network should

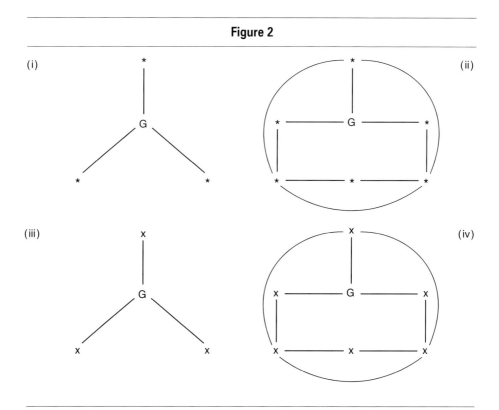

Figure 2

Table 2: Network characteristics

Characteristics of members (dots)	Characteristics of relations (lines)
1. Knowledge/information	1. Centrality
2. Legitimacy	2. Number of connections
3. Ability to conditionally change others incentive structures	3. Inclusiveness
4. Ability to unconditionally change others incentive structures	4. Rules of Interaction
	5. Embeddedness
5. Reputation	

not be overdrawn. The power of members is dependent upon the powers of other members given the relationship between them. Similarly the type of relationship members have will be dependent upon their resources. Nevertheless this *analytic* division into members' characteristics and network characteristics can enable us to keep in clearer view the relationship of variables in any given explanation and avoid the confusion of dependent and independent variables.[47]

Sociological network analysis has been used in four major ways.[48] First, variation in the structural ties between network members has been measured as a function of the individual properties of members and the wider society.[49] Secondly, sociologists have studied differences in individual behaviour or psychological health as a function of network characteristics.[50] Thirdly, the behaviour of a group is analysed as a function of the network in which the group operates.[51] Finally, studies have suggested that network characteristics may overcome other features of a group, such as overcoming the 'law of large numbers' under certain forms of network and that certain types of network allow for the easier transmission of information.[52]

Some of the theoretical advances in network theory are of a great importance and are intimately linked with bargaining models of power. Granovetter's early argument that the embeddedness of transactions in recurrent relations and networks increase the use of informal contracts,[53] has been extended to prove that embeddedness allows the development of trust and reciprocity in multi-period games.[54] The density of a network therefore affects the degree and speed at which cooperation may develop. This may help to explain the role of community in cooperative relations and the fact of density rather than small-size *per se* may be the important variable.[55] These formal developments in sociological network and game theory generate a set of research questions for political scientists investigating policy networks. How far the sociological approaches to network mapping can be used by political scientists or how far the formal results can be directly translated into quantitative empirical studies is more open to question. The limitations of the sociological approach to policy networks are best illustrated with reference to one or two of the better examples of its application in political settings.

Laumann and Pappi applied network analysis to élite structures to map a power élite using more advanced techniques than Hunter's, though the relationship between the élite maps and policy outcomes remain unclear.[56] Later work has

Figure 3: Event Linkages on Basis of Participation Patterns

		Event B	
		Participate	Not participate
Event A	Participate	a	b
	Not participate	c	d

attempted to relate policy influences to these maps. Laumann *et al.* have attempted to map, in two-dimensions, the organizations involved in various policy domains.[57] The maps are constructed by identifying organizations with interests in a particular policy area and assessing the level of their activity. By using a method of identifying significant decisions in a policy area, they have attempted to see what linkages between organizations exist across sets of different issues within the same policy area.[58] Their method assumes an organization could (a) participate in the first event (*i*) and continue to participate in the second (*j*), (b) participate in the first but not the second, (c) not participate in the first but participate in the second, (d) not participate in either. This can be represented in a matrix as in Figure 3. The relationship between events *i* and *j* is then given by Yule's $Y = (a.d/b.c) - 1/(a.d/b.c) + 1$. Where Y is positive the organizations tend to participate in the same events; where Y is negative organizations non-activity in one event is non-randomly associated with activity in the other. This can demonstrate the degree to which interests overlap in some policy domains. Following up this work, Laumann *et al.* then attribute a pro or con attitude towards each event on the basis of interview evidence. Comparing attitudes to participation Laumann *et al.* conclude that technocratic and strategic rather than ideological considerations drive participation. They then map their organizations by blockmodelling on two-dimensional space according to organizations taking up opposing or supporting positions. A description drawn from one of their maps shows its usefulness and its limitations:

> we find the American Agricultural Movement at the extreme lower lefthand side of the space diametrically opposite the National Cattlemen's Association at the upper righthand corner ... and the Environmental Defense Funds in the lower righthand corner, thus forming an equilateral triangle of opposing interests ... The Farm Bureau, like its more politically radical neighbor in the space, the American Agricultural Movement, represents grain producers. The Cattlemen's interests are generally aligned with those groups that process and consume grain, including the Milk Producers, General Mills, the Grocery Manufacturers Association, and so forth. The Environmental Defense Fund is the most active of the labor, environmental, and consumer groups that challenge, among other things, the farmers' use of pesticides and water.[59]

In other words, the years of hard data collection and formal analysis has yielded results which look plausible given what we already know about the groups concerned. This is too harsh: the paradox of formal analysis is that it must yield results which by and large fit with what we know by descriptive methods – otherwise we know something has gone wrong with our formal analysis. What we require to justify formalism is some surprising results, or paradoxical conclusions, which then justify closer qualitative analysis. Laumann *et al.* can claim some success in this regard. Their most interesting finding is that organizational coalition-building is highly unstable and in the Agriculture, Health and Energy domains there is no single partition which might coincide with a left-right ideological cleavage. Only in the Labor domain is there such a cleavage. They suggest that descriptive approaches probably exaggerate the degree of stability of participation, consensus and cleavage in policy-making. In fact we would predict this conclusion by applying some of the results of formal theorizing about government coalition building.[60] We know that as the number of ideological cleavages increases so does the expected instability of any coalition. In this case, though there is no need for formal coalitions, we should still expect the instability of informal alliances to increase with the number of cleavages.

The fruition of this approach is seen in *The Hollow Core*.[61] This book utilizes the formal network approach within a more discursive discussion of the policy process. Building on the techniques described above and using a series of smallest-space analyses the authors chart who bargains with whom in four policy domains. They are able to diagram the relationship of organizations within communication networks and the structure of conflict and cooperation comparing across the four policy domains. Whilst variations occur, they discover in all four domains that the networks vary in three-dimensional space with a hollow core – that is there are no policy influentials mediating or dominating at the centre. This a powerful use of formal network analysis, but even here caution must be applied when using it as an empirical analysis of various competing 'theories' of the state. By creating three-dimensional maps of communication networks through groups targeting different sets of government officials (within executive agencies and congressional committees) and through conflict and cooperation, the core may in fact be filled by the government agents as the termini of the network (that is, at which the communication is directed). As Heinz *et al.* acknowledge we cannot say whether these government agents act as interested participants, disinterested intermediaries or are 'captured' by certain groups.[62] Again therefore, the network analysis is more of a map of the policy process, than a fully fledged explanation of it.

Volker Schneider similarly uses three-dimensional mapping of organizations in two German policy domains – chemicals and telecommunications.[63] Demonstrating different structures in each he suggests that they seem to create a different mechanism of policy-making. In the first a corporatist picture of government emerges with the monopolistic Association of Chemical Producers and to a lesser degree a monopolistic trade union. In telecommunications a more pluralistic network is mapped. But why the maps are different is not explained by the network analysis itself. Rather we are left with the suggestion that the greater distributional conflict in telecommunications and the fact it is an emerging sector compared to the chemicals sector explains the different character of the networks.

Pappi and Knoke,[64] using James Coleman's exchange model of power,[65] also demonstrate the limitations of formal network approaches. They attempt to compare the relative power of functionally similar organizations within the Labour policy networks in Germany and the US, and the relative power of organizations within policy communities within the two networks. Again, despite an impressive attempt to quantitatively compare relative powers cross-nationally, the results are ultimately disappointing if not misleading. Coleman's is a constant-sum measure of power. But one of the most important, though least trumpeted, results from the policy network approach is how fragmented and separate groups (including government agencies) are able to act concertedly to wield more power than the sum of each member. Similarly, breaking up governance structures into differentiated quasi-governmental organizations within newly created policy communities can cause overall power loss.[66] Pappi and Knoke's numbers are not merely difficult to interpret, they are probably meaningless in terms of the concept of group and state power in mainstream discussion of state 'theory'.

A final example also reveals the limitations of formal network analysis. Using diagraph techniques Phillips maps the relationship between 33 national Canadian women's organizations.[67] She demonstrates that these diverse groups form a loosely coupled network bound by a collective identity of liberal feminism. She then tries to measure their influence in terms of their financial resources and network position by measuring their perceived impact as rated by a selected subset of government officials. In a multiple regression analysis size of budget was found to be a poor predictor of perceived influence whilst network position was found to be a strong influence. However, since network position is given in terms of centrality, and relative centrality is defined in terms of the number of ties involving a group divided by the total number of ties minus one, this is hardly surprising. Organizations which act as a conduit to government officials for other organizations (and therefore rightly identified by her method as more central) are almost bound to be *perceived* by government officials as being more influential. Government officials are hardly likely to identify as influential organizations with which they have few if any dealings, even if these peripheral groups *determine* the policies of the more centralized ones. The method of analysis here determined the results.

I do not wish to appear too sceptical about the usefulness of formal network analysis. If the properties of networks are to be clearly identified as causally efficacious then only this type of technique will demonstrate this. Any demonstration, no matter how weak, will then allow us to draw some inferences about broader structural effects even when these are not quantifiable. Furthermore, it is pernicious to damn a research programme too early in its life; only through attempting quantification with new techniques can we learn the limitations and try to overcome them in new and dynamic ways. However, there is a tendency amongst formal theorists to promise more than they can deliver.

Conclusions

Marin and Mayntz suggest that formal and informal network analysis need to be combined.[68] I have argued that only formal network analysis actually provides explanation in terms of the *properties of networks*. Informal network analysis would gain more by concentrating on the features of actors which bargaining theory teaches us are important. Thus we will learn more about the similarities and variances between policy networks. The resources actors use are in part determined

and constrained by structured networks and the properties formal network analysis
has elucidated. Quantification in the manner of the sociological network tradition
may enable us to see some of the general features which attach to network
structures. However, network analysis has proved inadequate in providing fully
determined causal analysis of particular networks in structural terms. Some network theorists simply believe this to be due to the state of the research programme
and the quality of the data recorded thus far. I have tried to argue that this is not
so. To promise that network analysis will eventually go beyond demonstrating
general features of networks will ultimately lead to disappointment. The quality of
the data is necessarily too poor for determinate predictions because collecting such
high quality data requires us to know the answers to the questions we are posing.
Such answers are themselves open to competing interpretations even for those
involved in the events. This is not an argument against formalism, but it is an
argument against too high expectations from it. Science may end in algebra, but
the nature of the data will ensure that social science will not end argument.

Notes

1 David Marsh and R. A. W. Rhodes, 'Policy communities and issue networks: beyond typology' in
David Marsh and R. A. W. Rhodes (eds), *Policy Networks in British Government*. Oxford: Oxford
University Press, 1992.

2 Michael M. Atkinson and William D. Coleman, 'Strong states and weak states: sectoral policy
networks in advanced capitalist economies', *British Journal of Political Science*, 19 (1989), 47–67;
Michael M. Atkinson and William D. Coleman, 'Policy networks, policy communities and the prob-
lems of governance', *Governance*, 5 (1992), 154–80; William D. Coleman, 'State traditions and compre-
hensive business associations: a comparative structural analysis', *Political Studies*, 38 (1990), 231–52;
William D. Coleman and Grace Skogstad, 'Policy Communities and Policy Networks: a Structural
Approach', in William D. Coleman and Grace Skogstad (eds), *Policy Communities and Public Policy in
Canada*. Toronto: Copp Clark Pitman, 1990; Martin Smith, *Pressure Power and Policy: State Autonomy and
Policy Networks in Britain and the United States*. Hemel Hempstead, Harvester Wheatsheaf, 1993.

3 Paul A. Sabatier, 'Knowledge, policy-oriented learning, and policy change: an advocacy coalition
framework', *Knowledge, Creation, Diffusion, Utilization*, 8 (1987), 648–92; Paul A. Sabatier, 'An advocacy
coalition framework of policy-change and the role of policy-oriented learning therein', *Policy Sciences*,
21 (1988), 129–68; Paul A. Sabatier and Neil Pelkey, 'Incorporating multiple actors and guidance
instruments into models of regulatory policy-making: an advocacy coalition framework', *Administration and Society*, 19 (1987), 236–63 and Paul A. Sabatier and Hank C. Jenkins-Smith (eds), *Policy
Change and Learning: An Advocacy Coalition Approach*. Boulder. Westview, 1993. For 'epistemic communities' see the essays in *International Organization*, 46, 1 (1992) [special issue Peter M. Haas (ed.),
Knowledge, Power and International Policy Coordination].

4 Due to misunderstanding of an earlier paper, Keith Dowding, 'Policy networks: don't stretch a good
idea too far', in Patrick Dunleavy and Jeffrey Stanyer (eds), *Contemporary Political Studies, 1994 vol. 1*
(Belfast, The Political Studies Association of the United Kingdom, 1994), where I was taken to be
lauding sociological network analysis I wish to reinforce this point. Sociological network analysis does
constitute a reasonable model since network characteristics do stand as independent variables. How
useful a model it will prove to be is, logically, a separate issue.

5 Ernest S. Griffiths, *The Impasse of Democracy*. New York: Harrison-Wilton, 1939.

6 David Truman, *The Governmental Process*. New York: Knopf, 2nd ed., 1971: Douglas Cater, *Power in
Washington*. New York: Random House, 1964; J. Leiper Freeman, *The Political Process*. New York:
Random House, 1965.

7 Cater, *Power in Washington*.

8 Charles O. Jones, 'American politics and the organization of energy decision-making', *Annual Review
of Energy*, 4 (1979), 99–121.

9 G. Peters, *American Public Policy*. Basingstoke, Macmillan, 2nd ed., 1986.

10 R. Ripley and G. Franklin, *Congress, the Bureaucracy and Public Policy*. Homewood, Dorsey, 2nd ed.,
1984, p. 16.

11 H. Heclo, 'Issue networks and the executive establishment', in A. King (ed.), *The New American Political System*. Washington, DC, American Enterprise Inc., 1978.

12 Hugh Heclo and Aaron Wildavsky, *The Private Government of Public Money*. London: Macmillan, 1974.

13 J. J. Richardson and A. G. Jordan, *Governing under Pressure: British Politics in a Post-Parliamentary Democracy*. Oxford: Martin Robertson, 1979; A. G. Jordan and J. J. Richardson, *Government and Pressure Groups in Britain*. Oxford: Clarendon, 1987; A. G. Jordan and J. J. Richardson, *British Politics and the Policy Process*. London: Unwin Hyman, 1987.

14 See A. G. Jordan, 'Sub-governments, policy communities and networks: refilling the old bottles?', *Journal of Theoretical Politics*, 2 (1990), 319–38, for the history of their approach.

15 Jeremy J. Richardson, William A. Maloney and Wolfgang Rudig, 'The dynamics of policy change: lobbying and water privatization', *Public Administration*, 70 (1992), 157–75.

16 Steven Wilks and Maurice Wright (eds), *Comparative Government-Industry Relations*. Oxford, Clarendon, 1987; Maurice Wright, 'Policy community, policy network and comparative industrial policies', *Political Studies*, 36 (1988), 593–614; Steven Wilks, 'Government-industry relations', *Public Administration*, 67 (1989), 329–39. Other publications from the initiative include A. Cawson, K. Morgan, D. Webber, P. Holmes and A. Stevens, *Hostile Brothers: Competition and Closure in the European Electronics Industry*. Oxford: Clarendon 1988: Wynn P. Grant, William Paterson and Colin Whitson, *Government and the Chemical Industry: a Comparative Study of Britain and West Germany*. Oxford: Clarendon, 1988. Hancher and M. Moran (eds), *Capitalism, Culture and Economic Regulation*, Oxford: Clarendon, 1989. For my criticisms of the Wilks-Wright model, see Keith Dowding 'Policy networks'.

17 See especially A. Cawson, P. Holmes and A. Stevens 'The interaction between firms and the state in France: The telecommunications and consumer electronic sectors', in Wilks and Wright, *Comparative Government-Industry Relations*; and Cawson *et al.*, *Hostile Brothers*.

18 David Marsh, 'Beyond new institutionalism: meso-level analysis is all very well but let's not lose sight of the macro questions' ECPR Joint Sessions, 30 March 4 April, 1992, Limerick.

19 More realistically one cannot have a theory about living creatures which does not apply to insects, though one may have a theory about warm-blooded animals which does not apply to insects. Even here, one would be seeking more fundamental theories, such as the difference warm blood makes. Analogously a theory about democratic states needs a more fundamental ('micro-level' if you like) theory about the behavioural difference democracy makes to the actions of institutions, groups, and so on.

20 Of those on offer only new right and Marxist approaches seem to avoid this criticism: see for example Patrick Dunleavy and Brendan O'Leary, *Theories of the State*. Houndmills: Macmillan, 1987.

21 See Marsh and Rhodes, 'Policy communities and issue networks' for this updated typology.

22 Rhodes, *Control and Power in Central-Local Relations*; R. A. W. Rhodes '"Power dependence" theories of central local relations: a critical assessment' in Goldsmith, *New Research in Central-Local Relations*; Rhodes, *Beyond Westminster and Whitehall*. I am rightly accused of ignoring the power dependence model in 'Policy networks' by R. A. W. Rhodes and David Marsh, 'Policy networks: "defensive" comments, modest claims, and plausible research strategies' paper to PSA Annual Conference, Swansea, March 1994. However, 'power-dependence' does not rate a citation in the index of either of the Marsh and Rhodes edited collections supposedly using the Rhodes model.

23 Rhodes, *Beyond Westminster and Whitehall*, p. 42.

24 See Dowding, *Rational Choice and Political Power* for discussion of these; the first four are based on the work of J. C. Harsanyi, 'Measurement of social power, opportunity costs and the theory of two-person bargaining games' and 'Measurement of social power in *n*-person reciprocal power situations', in his *Essays on Ethics, Social Behaviour and Scientific Explanation* Dordrecht, Reidel, 1976, the last on modern bargaining theory: see for example Eric Rasmusen, *Games and Information* Oxford, Blackwell, 1991. The key issue here is that concentrating upon bargaining resources, *however they are specified*, is more fruitful than trying to explain outcomes in terms of different types of network.

25 Rhodes, '"Power dependence" theories', p. 8.

26 This can also be applied to broad categories such as ideology: see Dowding, *Rational Choice and Political Power*, ch. 7; and Raymond Boudon, *The Analysis of Ideology*. Cambridge: Polity, 1989.

27 Dowding, *Rational Choice and Political Power*, ch. 3; Keith Dowding, 'Rational Mobilization' in Patrick Dunleavy and Jeffrey Stanyer (eds), *Contemporary Political Studies, 1994 vol. 2*.

28 Paul A. Sabatier, 'Policy Change over a Decade or More' in Sabatier and Jenkins-Smith (eds), *Policy Change and Learning*, p. 16.

29 This is another defining feature of Rhodes's work.

30 William J. Drake, 'Ideas, interests, and institutionalization: "trade in services" and the Uruguay round'; M. J. Peterson, 'Cetologists, environmentalists, and the international management of whaling'; Peter M. Haas, 'Banning chlorofluorocarbons: epistemic community efforts to protect stratospheric ozone'; Raymond F. Hopkins, 'Reform in the international food aid regime: the role of consensual knowledge'; Ethan Barnaby Kapstein 'Between power and purpose: central bankers and the politics of regulatory convergence'; and G. John Ikenberry, 'A world economy restored: expert consensus and the Anglo-American post-war settlement' all in *International Organization* 46, 1 (1992).

31 See especially James K. Sebenius, 'Challenging conventional explanations of international cooperation: negotiation analysis and the case of epistemic communities', *International Organization*, 46 (1992), 323–66.

32 John F. Munro, 'California water politics: explaining policy change in a cognitively polarized subsystem' in Sabatier and Jenkins-Smith, *Policy Change and Learning*.

33 Paul A. Sabatier, 'From Vague Consensus to Clearly Differentiated Coalitions: Environmental policy at Lake Tahoe, 1964–1985', in Sabatier and Jenkins-Smith, *Policy Change and Learning*.

34 Hank C. Jenkins-Smith and Gilbert K. St Clair, 'The Politics of Offshore Energy: Empirically Testing the Advocacy Coalition Framework' in Sabatier and Jenkins-Smith, *Policy Change and Learning*.

35 The different focus of institutional rational choice and the advocacy coalition framework seems apparent in Hank C. Jenkins-Smith, 'Alternative theories of the policy process: reflections on research strategy for the study of nuclear waste policy', *PS: Political Science and Politics* 24, (1991), 157–66.

36 Anthony E. Brown and Joseph Steward, Jr, 'Competing Advocacy Coalitions, Policy Evolution, Airline Deregulation', in Sabatier and Jenkins-Smith, *Policy Change and Learning*.

37 See Mark Wickham-Jones 'Monetarism and its critics: the university economists' protest of 1981' *Political Quarterly*, 6 (1992), 171 85.

38 Richard P. Barke 'Managing Technological Change in Federal Communications Policy: the Role of Industry Advisory Groups', in Sabatier and Jenkins-Smith, *Policy Change and Learning*.

39 Nigel Parton, *Governing the Family: Childcare, Child Protection and the State*. London: Macmillan, 1991, esp. ch. 6; c.f. Nigel Parton *The Politics of Child Abuse*. London: Macmillan, 1985.

40 Patrick Dunleavy, *The Politics of Mass Housing in Britain*. Oxford: Clarendon, 1981; and Patrick Dunleavy, 'Professions and policy change: notes towards a model of ideological corporatism', *Public Administration Bulletin*, 36 (1981), 3–16.

41 Paul A. Sabatier. 'Toward better theories of the policy process', *PS: Political Science and Politics*, 24 (1991), 147–56.

42 See Elinor Ostrom and Larry Kiser, 'The Three Worlds of Action', in Elinor Ostrom (ed.), *Strategies of Political Inquiry*. Beverly Hills: Sage, 1982.

43 David Knoke, *Political Networks: the Structural Perspective*. Cambridge: Cambridge University Press, 1990.

44 David Knoke and James H. Kuklinski, *Network Analysis*. Beverly Hills: Sage, 1982.

45 L. C. Freeman, 'Centrality in social networks: I conceptual clarification', *Social Networks*, 1 (1979); P. Bonacich, 'Technique for analysing overlapping memberships', in H. Costner (ed.), *Sociological Methodology, 1973*. San Francisco: Jossey Bass, 1972; P. Bonacich, 'Power and centrality: a family of measures', *American Sociological Review*, 52 (1987).

46 N. Christophides, *Graph Theory: an Algorithmic Approach*. New York: Academic, 1975; P. V. Marsden and N. Lin (eds), *Social Structure and Network Analysis*. Beverly Hills; Sage, 1982.

47 See my critique of Smith, *Pressure, Power and Policy* in Dowding 'Policy networks'.

48 Philippa Pattison, *Algebraic Models for Social Networks*. Cambridge, Cambridge University Press, 1993.

49 P. M. Blau, *Inequality and Heterogeneity: a Primitive Theory of Social Structure*. New York, Free, 1977; C. Fischer, *To Dwell Among Friends: Personal Networks in Town and City*. Chicago, Chicago University Press, 1982; C. Fischer, R. M. Jackson, C. A. Steuve and L. McAllister Jones, *Networks and Places: Social Relations in the Urban Setting*. New York, Free, 1977; B. Wellmen, 'The community question: the intimate networks of East Yorkers', *American Journal of Sociology*, 84 (1979), 1201 31.

50 R. C. Kessler, R. H. Price and C. B. Wortmann, 'Social factors in psychopathology', *Annual Review of Psychology*, 36 (1985), 531 72; S. Cohen and S. L. Syme (eds), *Social Support and Health*. New York; Academic, 1985; M. Granovetter, 'Economic action and social structure: the problem of embeddedness', *American Journal of Sociology*, 91 (1985), 481–510; W. E. Baker, 'The social structure of a national securities market', *American Journal of Sociology*, 89 (1983), 775–811; K. E. Campbell, P. V. Marsden and J. S. Hurlbert, 'Social resources and socioeconomic status', *Social Networks*, 8 (1986), 97–117.

51 E. O. Laumann and F. U. Pappi, *Networks of Collective Action: a Perspective on Community Influence Systems*. New York: Academic, 1976.

52 M. Granovetter, *Getting a Job: a Study of Contacts and Careers*. Cambridge MA: Harvard University Press, 1974; N. Friedkin, 'A test of the structural features of Granovetter's strength of weak ties', *Social Networks*, 2 (1980), 411–20; N. Lin and M. Dumin, 'Access to occupations through social ties', *Social Networks*, 8 (1986), 365 85; N. Lin, W. M. Ensel and J. C. Vaughn, 'Social resources and strength of ties: structural factors in occupational status attainment', *American Sociological Review*, 46 (1981), 393–76.

53 M. Granovetter, 'Economic action and social structure'.

54 W. Raub and J. Weesie, 'Reputation and efficiency in social interactions: an example of network effects', *American Journal of Sociology*, 96, (1990), 626–54; J. Weesie and W. Raub, 'The management of trust relations', paper presented at World Congress of Sociology, Bielefeld, July (1994).

55 Size is important to the community arguments of Michael Taylor, *Community, Anarchy and Liberty*. Cambridge: Cambridge University Press, 1982, and *The Possibility of Cooperation*. Cambridge: Cambridge University Press, 1987. Of course, empirically small size and density may well be correlated.

56 F. Hunter, *Community Power Structure*. Chapel Hill: University of North Carolina Press, 1953; Laumann and Pappi, *Networks of Collective Action*.

57 Edward O. Laumann and John P. Heinz with Robert Nelson and Robert Salisbury, 'Organizations in political action: representing interests in national policy-making' in Marin and Mayntz, *Policy Networks*; John P. Heinz, Edward O. Laumann, Robert L. Nelson and Robert H. Salisbury, *The Hollow Core: Private Interests in National Policy Making*. Cambridge MA: Harvard University Press, 1993.

58 Edward O. Laumann and David Knoke, *The Organizational State: Social Choice in National Policy Domains*. Madison, University of Wisconsin Press, 1987, ch. 1.

59 Laumann *et al.*, 'Organizations in political action', pp. 87–8.

60 See Michael Laver and Norman Schofield, *Multiparty Government: the Politics of Coalition in Europe*. Oxford: Oxford University Press, 1990 for a general review of the literature.

61 Heinz *et al. Hollow Core*.

62 Heinz *et al. Hollow Core*, pp. 377–8.

63 V. Schneider, 'Control as a Generalized Exchange Medium within the Policy Process? A Theoretical Interpretation of a Policy Analysis on Chemicals Control' in Bernd Marin (ed.), *Governance and Generalized Exchange: Self-Organizing Networks in Action*. Frankfurt: Campus, 1990; V. Schneider and R. Werle, 'Policy Networks in the German Telecommunications Domain' in Marin and Mayntz, *Policy Networks*; V. Schneider, 'The structure of policy networks: a comparison of the "chemicals control" and "telecommunications" policy domains in Germany', *European Journal of Political Research*, 21 (1992), 109–29.

64 F. U. Pappi and D. Knoke, 'Political Exchange in the German and American Labour Policy Domains' in Marin and Mayntz, *Policy Networks*.

65 James S. Coleman, *Foundations of Social Theory*. Cambridge MA: Belknapp, 1990.

66 Keith Dowding, Patrick Dunleavy, Desmond King and Helen Margetts, 'Rational choice and community power structures', *Political Studies* 43, 2 (1955), 265–77.

67 Susan D. Phillips 'Meaning and structure in social movements: mapping the network of national Canadian women's organizations', *Canadian Journal of Political Science*, 24 (1991), 755–81.

68 Bernd Marin and Reynate Mayntz, 'Introduction: Studying Policy Networks', in Marin and Mayntz, *Policy Networks*.

Notes on Contributors

James Alt is Frank G. Thomson Professor of Government at Harvard University. His publications include *Perspectives on Positive Political Economy* (Cambridge University Press, 1990) and numerous articles on political economy issues.

Malcolm Anderson was Professor of Politics at the University of Edinburgh, until he retired in 1998. His recent publications include *Frontiers: Territory and State Foundation in the Modern World*.

Brian Barry is Arnold A. Saltzman Professor of Philosophy and Political Science at Columbia University, New York. His recent publications include the first two volumes of a three-volume Treatise on Social Justice, published in 1989 and 1995 and *Culture and Equality: An Egalitarian Critique of Multiculturalism*, published in 2000.

R. J. Bhansali is Professor of Statistics at the University of Liverpool and Fellow, Institute of Mathematical Statistics, Fellow, American Statistical Association. He is the author of numerous articles and chapters on Time Series Analysis, especially on Spectral Analysis, Prediction Theory and Model Selection.

Paul Bissell was Research Officer on an ESRC-funded project on Conservative Party Members during 1992–3, and now works in business.

G. D. H. Cole (1889–1959) was a Fellow of All Souls, Oxford, Chichele Professor and Social and Political Thought, and an English Guild Socialist. He was the author of numerous books including *Guild Socialism Re-Stated* (1920), *Social Theory* (1920) and the multi-volume *A History of Socialism* (1958).

Diane Coole is Professor of Political Philosophy at Queen Mary and Westfield College, London. Her publications include *Women in Political Theory* (1993) and *Negativity and Politics* (2000).

Ivor Crewe is Vice Chancellor of the University of Essex, where he was previously Professor of Government. His recent publications (with co-authors) include *Political Communications: why Labour won the general election of 1997* (2000) and *Was it Blair who won it?: leadership effects and the 1997 British general election* (1998).

Karl Deutsch (1912–1992) was Professor of Political Science at a number of American universities, the last being Harvard. His publications included *The Nerves of Government: models of political communication and control* (1963) and *Politics and Government: how people decide their fate* (1980).

Published by Blackwell Publishers, 108 Cowley Road, Oxford OX4 1JF, UK and 350 Main Street, Malden, MA 02148, USA

Keith Dowding is Professor of Political Science at the London School of Economics and Political Science. His publications include *Rational Choice and Political Power* (1991) and *The Civil Service* (1995).

Graeme Duncan was Dean of Humanities and Social Sciences at LaTrobe University in Australia until 1998 when he retired.

John Dunn is Professor of Political Theory at Cambridge University and a Fellow of Kings College. His recent publications include *Political Obligation in its Historical Context* (1980) and *Interpreting Political Responsibility* (1990).

C. A. E. Goodhart is Norman Sosnow Professor of Banking and Finance at the London School of Economics and Political Science. His recent publications include *Myths about the Lender of Last Resort* (1999) and *Recent Developments in Central Banking: some special features of the monetary policy committee and of the European system of Central Banks* (1999).

B. D. Graham is Visiting Research Professor in Politics at the University of Sussex. His recent publications include *Representation and Party Politics: a comparative perspective* (1993) and *Choice and Democratic Order: the French Socialist Party, 1937–1950* (1994).

Steven Lukes is Professor of Sociology at New York University and will be Centennial Visiting Professor at the London School of Economics from January 2001. His most recent publications include: *Moral Conflict and Politics* (1991) and *The Curious Enlightenment of Professor Caritat* (1995).

J. P. Nettl (1926–68) worked principally at the University of Leeds before his untimely death in an aircraft accident. His publications included *Political Mobilization: a sociological analysis of methods and concepts.* (1967); *Rosa Luxemburg.* (1969) and *International Systems and the Modernization of Societies* (co-authored, 1968).

Michael Oakeshott (1901–90) was Fellow of Gonville and Caius College, Cambridge, and succeeded Harold Laski as Professor of Political Science at the London School of Economics and Political Science in 1951 where he remained until his retirement in 1967. He was author of *Experience and its Modes* (1933), *Rationalism in Politics and other Essays* (1962) and *On Human Conduct* (1975).

Nelson Polsby is Heller Professor of Political Science at the University of California, Berkeley. His publications include *Community Power and Political Theory* (1980), *Congress and the Presidency* (1986), *New Federalist Papers* (with others, 1997) and *Presidential Elections* (originally with Aaron Wildavsky, 2000).

Jeremy Richardson is Nuffield Professor of Comparative European Politics, Director of the Centre for European Politics, Economics and Society, and a Fellow of Nuffield College, University of Oxford. His recent publications include *European Union: Power and Policy Making* (1996) and (with William Maloney) *Managing Policy Change in Britain. The Politics of Water* (1995).

Gillian Rose, (1947–95), was Professor of Social and Political Thought at the University of Warwick. She wrote numerous books on modern European social and political theory, as well as the moving philosophical memoir *Love's Work* (1995) written whilst she was struggling with cancer.

Bo Särlvik, who died in 1998, was a prominent Swedish political scientist specializing in electoral analysis, who was also Professor of Government for some years at the University of Essex. His major publications included the co-authored *Decade of Dealignment: the Conservative victory of 1979 and electoral trends in the 1970s* (1983).

Patrick Seyd is Professor of Politics at the University of Sheffield. His recent publications (co-authored) include *Labour's Grass Roots* (1992); *True Blues: the politics of Conservative Party membership* (1994) and *Labour and Conservative Party Members 1990–92* (1996).

Hillel Steiner is Professor of Political Philosophy at the University of Manchester. The author of numerous journal articles on right, liberty, justice and moral reasoning, his books include *An Essay on Rights* (1994).

Paul Whiteley is Professor of Politics at the University of Sheffield. His recent publications (co-authored) include *Labour's Grass Roots* (1992); *True Blues: the politics of Conservative Party membership* (1994) and *Labour and Conservative Party Members 1990–92* (1996).

F. M. G. Willson was Fellow of Nuffield College, Oxford and worked throughout his life on a range of public administration topics. His publications included *The Organization of British Central Government, 1914–56* (1957), co-authored with D. N. Chester.

Sources for Contributions

The following papers are all from *Political Studies:*

1. G. D. H. Cole 'What is Socialism? Parts 1 and 2' Vol. 1 Nos. 1 and 2 February and June 1953 pp. 21–33 and pp. 175–183.

2. John Dunn 'Justice and the Interpretation of Locke's Political Theory' Vol. 16 No. 1 March 1968 pp. 68–87.

3. Michael Oakeshott 'The Vocabulary of a Modern European State' Vol. 23 Nos 2 and 3 June–September 1975 pp. 319–341.

4. Gillian Rose 'How is Critical Theory Possible? Theodor W. Adorno and concept formation in sociology' Vol. 24 No. 1 March 1976 pp. 69–85.

5. Hillel Steiner 'Liberty and Equality' Vol. 29 No. 4 December 1981 pp. 555–569.

6. Diana Coole 'Constructing and Deconstructing Liberty: A feminist and poststructuralist analysis' Vol. 41 No. 1 March 1993 pp. 83–95.

7. F. M. G. Willson 'The Routes of Entry of New Members of the British Cabinet, 1868–1958' Vol. 7 No. 3 September 1959 pp. 222–232.

8. J. P. Nettl 'Consensus or Elite Domination: the case of business' Vol. 13 No. 1 March 1965 pp. 22–44.

9. James Alt, Ivor Crewe and Bo Särlvik 'Angels in Plastic: The Liberal surge in 1974' Vol. 25 No. 3 September 1977 pp. 343–368.

10. Paul Whiteley, Patrick Seyd, Jeremy Richardson and Paul Bissell 'Thatcherism and the Conservative Party' Vol. 42 No. 2 June 1994 pp. 185–203.

11. Nelson Polsby 'Towards an Explanation of McCarthyism' Vol. 8 No. 3 September 1960 pp. 250–271.

12. Karl Deutsch 'The Propensity to International Transactions' Vol. 8 No. 2 March 1960 pp. 147–155.

13. Graeme Duncan and Steven Lukes 'The New Democracy' Vol. 11 No. 2 June 1963 pp. 156–177.

14. Malcolm Anderson 'The Myth of the "Two Hundred Families"' Vol. 13 No. 2 June 1965 pp. 163–178.

15. B. D. Graham 'Theories of the French Party System under the Third Republic' Vol. 12 No. 1 March 1964 pp. 21–32.

16. C. A. E. Goodhart and R. J. Bhansali 'Political Economy' Vol. 18 No. 1 March 1970 pp. 43–106.

17. Brian Barry 'Is it better to be powerful or lucky?: Part 1' Vol. 28 No. 2 June 1980 pp. 183–194.

18. Keith Dowding 'Model or Metaphor? A Critical review of the Policy Network Approach' Vol. 43 No. 1 March 1995 pp. 136–158.

BRITISH POLITICAL SCIENCE: FIFTY YEARS OF POLITICAL STUDIES

INDEX